Assistive
TECHNOLOGY

SAGE was founded in 1965 by Sara Miller McCune to support the dissemination of usable knowledge by publishing innovative and high-quality research and teaching content. Today, we publish over 900 journals, including those of more than 400 learned societies, more than 800 new books per year, and a growing range of library products including archives, data, case studies, reports, and video. SAGE remains majority-owned by our founder, and after Sara's lifetime will become owned by a charitable trust that secures our continued independence.

Los Angeles | London | New Delhi | Singapore | Washington DC

Assistive
TECHNOLOGY

EMILY C. BOUCK
Michigan State University

Los Angeles | London | New Delhi
Singapore | Washington DC

Los Angeles | London | New Delhi
Singapore | Washington DC

FOR INFORMATION:

SAGE Publications, Inc.
2455 Teller Road
Thousand Oaks, California 91320
E-mail: order@sagepub.com

SAGE Publications Ltd.
1 Oliver's Yard
55 City Road
London EC1Y 1SP
United Kingdom

SAGE Publications India Pvt. Ltd.
B 1/I 1 Mohan Cooperative Industrial Area
Mathura Road, New Delhi 110 044
India

SAGE Publications Asia-Pacific Pte. Ltd.
3 Church Street
#10-04 Samsung Hub
Singapore 049483

Acquisitions Editor: Theresa Accomazzo
eLearning Editor: Robert Higgins
Editorial Assistant: Georgia McLaughlin
Production Editor: Libby Larson
Copy Editor: Jared Leighton
Typesetter: C&M Digitals (P) Ltd.
Proofreader: Eleni Georgiou
Indexer: Maria Sosnowski
Cover Designer: Karine Hovsepian
Marketing Manager: Johanna Swenson

Printed in the United States of America

Library of Congress Cataloging-in-Publication Data

Bouck, Emily C., author.

Assistive technology/Emily C. Bouck.

Los Angeles: Sage Publications, 2016. | Includes bibliographical references and index.

LCCN 2015029117 |
ISBN 978-1-4833-7443-7 (pbk.: alk. paper)

Subjects: LCSH: Children with disabilities—Education—United States. | Students with disabilities—Services for—United States. | Special education—Technological innovations—United States. | Self-help devices for people with disabilities.

Classification: LCC LC4019 .B67 2016 | DDC 371.9—dc23
LC record available at http://lccn.loc.gov/2015029117

This book is printed on acid-free paper.

16 17 18 19 10 9 8 7 6 5 4 3 2 1

Brief Contents

Detailed Contents

Preface

I became interested in educating students with disabilities—and later their teachers—one summer, early in my college experience, when I decided to become a one-on-one inclusion counselor for a young girl with autism spectrum disorder. Prior to that summer, I had limited experiences with students or adults with disabilities, and looking back, I could not quite tell you what actually prompted me to apply for and accept the job. However, it was one of my best decisions. That summer experience put me on the path to my lifelong interest and career in special education and even my passion for assistive technology. The young girl and I both spent the summer learning a lot, especially me, as I learned to appreciate the low-tech assistive technology I had to work with each day in our day camp setting.

I was prompted to tell this story as one of my desires throughout this textbook was to make sure I was addressing the range of assistive technology that exists to support students with disabilities, including the low-tech options, often considered less glamorous. However, I am committed to helping future and current educators understand and see the value in all types and levels of assistive technology, regardless of any of the constraints of their context. Throughout this textbook, I provide readers with text and images about the range of assistive technology they can use to support students with disabilities, from low tech up to high tech and from free to for-purchase options. I also wanted to try to keep the textbook current and, to the maximum extent possible, forward thinking. To that end, the chapters provide the reader with Web 2.0 and/or app-based assistive technology options to consider, given the current (and predicted future) trend in education toward more mobile and personalized technology, such as tablets.

This textbook on assistive technology is intended to help educators better understand assistive technology and how it can support students with disabilities, from early childhood through transition into adulthood. To do so, *Assistive Technology* focuses on presenting different options to support students by considering the purpose or support the technology can provide (e.g., vision, behavior, instructional aid, and computer access) and not basing it on a student's disability categorization (e.g., learning disability or orthopedic impairment). The textbook is also written to support both the intended reader as well as the intended instructor. To that end, I tried to make it both grounded in research (and provided actual research studies) as well as readable, engaging, and grounded in life by presenting stories from practice (i.e., Case Studies). As

I believe to truly learn about assistive technology, one must also interact with it to the best of one's ability, the textbook contains both Extension Activities, where students and instructors—separately or together—can view engaging videos pulled from the Web about uses of assistive technology, and Application Activities, where students are encouraged to interact with free (or free trials of) Web 2.0 or app-based assistive technology options. I hope you enjoy reading and using this textbook as much as I enjoyed writing it.

Audience

Assistive Technology was written for multiple audiences, including those seeking to become assistive technology specialists, preservice and in-service special education teachers, and preservice and in-service general education teachers. An understanding and knowledge of assistive technology is of utmost importance for those teaching and supporting students with disabilities. As the rate of inclusion for students with disabilities continues to increase, the need for general educators to also have knowledge and familiarity with assistive technology increases. Of course, this textbook can support anyone who needs to better understand assistive technology and how it supports early-childhood through transition-aged students with disabilities in school-based settings (e.g., occupational therapists, instructional technologists, and speech-and-language pathologists). Hopefully, this book can also serve as a resource for parents who are seeking additional information about assistive technology to support their own children in terms of access and achievement.

Organization of the Text

This textbook is organized into 10 chapters (see below). The 10 chapters are not, for the most part, organized around disability categories (e.g., "Assistive Technology for Students with Learning Disabilities" or "Assistive Technology for Students with Orthopedic Impairments"). Rather, the content and chapters are organized around the purposes for assistive technology (e.g., "Assistive Technology as Instructional Aids" and "Assistive Technology for Computer Access"). Hence, in the chapter "Assistive Technology as Instructional Aids," for example, you will find references to assistive technology to support students with learning disabilities but also students with more severe disabilities, such as students with moderate or severe intellectual disability. As you will note, the chapters in the textbook, outside of Chapter 1 and perhaps Chapter 2, are not structured in such a manner that one must teach or experience the content in the order of the chapters. Instead, the textbook is organized so that individual instructors can teach the chapters, and others can interact with the book in their particular order of choosing.

Chapter 1: Assistive Technology Background

Chapter 2: (Assistive) Technology Frameworks

Chapter 3: Assistive Technology for Communication

Chapter 4: Assistive Technology for Mobility and Positioning

Chapter 5: Assistive Technology for Computer Access

Chapter 6: Assistive Technology for Vision and Hearing

Chapter 7: Assistive Technology to Support Behavior and Organization

Chapter 8: Assistive Technology as Instructional Aids

Chapter 9: Assistive Technology to Enhance Independence and Transition

Chapter 10: Assistive Technology for Young Children

Features

Each chapter is similarly structured at the beginning and the end. Each chapter begins with a brief overview of the content covered as well as **Chapter Objectives**. Each chapter ends with **Extension Activities**, **Application Activities**, **Discussion Questions**, **Resources/Additional Information**, and **Suggested Enrichment Readings**. Each chapter also contains many pictures and images of different technology to help connect the reader visually with the technology being discussed. Additionally, the content in the chapters is grounded, to the extent possible, in research. Given the current, and appropriate, era of attention to research-based or research-supported practice, it is important for future and current educators to understand the research base, and at times lack thereof, behind assistive technology for students with disabilities.

Additional features of this textbook include its focus on Web 2.0 and app-based assistive technology, attention to free or low-cost technology, and a consistent focus on the continuum of technology with special attention to low-tech options. Each chapter includes a special section focused on Web 2.0 and app-based assistive technology relative to the purpose being discussed (e.g., vision and hearing or instructional aids). Web 2.0 resources and apps are also mentioned throughout each chapter as appropriate. Given the increased access and use of computers, the Internet, and mobile technologies (e.g., tablets), it is important that educators supporting students with disabilities understand the more traditional stand-alone versions of assistive technology as well as the increasingly popular online and app options.

Pedagogical Aids and High-Interest Features

My goal in writing this book was to create the kind of textbook I wanted to use as an instructor teaching a course on assistive technology as well as to be sensitive to the student readers. The features that excite me as a teacher educator include the Case Studies (at least one, but typically more), Perspectives, and Extension and Application Activities in each chapter.

- The **Case Studies** focus on students and teachers and provide a personal perspective of assistive technology and how it is being used to support students or by teachers to improve the educational experience of students.

- Each chapter contains multiple **Perspective** sections, which represent a range of different facets I wanted to highlight. For example, some Perspectives focus on highlighting the Research to Practice of a particular technology or type of technology. Others focus on a Technology Mindset and ask the reader to consider his or her perspective about a topic or technology prior to getting into the chapter, involve connecting the technology discussed to a curriculum, or further elaborate on a particular idea presented in the chapter.

- The **Extension Activities** and **Application Activities** are meant to help connect the reader to resources relevant to the content presented outside of the textbook, and both can be done in class, used for online instruction, or provided for students to engage with on their own time to further their understanding of the material. With the Extension Activities, students are often asked to watch a video—in class or on their own—that is relevant to the technology and/or topic being discussed in each chapter. With the Application Activities, students are meant to get their hands dirty, so to speak, in that they are encouraged to try out different free Web 2.0 or app technology referenced in each chapter. They might also be asked to read other material relevant to the technology being discussed.

Ancillaries and Accompanying Technology

The free open-access **Student Study Site** at **study.sagepub.com/bouck** features multimedia and web resources, eFlashcards, and student quizzes.

The password protected **Instructor Resource Site** at **study.sagepub.com/bouck** includes a test bank, PowerPoints, and more.

Acknowledgments

When I first started writing this book, it felt like such a solitary project, but it was quickly enriched by the teachers whose classrooms I visited while writing, those whose classrooms I had previously visited and recalled, and the reviewers who helped to guide the text to become what it is today. To all the teachers and students who allowed me into their classrooms and to observe their use of the range of assistive technology as well as to the educators who helped to form the Case Studies, I thank you. Although this textbook is rooted in the research behind the assistive technology, it is the practical elements, including the case studies and other examples from the field, that make the book come to life. Thank you to the following educators and educational institutions for inspiration and/or allowing me to observe current experiences, reflect about previous experience, and/or speak with you: Patti Fish, Whitney Bartlett, Matthew Wright, Alyssa Jenkins, Jordan Shurr, Pei-lin Weng, Jennifer Walters, Debra Squire, Robin Lowell, Angela Buckland, Lauren Sullivan, Rebecca Olson, Portland Public Schools, Lafayette Public Schools, Traverse City Public Schools, Williamston Public Schools, Heartwood School, Indiana State School for the Blind, Washington State School for the Blind, "Z" Frank Apachi Day Camp, Keshet, and the St. Louis Center. I would also like to thank my family and friends, and those of my children, whose names I used as pseudonyms throughout the book.

I would also like to express my appreciation for my editor, Theresa Accomazzo, and her editorial assistant, Georgia McLaughlin, for guiding me through the process. I would also like to acknowledge the multiple reviewers who reviewed different chapters as well as the initial prospectus. All their input strengthened the textbook, and I know it became better as I saw it through their eyes. Thank you to Dave Edyburn, University of Wisconsin–Milwaukee; Rebecca Barr Evers, Winthrop University; Sara Flanagan, University of Kentucky; Kimberly Floyd, West Virginia University; Patricia Ging, Tennessee Wesleyan College; Rebecca Hines, University of Central Florida; Alice Kozen, Niagara University; Hwa Lee, Bradley University; Yeunjoo Lee, California State

University–Bakersfield; Mike Marotta, Felician College; Karen McCaleb, Texas A&M University–Corpus Christi; Trisha Nishimura, Whittier College; Jasmine Ramirez, Miami Dade College; Scott Sparks, Ohio University; Terri Cooper Swanson, Pittsburg State University; and Gardner Umbarger, Saginaw Valley State University. Finally, in support of the editing of this book, I would like to thank Mary Bouck for reading all chapter drafts.

About the Author

Emily C. Bouck is an Associate Professor of Special Education in the Department of Counseling, Educational Psychology, and Special Education at Michigan State University. She received her doctorate in special education from Michigan State University. Dr. Bouck is the author of numerous peer-reviewed journal articles and chapters relating to her two main areas of research: mathematics education for students with disabilities and functional life skills education for students with disabilities, with a central theme of assistive technology throughout both areas. She has contributed a chapter on assistive technology to Richard Gargiulo's *Special Education in Contemporary Society*, published by SAGE, and will be brought on as the co-author for the sixth edition. Dr. Bouck is a Past President of the Division on Autism and Developmental Disabilities of the Council for Exceptional Children and has also been active in the Technology and Media Division of the Council for Exceptional Children. Dr. Bouck has taught courses on assistive technology; social, legal, and ethical issues in special education; special education methods; and doctoral seminars. She has experience working with a range of students with disabilities in school settings from preschool through age 26.

Assistive Technology Background

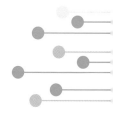

Chapter 1 presents background information to help the reader understand assistive technology for students with disabilities, including understanding the categorization of assistive technology and aspects of legislation. Chapter 1 sets the stage for the remaining chapters that will present assistive technology aligned with issues of disability or age. Chapter 1 concludes by discussing Universal Design for Learning (UDL), including the relationship between UDL and assistive technology.

Technology—widely defined as tools—has been present in society since the beginning. Technological innovations, ranging from stone tools to crayons and to the Internet and iPads, helped shape society and continue to do so (Mishra & the Deep-Play Research Group, 2012). Recent research suggests many young individuals as well as adults are increasingly using more sophisticated (i.e., modern, digital) technology in their everyday lives, such as cell phones, computers, and MP3 players (Banks 2008; Madden, Lenhart, Duggan, Cortesi, & Gasser, 2013; Rideout, Foehr, & Roberts, 2010). Aside from daily life, technological innovations also helped to shape education and teaching and learning. In terms of digital and modern technology, such as computers and the Internet, access in schools dramatically increased over the last two decades, with an average student to instructional computer ratio of 3:1 in all public schools and 98% of all public schools having Internet access (National Center for Education Statistics, 2013).

Technology in education is often referred to as **educational technology**, "the application of technology to teaching and learning" (Edyburn, 2013, p. 9). Technology in education can be broadly defined, including today's

Chapter Objectives

After reading the chapter, the reader will be able to do the following:

1. Explain the different categorizations of assistive technology devices

2. Identify the history of assistive technology in federal legislation

3. Describe key historical and current issues involving assistive technology

4. Discuss mobile technology apps and provide a resource for evaluating apps

5. Explain the principles of Universal Design for Learning

6. Articulate the relationship between Universal Design for Learning and assistive technology

modern conceptualizations of technology (e.g., computers, the Internet, iPads), as well as some of the original tools used in schools (e.g., the slate and chalk) (Blackhurst, 2005a; Mishra & Koehler, 2009). The broad category of educational technology can be subdivided into different types: (a) technology of teaching (i.e., instructional approaches); (b) medical technology (i.e., devices involving one's health); (c) productivity technology (i.e., tools for creating products); (d) information technology (i.e., tools that provide access to information); (e) instructional technology (i.e., tools that support learning); and (f) assistive technology (i.e., devices to support the independence and access of students with disabilities) (Blackhurst, 2005a, 2005b) (see Table 1.1).

Assistive Technology
· ·

Assistive technology is essentially technology to support individuals with disabilities. However, while assistive technology is typically considered devices and tools, it actually refers to *devices* as well as *services* to assist in the selection, acquisition, and maintenance of those devices. An **assistive technology device**, as defined by the Technology-Related Assistance for Individuals with Disabilities Act of 1988—called the Tech Act—(Pub. L. 100-407), is "any item, piece of equipment, or product system, whether acquired commercially, modified, or customized, that is used to increase, maintain, or improve functional capabilities of individuals with disabilities" (29 U.S.C. § 2202[2]). An **assistive technology service** refers to "any service that directly assists an individual in the selection, acquisition, or use of an assistive technology device" (Pub. L. 100-407). Specifically, more in-depth, the definition of assistive technology service addresses the following:

(a) The evaluation of the needs of a child with a disability, including a functional evaluation of the child in the child's customary environment;

(b) Purchasing, leasing, or otherwise providing for the acquisition of assistive technology devices by children with disabilities;

(c) Selecting, designing, fitting, customizing, adapting, applying, maintaining, repairing, or replacing assistive technology devices;

(d) Coordinating and using other therapies, interventions, or services with assistive technology devices, such as those associated with existing education and rehabilitation plans and programs;

(e) Training or technical assistance for a child with a disability or, if appropriate, that child's family; and

(f) Training or technical assistance for professionals (including individuals providing education or rehabilitation services), employers, or other individuals who provide services to, employ, or are otherwise substantially involved in the major life functions of that child (Individuals with Disabilities Education Improvement Act, 2004, 20 U.S.C. 1401(2) § 300.6; U.S. Department of Education, n.d.).

Table 1.1 Examples of Six Distinct Types of Educational Technology

Technology of Teaching	Medical Technology	Productivity Technology	Information Technology	Instructional Technology	Assistive Technology
• Direct instruction • Problem-based learning	• Cochlear implants • Feeding tubes	• Microsoft Word • Presentation tools (e.g., PowerPoint)	• The Internet	• Educational computer software • SMART Boards	• Speech-to-text • Seat cushions

Source: Adapted from "Perspectives on Applications of Technology in the Field of Learning Disabilities," by A. Blackhurst, 2005, *Learning Disability Quarterly,* 28(2), pp. 175–178.

Assistive Technology Services

Assistive technology services are multifaceted but generally involve the selection, acquisition, implementation, and maintenance of assistive technology devices (see Figure 1.1). While assistive technology services may be provided by an **assistive technology specialist**, these specially trained **related service** providers are not available in every local educational agency (LEA). When LEAs do not have access to an assistive technology specialist, special education teachers, speech-language pathologists, occupational therapists, and/or instructional technologists may be responsible for providing assistive technology services (Edyburn, 2004; Marino, Marino, & Shaw, 2006).

Quality Indicators for Assistive Technology Services. As noted, assistive technology services are multifaceted. To help support educators' delivery of high-quality assistive technology services, the Quality Indicators for Assistive Technology Services (QIAT) were developed (see new website: http://www.qiat.org/ index.html (Zabala et al., 2000; Zabala & Carl, 2005). QIAT focuses on assistive technology service development, delivery, and evaluation for students as well as for family members and school personnel supporting the student. To address a shortage of attention on assistive technology services, the QIAT Consortium was founded, which developed the quality indictors (Zabala et al., 2000). QIAT exists for (a) consideration of a student's needs for assistive technology, (b) assessment

- Assessment/evaluation
- Lending library trials
- Determining goals

- Purchasing
- Borrowing
- Making

Selection

Acquisition

Maintenance

Implementation

- Monitoring, including additional training
- Fixing
- Ongoing assessment

- Training students, educators, families
- Ongoing assessment

Source: E. Bouck. Adapted from *Special Education in Contemporary Society: An Introduction to Exceptionality* (5th ed.) by R. M. Gargiulo, 2015. Copyright 2015 by SAGE Publications.

for assistive technology, (c) documentation of assistive technology devices and services in the IEP, (d) assistive technology implementation, (e) effectiveness evaluation of assistive technology devices and services, (f) transition relative to assistive technology, (g) assistive technology professional development and training, and (h) administrator support and leadership for assistive technology.

The QIAT can be very useful for IEP teams as well as other educators involved with assistive technology decision-making and for implementation and monitoring. (Room precludes the reproduction of all the indicators in this textbook.) At the QIAT website, downloadable Microsoft Word and PDF documents exist for each of the eight areas (see http://www.qiat.org/indicators. html). In addition, QIAT matrices are available for self-evaluation of the

Case Study 1.1

Jordan is an assistive technology consultant for his county's special education cooperative (i.e., the three school districts in the county where he works collaborate around special education services, including the location of programs and related service providers). While Jordan is not an assistive technology specialist, he does many of the same tasks. For example, Jordan works with students and teachers in grades preK–12 with mild through severe disabilities and needs. He helps to evaluate and write the assessment reports for students. He also works with the state lending library to obtain device trials and then helps to implement those devices as well as maintain them once they are selected for an individual student. Jordan also attends IEP

iStock/asiseeit

meetings for students who need or may need assistive technology services. Finally, Jordan sees his role as a resource for direct service providers, such as teachers. He not only provides formal and informal training (i.e., creates videos on how to use different technology that are housed on a website educators have access to), but he will meet with teachers about issues relative to assistive technology.

application of QIAT in schools (QIAT Consortium, 2012). The matrices allow teams to assess themselves on the QIAT, ranging from unacceptable to promising practices for each indicator for each of the eight areas.

Assistive Technology Device Categorization

Given the broad definition of assistive technology devices that appears in federal legislation (i.e., "any item, piece of equipment, or product system"), it is helpful to view assistive technology in different categorizations. Two common ways assistive technology is categorized are by level of technology and then purpose of technology. In terms of level of technology, one can categorize assistive technology devices as no tech, low tech, medium or mid tech, and high tech (Blackhurst, 1997; Edyburn, 2005; Johnson, Beard, & Carpenter, 2007; Vanderheiden, 1984) (see Table 1.2 for examples of assistive technology devices across the level of technology categorization). Of note, there is not agreement on the number of categories (e.g., two, three, four), nor is there universal acceptance on particular devices being strictly in one category versus another. For this book, we will discuss assistive technology as occurring within four categories: no tech, low tech, mid tech, and high tech.

No-tech is what it intuitively sounds like—no-technology assistive technology. No-tech assistive technology often can involve the implementation of a teaching strategy, such as mnemonics (e.g., HOMES for remembering the Great Lakes—Huron, Ontario, Michigan, Erie, and Superior) (Behrmann & Jerome, 2002; Blackhurst, 1997). Others also consider no-tech assistive technology to include other related services, such as occupational therapy (National Assistive Technology Research Institute, 2001). Low-tech (or light tech) assistive technologies are typically devices or tools without a power source (Behrmann & Schaff, 2001; Blackhurst, 1997). Generally, low-tech assistive technology devices require little training and have a lower cost.

Mid-tech or medium-tech assistive technology devices are those tools that typically require a power source—such as a battery—as well as increase in cost and potential training needed for implementation or operation. Finally, high-tech assistive technologies are the most sophisticated assistive technology devices. Originally, high-tech assistive technology was associated with computers and computer programs (e.g., text-to-speech, word prediction) but also include

Table 1.2 Examples of Assistive Technology Devices by Categorization

No-Tech AT	Low-Tech AT	Mid-Tech AT	High-Tech AT
• Mnemonics (Please excuse my dear Aunt Sally for PEDMAS: Parenthesis, Exponents, Multiplication & Division, Addition & Subtraction) • Graphic organizers	• Pencil grips • Raised lined paper • Highlighter tape • Large print text • Grabbers	• Calculators • Audio recorder • Switches • Books on tape • Talking spell checkers or dictionaries	• Text-to-speech • Smartphone or tablet and their apps • Digital textbooks (supported eText) • Power wheelchairs

Source: E. Bouck. Adapted from *Special Education in Contemporary Society: An Introduction to Exceptionality* (5th ed.) by R. M. Gargiulo, 2015. Copyright 2015 by SAGE Publications.

The previous quote about new technologies revolutionizing eduation but not succeeding actually comes from an 1988 article by Peter Lewis in *The New York Times*, which he attributes to the introduction of the blackboard. However, the quote could be applicable to a number of technologies that you might have guessed, such as SMART Boards, iPads, computers, or LCD projectors. There are a few points from the quote worthy of consideration. One, technology is not just computers or sophisticated devices, and neither is assistive techology. Technology is also pencils, black and/or whiteboards, and crayons, and assistive technology is also pencil grips, raised-line papers, and seat cushions. Another point is that one technology will not revolutionize education. Technologies are tools. Assistive technology can benefit and assist students with disabilities, but students still need teachers to teach and be active contributors to their learning. The third and final point is that, unfortunately, teachers are often blamed when technology does not produce the anticipated results. However, it is important to understand that for teachers to implement technology—or assistive technology—they need training on not just how to use the technology but also how to use it in an effective and efficient way to meaningfully integrate it into their teaching and student learning. Implementing technology for the sake of implementing technology is not the goal. Implementing technology because it fits with one's pedagogical perspective (i.e., approach to teaching) and helps to deliver content is the goal (Mishra & Koehler, 2009).

smartphones as well as mobile tablets. High-tech assistive technologies generally are the most expensive devices as well as the ones necessitating the most training (Blackhurst, 1997; Edyburn, 2005; Johnson et al., 2007; Vanderheiden, 1984). Although high-tech assistive technology devices can be very appealing (e.g., iPads and iPad apps), when considering assistive technology for students, one typically begins with low-tech. Low-tech assistive technology devices are typically less stigmatizing or attention-drawing and are easier to implement (Behrmann & Schaff, 2001; Blackhurst, 1997).

Aside from level of technology, another way to categorize assistive technology devices is by their purpose. Similar to the categorization via level, there is not a universally accepted and used purpose categorization. Two common categorization systems are the one proposed by Bryant and Bryant (2003, 2012) and the one proposed by the Wisconsin Assistive Technology Initiative (WATI) (Gierach, 2009) (see Table 1.3 for examples of assistive technology devices across the technology purpose categorization). Bryant and Bryant's classification system

Table 1.3 Example Assistive Technology Devices by Purpose

Bryant and Bryant Purposes of AT	Wisconsin Assistive Technology Initiative Categories of AT	Examples
Positioning	Seating, positioning, and mobility	• Adjustable height desks • Custom wedges
Mobility		• Wheelchair • Gait trainer
Augmentative and alternative communication (AAC)	Communication	• Picture Exchange Communication Symbols • Proloquo2Go® app
Computer access	Computer Access	• Alternative keyboard • Speech/voice recognition
Adaptive toys and games	Recreation and leisure	• Switch-operated battery toys • Larger or Braille playing cards
Adaptive environments	Activities of daily living	• Adapted utensils and dishes • Talking microwave
Instructional aids	Motor aspects of writing and composition of written material	• Speech-to-text • Raised-line paper • Word prediction • Portable spell checker
	Reading	• Reading Pen • Highlighter strips
	Mathematics	• Concrete or virtual manipulatives • Calculator
	Organization	• Watchminder • Daily planner
	Vision	• Braille notetaker • eText or digital text
	Hearing	• Cochlear implant • FM system

Source: AssistiveWare® (2014); Bouck and Flanagan (2009); Bryant and Bryant (2003); Gierach (2009); Johnson, Beard, and Carpenter (2007). Adapted from *Special Education in Contemporary Society: An Introduction to Exceptionality* (5th ed.) by R. M. Gargiulo, 2015. Copyright 2015 by SAGE Publications.

involves seven purposes: positioning, mobility, augmentative and alternative communication (AAC), computer access, adaptive toys and games, adaptive environments, and instructional aids. WATI organized assistive technology by potential tasks, including seating, positioning, and mobility; communication; computer access; motor aspects of writing and composition of written material; reading; mathematics; organization; recreation and leisure; activities of daily living; vision; hearing; and multiple challenges (Gierach, 2009). Table 1.3 highlights the similarities of the two approaches.

Positioning, seating, and mobility refer to posture, positions, and movement. Throughout the day individuals—including students with disabilities—are in different positions, including sitting, standing, and walking. For students with disabilities with motoric challenges or physical challenges, assistive technology for positioning, seating, or mobility can be implemented to address such challenges. These assistive technology devices and tools can help an individual be in the best position (e.g., height of a desk or chair, a wedge, seat cushion, or ball [as a seat]) and move throughout an environment (e.g., wheelchair, gait trainer, white cane) (Stindt, Reed, & Obukowicz, 2009). Note that assistive technology for positioning, seating, and mobility will be discussed in detail in Chapter 4.

Assistive technology for communication is referred to as augmentative and alternative communication. In other words, assistive technology can augment (i.e., supplement) an individual's verbal speech or serve as an alternative to verbal speech. However, with any AAC system selected, verbal speech production is still a goal, and AAC devices are an effective means of supporting verbal speech production (Cumley, Maro, & Stanek, 2009; Millar, Light, & Schlosser, 2006). AAC devices, like all assistive technology, exist on a continuum from low-tech (e.g., using pictures or symbols to communicate) to high-tech (e.g., a speech output app on a smartphone or mobile tablet). Augmentative and alternative communication will be discussed in greater detail in Chapter 3.

Assistive technology for computer access refers to ways to access a computer or computer-like device. While the majority of individuals may access a computer with a keyboard or a mouse, this may not be an option for all individuals with disabilities. Alternative ways to access computers exist, including using voice controls (voice or speech recognition), a joystick, or a variety of switches. Some of the alternative ways to access a computer or computer-like device, such as a mobile tablet or smartphone, may come as standard accessibility features with an operating system or device (e.g., sticky keys). Chapter 5 will present additional information on assistive technology for computer access.

Assistive technology for instructional purposes, including reading, writing, and mathematics, is an important consideration for students with disabilities and K–12 educators. In the K–12 school environment, assistive technology for instructional purposes might be the most common type of assistive technology a teacher encounters as they include assistive technologies for the provision of students accessing and participating in content area instruction. Assistive technology for reading can include books on tape, supported eText, and text-to-speech (Cumley, 2009). Assistive technology for writing can include word processors, pencil grips, raised-line paper, and speech-to-text (Nankee, Stindt, & Lees, 2009; Swenson, Wirkus, & Obukowitz, 2009). Examples of mathematics assistive technology include calculators and manipulatives (Obukowicz, 2009). Assistive technology for instructional aids will be discussed primarily in Chapter 7.

Although assistive technology for instructional purposes can be important for the success of a student with a disability, assistive technology for recreation and leisure (i.e., adaptive toys and games) as well as well for daily living (i.e., adaptive environments) is also important in and beyond formal schooling. Assistive technology for recreation and leisure can assist individuals with disabilities across the age span in meaningfully participating in social or fun activities. Assistive technology to support leisure and recreation can include adaptive playing cards (e.g., Braille) as well as a holder for the playing cards. Switches can also be used to make battery-operated toys run for young children with disabilities (Comer, 2009). Adaptive utensils and dishes are examples of assistive technology for daily living (Gierach & Stindt, 2009). In addition, tools or devices can adapt the environment to enable an individual with disabilities to be more independent in his/her environment. For example, smoke detectors can flash as opposed to beep, lights can turn on and off via clapping as opposed to a switch, and a microwave can give verbal prompts. Chapter 9 will provide additional information regarding assistive technology for leisure and recreation as well as daily living.

Organization-focused assistive technology is technology to support students' executive functioning, including self-management and self-monitoring, memory, and organization of materials and time (Obukowicz, Stindt, Rozanski, & Gierach, 2009). Assistive technology for organization ranges from daily organizers that may be used by all students to paper-and-pencil self-monitoring or technology-based self-monitoring (e.g., iPad apps). Within the self-management aspect, fidget toys (e.g., silly putty, Koosh ball) can also serve as an assistive technology. Assistive technology to support behavior will be discussed in Chapter 8.

Finally, assistive technology can support the sensory tasks related to vision and hearing, particularly focused on students identified with a visual impairment— including blindness—and/or a hearing impairment, including deafness. Assistive technology focused on supporting students with vision or hearing can cut across other domains, such as instructional assistive technology as well as assistive technology for daily living. Examples of assistive technology to support students with visual impairments include Braille, supported eText, and closed-circuit television (CCTV) (Wiazowski, 2009). Examples of assistive technology to support students with hearing impairments include hearing aids, real-time captioning, and FM (personal frequency modulation) systems (Heckendorf, 2009). Assistive technology focused on vision and hearing is discussed in Chapter 6.

Case Study 1.2

Matt is a special education teacher at a state-accredited residential and day school that serves students between the ages of 6 and 21. Matt works with students who have learning disabilities and/or emotional behavior disorders who struggle in a typical school setting as well as students with intellectual disability and students with autism spectrum disorder. Matt's students with learning disabilities and/or emotional behavior disorders are not reading or writing on grade level. For his older students who still struggle with handwriting, he makes pencil grips or weighted pencils available and feels that pencil grips benefit his students. For his younger students who struggle with reading, Matt takes advantage of books on tape or electronic books played through an MP3 player. Matt's school also has more sophisticated technology to support students with more intense needs. Every classroom

iStock/SolStock

in Matt's school has an iPad, and Proloquo2Go® is used for students with communication needs. At Matt's school, most of the assistive technology needs and decisions for individual students are made by the school's occupational therapists or speech-language pathologists.

Assistive Technology Legislation for Education

Assistive technology is actually a life-span support, meaning assistive technology can benefit newborns through school-aged children and beyond through an individual's adulthood. An individual's need for assistive technology might also vary across one's life. As all individuals age, they may be more in need of particular assistive technology devices (e.g., hearing aids). Given the practical application of assistive technology across a life span, assistive technology is addressed in multiple pieces of federal legislation.

The Tech Act. Assistive technology was actually first defined in the 1988 Technology-Related Assistance for Individuals with Disabilities Act (i.e., the Tech Act; Pub. L. 100-407; 29 U.S.C. §§ 3001–3007). The definitions of assistive technology devices and services persist through other important legislation involving individuals with disabilities, including the Americans with Disabilities Act (1990), the Individuals with Disabilities Education Act (1990, 1997, 2004), and the Assistive Technology Act (1998; Petcu, Yell, & Fletcher, 2014). The Tech Act not only defined assistive technology devices and services (please refer to earlier in the chapter) but also provided federal money to states through grants to provide services and increase awareness regarding assistive technology (Blackhurst, 2005a).

The reauthorization of the Tech Act in 1994 (Pub. L. 103-218) continued funding to states regarding assistive technology (Crowl & Franklin, 1994). In 1998, the Tech Act ended and the Assistive Technology Act (Pub. L. 105-394) was passed; the Assistive Technology Act was reauthorized again in 2004 (Pub. L. 108-364). The Assistive Technology Act also provided funding to states regarding assistive technology. Specifically, the funding created permanent technology-related assistance programs in each state. Each state's Assistive Technology Act program supports individuals with disabilities across the life span and involves loan programs for devices. Each state program also provides training, technical assistance, and public awareness (National Assistive Technology Technical Assistance Partnership, n.d.) (see http://www.resnaprojects.org/allcontacts/statewidecontacts.html).

The IDEA. The Individuals with Disabilities Education Act, first passed in 1975 and called the Education for All Handicapped Children Act (Pub. L. 94-142), is the federal law that governs the education of students with disabilities. Assistive technology by definition did not appear in the IDEA law until 1990; the definitions of assistive technology devices and services were adopted from the Tech Act of 1988 (Blackhurst, 2005a). In the 1997 reauthorization of the IDEA, greater emphasis was placed on individualized education program teams to consider assistive technology. While previously, IEP teams generally considered and included assistive technology for students with more severe or low-incidence disabilities (e.g., students with visual impairments, students with multiple disabilities), the 1997 reauthorization of the IDEA required IEP teams to consider assistive technology for students with more high-incidence disabilities (e.g., students with learning disabilities) (Edyburn, 2000; Quinn et al., 2009). Assistive technology is one the five special considerations in IEP development, along with behavior considerations, if the student is blind or visually impaired, if the student is deaf or hard of hearing/has communication needs and if a student has limited English proficiency (Yell, 2012).

IEP asks in AT is needed/appropriate

In an IEP, assistive technology can be included in multiple places. One of the most common places an IEP team might note assistive technology device needs is under supplementary aids, as a supplementary aid or listed as an accommodation. Assistive technology services can be listed under the direct services portion of an IEP. In addition, IEP teams may need to consider assistive technology device needs as an accommodation relative to the participation of students with disabilities in the state's accountability system.

The IDEA was last reauthorized in 2004; the name changed to the Individuals with Disabilities Education Improvement Act (Pub. L. 108-446). Relative to assistive technology, IDEA (2004) created exclusion criteria. Specifically, the legislation stipulated that schools were not responsible for providing or maintaining surgically implanted assistive technology (e.g., cochlear implants) (see Chapter 6 for additional information). In other words, schools do not assume the financial burden.

IDEA 2004 also included the National Instructional Materials Accessibility Standard (NIMAS). NIMAS stipulates that students with **print disabilities** (i.e., generally considered students with visual impairments, reading-based disabilities, and physical disabilities) were to be provided with accessible instructional materials (National Center on Accessible Instructional Materials, 2011). NIMAS suggested accessible materials include such options as large print, Braille, audio, or digital text. NIMAS stipulated that books for educational purposes, such as textbooks, need to be offered by state educational agencies (SEAs) or local educational agencies in a file format compliant with the one specified in NIMAS. Hence, students for whom digital text is appropriate could be granted digital textbooks at no cost. Please see the National Instructional Materials Access Center for additional information regarding NIMAS (http://www.nimac.us/) and the National Center for Accessible Instructional Materials (http://aim.cast.org/) for additional information regarding **accessible instructional materials** (AIM).

Section 504. Section 504 of the Rehabilitation Act of 1973 also contained provisions regarding assistive technology and education. Section 504 of the Rehabilitation Act of 1973 essentially prohibited discrimination against individuals with disabilities by entities that receive federal funding, including public K–12 schools and institutions of higher education (Yell, 2012). Individuals with disabilities, which are more broadly defined than the definitions for the 13 disability categories covered under the IDEA, are granted physical access to programs and activities as well as the right to receive reasonable accommodations. Reasonable accommodations in school as well as in postsecondary education and employment can include assistive technology.

[handwritten note: 504 Plan can included AT]

Section 508. Section 508 of the Reauthorization Rehabilitation Act of 1998 contains provisions relative to technology and individuals with disabilities. Section 508 stipulates that federal agencies must provide accessible electronic and information technology goods and services to individuals with disabilities (WebAIM, 2015). Specifically covered under Section 508 is that government websites are accessible to individuals with disabilities, such as through the use of screen readers by individuals with visual impairments (DO-IT, 2015).

The Americans with Disabilities Act. The Americans with Disabilities Act (ADA) is a federal law passed in 1990, and its focus was to prevent discrimination against individuals with disabilities. Unlike Section 504, ADA covers both private as well as public organizations (Kinsell, 2014). ADA regulates the provision of assistive technology as a means of an accommodation, including the range of no-tech, low-tech, mid-tech, and high-tech. For example, ADA involves accessible telecommunications, including provision of hearing aid–compatible phones (Kinsell, 2014).

History of Assistive Technology

Although the definition of assistive technology did not occur in federal legislation until 1988 (i.e., the Tech Act of 1988), nor were IEP teams required to consider assistive technology for *all* students with disabilities until after the reauthorization of the Individuals with Disabilities Education Act of 1997, assistive technology existed. For example, in 1932 Louis Braille published the Braille code for individuals who were blind. Other inventions preceding federal legislation included electric amplifying devices for individuals with hearing impairments in 1900 and the talking calculator in 1975 (Blackhurst, 2005a; Nazzaro, 1977). Outside of assistive technology for students with more sensory impairments, access also predated mandated legislation. For example, the first technology specifically designed for students with severe physical disabilities as a means of communication was developed in 1963 (Glennen, 1997; Vanderheiden & Grilley, 1976).

Current Issues of Assistive Technology

Assistive technology benefits students with disabilities; assistive technology can also promote independence, encourage empowerment, and level the playing field (Edyburn, Higgins, & Boone, 2005). For example, students who cannot or struggle to use their voice to communicate can be given augmentative and alternative communication devices (e.g., picture symbols or voice output device). Students who struggle with access to a computer through traditional means (e.g., keyboard or mouse) can use speech or voice recognition. And students who struggle with independently reading text can have text presented digitally and read to them. Yet these positives of technology must be understood in light of the challenges or negative facets. In other words, one cannot embrace technology without understanding its limitations.

Despite assistive technology's potential benefits, challenges still exist to its use, with access being a major issue. Although school districts are required to pay for assistive technology if it is listed in a student's IEP (with the exception of surgically implanted assistive technology), the assistive technology still needs to be written into the student's IEP (see Chapter 2 for additional information on assistive technology and IEPs). This means IEP team members need to have information about assistive technology and the different options available to support students with disabilities in independence, access, and success. Recently, Okolo and Diedrich (2014) found special educators and general educators reported less knowledge about assistive technology than presumed ideal, given the frequency with which students with disabilities are included in general education settings. The lack of access may be particularly true for students with more high-incidence disabilities, such as learning disabilities (Bouck, Maeda, & Flanagan, 2012; Edyburn, 2000).

In addition to access, students themselves can hamper assistive technology use. Students may abandon or select not to use an assistive technology device due to stigmatization (Alper & Raharinirina, 2006). Chapter 2 will present frameworks for assistive technology decision-making to help select assistive technology devices that fit with the student and his/her needs. Finally, a critical feature for successful use and implementation of assistive technology is training after making an assistive technology decision. Students, all teachers involved with the particular student and device, parents, and other related service providers need to be sufficiently trained on how to use the technology as well as how to meaningfully implement or integrate it into the student's learning (McGregor & Pachuski, 1996; Riemer-Reiss & Wacker, 2000).

If IEP team does not have knowledge of tech. available, cannot provide access to student.

Watson, Ito, Smith, and Andersen (2010) evaluated the effect of assistive technology on student outcomes. Using a small sample size of newly referred students for assistive technology with a repeated-measures quasi-experimental design, Watson et al. (2010) found no assistive technology abandonment occurred within one year when assistive technology was implemented following a team approach. The authors also found gains in student performance after implementation of the assistive technology.

Universal Design for Learning

A conceptual framework related to but not about assistive technology is Universal Design for Learning. UDL actually originates from the field of architecture and the concept of universal design. With universal design, buildings, products, and services (e.g., sidewalks) are designed to be accessible from the beginning; in other words, individuals with varying abilities or needs can use them. Examples of universal design in architecture include curb cuts in sidewalks as well as elevators in buildings and closed captioning on television. These features are then accessible to individuals challenged with mobility, such as individuals who use a wheelchair for mobility, as well as individuals with visual impairments and hearing impairments. However, these features also benefit others (e.g., curb cuts benefit individuals pushing strollers or pulling suitcases).

UDL is good for ALL

Universal Design for Learning is an extension of universal design; it is the application of inherent accessibility to education (see the National Center on Universal Design for Learning [http://www.udlcenter.org/] and the Center for Applied Special Technologies [CAST; http://www.cast.org/our-work/about-udl .html]). In other words, it is an educational conceptual framework focused on making curriculum (i.e., teaching and learning) accessible to all learners—a framework so all learners can access and experience success in school by providing options. UDL is not a one-size-fits-all model but rather focuses on removing barriers for learners (Hitchcock, Meyer, Rose, & Jackson, 2002; Rose, Hasselbring, Stahl, & Zabala, 2005; Rose & Meyer, 2002). UDL is framed around seven features (see Table 1.4) and three principles: multiple means of representation or presentation, multiple means of engagement, and multiple means of expression (Council for Exceptional Children [CEC], 2005). Multiple means of representation or presentation refers to an educator presenting information in different formats, such as both verbally reading and/or saying

Table 1.4 Features of UDL

Features	Description
Equitability	The needs of all students are met
Flexibility	The diversity students bring to learning is embraced
Simple and intuitive	Teaching and learning is accessible and adjustable
Multiple means of presentation	Educators use different ways to teach
Success-oriented	Barriers are removed, and student learning is supported
Appropriate level of student effort	Educators adjust their teaching and assessing
Appropriate environment for learning	The environment is accessible and encourages learning for all

Source: Based on CEC, 2005.

something while also having that information available in writing to students. Multiple means of engagement refers to students actively choosing how they participate with the material they are learning, such as by using concrete or virtual manipulatives or working individually or in small groups. Finally, multiple means of expression indicates there is more than one way to express or show what one has learned. For example, one student might write a paper while another student creates a poster and a third a video depicting his or her understanding of a class novel.

UDL involves providing *all* students access to learning by promoting options and choice in how they engage in their learning, how they express learning, and how the information to be learned is presented. A key element is the choice provided to students as well as making the choices available to *all* students, rather than applying them as accommodations to individual students.

Assistive technology and UDL are closely related. While using assistive technology in and of itself does not ensure that UDL is being implemented, technology does play a large role in providing UDL. In other words, technology, such as assistive technology, can provide many options for allowing educators to provide multiple means of representation, engagement, and expression. Yet assistive technology is typically considered for an individual student to enable him/her to maintain, improve, or increase in his/her functional capabilities—including but not limited to academics—and assistive technology decision-making is done via a team, such as the IEP team. UDL, on the other hand, is implemented by a teacher through his/her own initiative or that of the local education agency. UDL is focused on providing accessibility for a wide range of students through providing multiple options. UDL is not focused on a particular student but the entire learning environment (Rose et al., 2005; Messinger-Willman & Marino, 2010).

To illustrate the distinction, consider the following scenario. Mr. Nowak and Ms. Lang are both teachers of the same content area in the same secondary school and both have inclusive classrooms. In both classrooms, there is at least one student with a disability whose IEP includes text-to-speech or supported eText as an assistive technology supplementary aid. Ms. Lang allows the student whose IEP includes read-aloud accommodations via technology to use the technology as needed relative to reading, such as using Natural Reader to read materials on the computer as well as the Reading Pen to read printed textbooks when the digital version and the reader are not convenient. In contrast, Mr. Nowak seeks a grant to purchase multiple Reading Pens and makes them available during class. He also secured Natural Reader as well as a few other text-to-speech options on the three computers in his classroom. Mr. Nowak allows his students to select the method in which they wish to engage in their in-class reading, such as through technology (e.g., Reading Pens, text-to-speech software on the computers), reading with a peer, or reading to oneself. Mr. Nowak is implementing UDL to reduce the barriers to learning for all students and encouraging choice; Ms. Lang is implementing an IEP as written in accordance with the law.

UDL implementation can look different in different settings or contexts, and UDL implementation can be challenging. Knowing what UDL is and knowing how to implement UDL are two very different things. However, there are resources available to help educators implement UDL in their practice. For example, the National Center on Universal Design for Learning provides guidelines and checkpoints for the three major principles of UDL. Within each checkpoint of each guideline for each of the three principles (e.g., multiple means of representation, engagement, and expression), the UDL Center provides examples for implementation (see Table 1.5 for a sample from the center's website). The center also provides access to toolkits to aid in implementation and free online modules on UDL. In addition, the Center for Applied Special Technologies offers learning tools that support UDL implementation in classrooms (see Table 1.6 and http://www.cast.org/learningtools/index.html). These learning tools are both for students (e.g., UDL Book Builder) as well as for educators (e.g., UDL Exchange).

Table 1.5 Sample National Center on Universal Design for Learning Implementation Examples

Principle 1: Multiple means of representation	Guideline 1: Provide options for language, mathematical expressions, and symbols	Checkpoint 2.5: Illustrate through multiple media	Examples: Virtual manipulatives through National Council of Teachers of Mathematics Illuminations; online museums, Wordle;

Source: Adapted from National Center for Universal Design for Learning (http://www.udlcenter.org/implementation/examples/examples2_5) © CAST, Inc. 2012

Table 1.6 UDL Resources

Resource	Description	Website
UDL Implementation Examples	Examples of tools to support implementation	http://www.udlcenter.org/implementation/examples
UDL Toolkits	Open-source software for creating and developing web content following the principles of UDL	http://udl-toolkit.cast.org/home
CAST UDL Online Module	Two free modules explaining UDL	http://udlonline.cast.org/home
UDL Studio	Users create or use others' UDL projects	http://udlstudio.cast.org/
UDL Exchange	Educators create and share instructional resources for implementing UDL	http://udlexchange.cast.org/home
UDL Curriculum Toolkit	Educators develop web-based curriculum following UDL	http://udl-toolkit.cast.org/home
UDL Curriculum Self-Check	Educators can check to see if their curriculum follows UDL principles	http://udlselfcheck.cast.org/
UDL Book Builder	Digital books using UDL principles	http://bookbuilder.cast.org/
CAST Science Writer	Online science lab and class writing support tool	http://sciencewriter.cast.org/
UDL Editions	Supports students accessing text through digital media and scaffolds	http://udleditions.cast.org/
CAST Strategy Tutor	Supports students researching online	http://cst.cast.org/cst/auth-login
iSolveIt	iPad apps to develop logical thinking and reasoning skills based on UDL	http://isolveit.cast.org/home

Source: Adapted from http://www.cast.org/learningtools/

Perspectives of Assistive Technology in This Textbook

Although one cannot predict the future for assistive technology, there are trends in technology in general that assistive technology is likely to follow. For example, everyday technology is becoming more mobile, smaller, faster, and personalized

(Bolkan, 2012). Assistive technology is also following suit. Increasingly, mobile tablet or smartphone apps are devoted to individuals with disabilities, special education, and assistive technology. One can search iTunes, Android apps, or even Chrome apps for any of these terms and find hundreds of apps, ranging from free to hundreds of dollars. Mobile tablets and apps are likely to be increasingly used in the education of students with disabilities. This textbook will showcase mobile technologies and their apps to help current and future educators have the most up-to-date information possible. However, one technology (i.e., mobile technologies and their apps) does not revolutionize education and will not be the answer to everything. While this textbook will discuss apps for mobile devices as well as Web 2.0 technologies educators can use, it will also focus on low-tech and mid-tech technologies that do not require computers or mobile devices. A key principle in assistive technology is to start low-tech and then consider more advanced or sophisticated technology. Please remember that technology is great, but it is not the solution to every problem, and assistive technology devices must be carefully selected, as we will discuss in Chapter 2.

Mobile Devices and Apps

Given the focus in and out of schools today on mobile technologies and apps, they will be presented as assistive technology and technology considerations throughout this textbook. However, we feel that successful use of apps for mobile devices begins with educators thinking critically about the apps they are or may be using and determining if they are not only worth the cost but also if they provide the experiences or learning they want students to achieve. While free apps can be great for cash-strapped educators, you may get what you pay for in terms of experiences. On the other hand, there is not necessarily a correlation between the cost of an app and the app's quality. We strongly encourage educators to not just perform a search on Google or another search engine for "apps for autism" or "reading apps" or even to just accept the education or special education lists on iTunes or Google Play for Android. Instead, we encourage educators to scrutinize the apps they are considering. While a standard rubric or model does not exist for evaluating apps for students in general—or students with disabilities specifically—options do exist. We encourage educators to visit the blog Learning in Hand with Tony Vincent (see http://learninginhand.com/blog/ways-to-evaluate-educational-apps.html) to explore the different rubrics available and select one they feel they can use for making decisions regarding apps or other software. Or educators may select to use the Apps Consideration Checklist (TAM, 2012), available from the publication *Apps for All Students* (2012) from the Technology and Media Division (TAM) of the Council for Exceptional Children (see Tammaro & Jerome, 2012). A sample app evaluation rubric is also provided in Figure 1.2 by Harry Walker (2010).

Figure 1.2 App Evaluation Rubric

Evaluation Rubric for iPod Apps

Domain	1	2	3	4
Curriculum Connection	Skill(s) reinforced in the app are not clearly connected to the targeted skill or concept	Skill(s) reinforced are prerequisite or foundation skills for the targeted skill or concept	Skill(s) reinforced are related to the targeted skill or concept	Skill(s) reinforced are strongly connected to the targeted skill or concept
Authenticity	Skills are practiced in a rote or isolated fashion (e.g., flashcards)	Skills are practiced in a contrived game/simulation format	Some aspects of the app are presented in an authentic learning environment	Targeted skills are practiced in an authentic format/problem-based learning environment
Feedback	Feedback is limited to correctness of student responses	Feedback is limited to correctness of student responses and may allow for student to try again	Feedback is specific and results in improved student performance (may include tutorial aids)	Feedback is specific and results in improved student performance; Data is student performance; Data is available electronically to student and teacher
Differentiation	App offers no flexibility (settings cannot be altered)	App offers limited flexibility (e.g., few levels such as easy, medium, hard)	App offers more than one degree of flexibility to adjust settings to meet student needs	App offers complete flexibility to alter settings to meet student needs
User Friendliness	Students need constant teacher supervision in order to use the app	Students need to have the teacher review how to the use the app on more than one occasion	Students need to have the teacher review how to use the app	Students can launch and navigate within the app independently
Student Motivation	Students avoid the use of the app or complain when the app is assigned by the teacher	Students view the app as "more schoolwork"and may be off-task when directed by the teacher to use the app	Students will use the app as directed by the teacher	Students are highly motivated to use the app and select it as their first choice from a selection of related choices of apps

Source: Adapted from "Evaluation Rubric for iPod Apps," by H. Walker, 2010. Retrieved from http://learninginhand.com/blog/evaluation-rubric-for-educational-apps.html. Copyright 2010 by Harry Walker.

KEY TERMS

accessible instructional
   materials, p. 14

assistive technology
   device, p. 2

assistive technology
   service, p. 3

assistive technology
   specialist, p. 4

educational technology, p. 1

print disabilities, p. 14

related service, p. 4

EXTENSION ACTIVITIES

- Have students complete the IRIS Center Module on Assistive Technology (http://iris .peabody.vanderbilt.edu/module/at/)

- Show in class—or have students watch individually outside of class—the video from Don Johnston Incorporated on YouTube titled "The Case Against Assistive Technology" (see https://www.youtube .com/watch?v=lNs88Ki1WSo). Engage in a discussion regarding what are the barriers to assistive technology implementation in schools and how educators can overcome those barriers. Engage in an open discussion regarding the assumptions or misconceptions regarding assistive technology (e.g., unfair, cheating) and if these are valid arguments.

- Show in class—or have students watch individually outside of class—the video from Edutopia titled "How Assistive Technology Enables Dreams" (see http://www.edutopia .org/assistive-technology-enabling-dreams-video). What assistive technology was shown in the video? And what benefits did that assistive technology provide to the students with disabilities?

- Show in class—or have students watch individually outside of class—the following video produced by a state technology center titled "Understanding Assistive Technology: Simply Said" (see http://bit.ly/1e4SFd8). After students have explored their own state options, discuss what resources and supports they can get as educators—or their students may be able to get as individuals—from such statewide programs.

- Outside of class, have students select a UDL learning tool from CAST (see http:// www.cast.org/learningtools/; UDL Book Builder, CAST Science Writer). Have students register and explore the tool they selected. Students can share their reactions and perceptions of the UDL learning tool in a face-to-face discussion or via an online discussion.

APPLICATION ACTIVITIES

- As mentioned in the text, each state has an Assistive Technology Act Program; a list of state programs with links can be found on the RESNA Catalyst Project website (see http://www.resnaprojects.org/allcontacts/ statewidecontacts.html).

Find your state's program and explore its website. What services or supports does it offer to individuals? To preK–12 educators?

- In addition to Assistive Technology Act Programs, states may also offer statewide projects focused on assistive technology and/or accessible instructional materials focused directly on K–12 public schools. For example, PATINS (http://www.patinsproject .com/) supports the state of Indiana and MiTS (http://mits.cenmi.org/) the state of Michigan. Search and find your state's project. (See, for example, state information from the National Center on Accessible Instructional Materials [http://aim.cast .org/learn/policy/state#.U_3aQUh2naG] or State Leaders of Assistive Technology in Education [http://www.slatenetwork.org/ view.php?nav_id=4], and determine what services and supports it offers both in terms of direct resources as well as professional development.)

- The *Journal of Special Education Technology* (JSET) (see http://www.tamcec.org/jset/) is the journal of the Division of Technology and Media of the Council for Exceptional Children. It publishes research related to technology (e.g., assistive technology) for students with disabilities. Determine if your school or university has an electronic or hard-copy subscription to JSET and find a recent article. Read the article and discuss with your class recent research regarding assistive technology for students with disabilities.

- Visit the website Learning in Hand with Tony Vincent (see http://learninginhand.com/blog/ ways-to-evaluate-educational-apps.html), and explore the different rubrics for making decisions regarding apps. Then, select an app that you might consider using for students with disabilities in any fashion (e.g., mathematics, reading, social-emotional development, social skills) from your app store (iTunes or Android apps)—it can be a free app—and evaluate it using the rubric you selected.

DISCUSSION QUESTIONS

1. What is an example of a low-tech assistive technology? A medium- or mid-tech assistive technology? A high-tech assistive technology? What makes an assistive technology low-tech versus high-tech?

2. What is the federal legislation definition of an assistive technology device? Interpret that definition for everyday use. What makes something assistive technology?

3. What are examples of assistive technology services under the federal legislation definition?

4. What changes were made in the reauthorization of the Individuals with Disabilities Education Act in 2004 regarding assistive technology?

5. What are some current challenges with assistive technology, and how might those challenges be overcome?

6. What are the three main principles of UDL, and how can a teacher implement those in a classroom?

RESOURCES/ADDITIONAL INFORMATION

Please consider the following websites for additional information or resources.

- Wisconsin Assistive Technology Initiative—Free Publications (http://wati.org/?page Load=content/supports/free/index.php)

- National Center on Technology Innovation (http://www.nationaltechcenter.org/)

- The National Center on Accessible Information Technology in Education (AccessIT) (http://www.washington.edu/accessit/)

- The QIAT Consortium (http://www.qiat.org/indicators.html)

- Watch in class, or have students individually watch outside of class, the following presentation by Dr. David Rose from CAST titled "Dr. David Rose on Universal Design for Learning" (see https://www.youtube.com/watch?v=yETe92mwoUE). While the video can be watched in it entirety, the first 12 minutes of the video explain UDL nicely.

- The National Center on Universal Design for Learning has a channel on YouTube that provides multiple videos that give examples of what UDL looks like in the classroom (see http://bit.ly/1J4UFiO)

SUGGESTED ENRICHMENT READINGS

- Edyburn, D. L. (2013). Critical issues in advancing the special education technology evidence-base. *Exceptional Children, 80*, 7–24.

- Petcu, S. D., Yell, M., & Fletcher, T. (2014). Assistive technology: Legislation and legal issues. *Exceptionality, 22*, 226–236.

- Readings identified by Dr. Dave L. Edyburn as the best of article of the year from 2004–2014 (see https://pantherfile.uwm.edu/edyburn/www/what/best.html).

(Assistive) Technology Frameworks

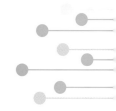

Chapter 2 presents frameworks, guides, and assessments relative to assistive technology decision-making. In particular, Chapter 2 will present specific frameworks for assistive technology consideration (e.g., the University of Kentucky Assistive Technology Project Toolkit), frameworks for decision-making (e.g., the SETT framework), and assistive technology assessments (e.g., Functional Evaluation of Assistive Technology). In addition, Chapter 2 will discuss assistive technology relative to the IEP. Chapter 2 will also present the TPACK and TAPE frameworks for assistive technology.

As discussed in Chapter 1, assistive technology can benefit students with disabilities. Assistive technology can enable them with greater access and success as well as increased independence. But, as alluded to in Chapter 1, selecting the right assistive technology for a student is important. Chapter 2 will discuss assistive technology decision-making, different strategies for making such decisions, and who needs to be involved in the decision-making process. In addition, assistive technology assessments will be discussed. The chapter will conclude with information on TPACK and repurposing technology to be assistive technology.

Assistive technology decision-making, like all decision-making relevant to the programming of a student identified with an IDEA disability, is typically made by the **individualized education program** (IEP) team. The law specifies the following individuals are to be members of a student's IEP team and must attend IEP meetings, unless their attendance is excused in writing by the parents and the school: a student's parents or

chapter Objectives

After reading the chapter, the reader will be able to do the following:

1. Explain the role of an assistive technology specialist

2. Identify different frameworks for assistive technology decision-making

3. Identify different guides to assistive technology decision-making

4. Identify different assistive technology assessments

guardian; at least one special education teacher; at least one general education teacher; a representative from the local education agency (LEA) who can commit the district to the services agreed upon; an individual to interpret any evaluations (e.g., school psychologist); and the student, as appropriate (Yell, 2012). Related service providers (e.g., speech and language therapists, occupational therapists, including **assistive technology specialists**, and/or individuals with expertise in assistive technology) can attend as needed but are not required (Yell, 2012).

An assistive technology specialist is a trained individual focused on providing assistive technology services. Specifically, an assistive technology specialist may assess a student's needs, secure the technology, train the student and others on the technology, consult with teachers and other educators with respect to the use of assistive technology, and monitor the technology implementation. In other words, the assistive technology specialist can be an individual specifically focused on assistive technology considerations and services for students with all disabilities. However, assistive technology decision-making is a team decision. While an assistive technology specialist (i.e., someone on the IEP team specifically devoted to assistive technology) might be ideal, such roles do not exist in every LEA. When IEP teams do not include an assistive technology specialist, other team members can fill that role, including special education teachers, instructional technologists, speech-and-language pathologists, and occupational therapists (Edyburn, 2004; Marino, Marino, & Shaw, 2006; Reed & Bowser, 2012).

Parents are important members of IEP teams and, by law, schools are to meaningfully involve them in the development of their child's educational programming, including issues of assistive technology decision-making (Yell, 2012). Given that some assistive technology devices travel from school to home and back to school, parental/family acceptance, parental/family willingness to implement at home, and family resources are factors in assistive technology decision-making (Parette, VanBiervliet, & Hourcade, 2000).

Assistive Technology Decision-Making

Assistive technology decision-making involves many steps. First, assistive technology needs to be considered, then an assessment should occur, followed by selecting, implementing, and evaluating. As discussed in Chapter 1, each IEP team is responsible for considering assistive technology for *each* student with a disability (Quinn et al., 2009). This means that regardless of a student's IDEA disability category, the IEP team must consider if s/he would benefit from assistive technology services or devices.

Assistive technology decision-making can be a daunting process for an IEP team, even with an assistive technology specialist. However, without an assistive technology specialist, IEP teams typically rely on special education teachers or related service providers (Marino et al., 2006). To help IEP teams meet the federal mandate regarding assistive technology considerations for *all* students with disabilities, as well as aid in making the best decisions to benefit students with disabilities, different tools exist: frameworks, guides (i.e., toolkits), and assessments for decision-making (see Table 2.1 for information on resources

Table 2.1   Resources for Assistive Technology Decision-Making

Decision-Making Guide/ Framework/Assessments	Resources
Guides	
University of Kentucky Assistive Technology Toolkit	http://natri.uky.edu/assoc_projects/ukat2/at_intro/IntroToAT.pdf
	Follows the Unifying Functional (Human Function) Model
	(Downloadable documents to assist in assistive technology decision-making)
National Assistive Technology Research Institute, Assistive Technology Planner	http://natri.uky.edu/atPlannermenu.html
	http://www.tamcec.org/publications/planning-tools/
	(Downloadable and able to purchase, respectively, a kit to make assistive technology decisions)
EdTech Points	http://www.educationtechpoints.org/manuals-materials/education-tech-points-manual (Manual can be purchased)
Assessments	
Assistive Technology Assessments and Decision-Making	http://www.wati.org/?pageLoad=content/supports/free/index.php
	http://sped.dpi.wi.gov/sped_at-wati-forms-fillable
	(Downloadable documents to assist in assistive technology decision-making and assessments from the WATI)
Functional Evaluation for Assistive Technology	http://www.nprinc.com/the-feat-functional-evaluation-for-assistive-technology/
	(Assessment for purchase)
Frameworks	
Student, Environment, Tasks, and Tools (SETT)	http://www.joyzabala.com/Documents.html
	(Downloadable documents to assist in implementing the SETT framework)
Matching Person and Technology	http://www.matchingpersonandtechnology.com/mptdesc.html
	(Online sample assessment items; full one can be purchased)

Source: Adapted from *Special Education in Contemporary Society: An Introduction to Exceptionality* (5th ed.) by R. M. Gargiulo, 2015. Copyright 2015 by SAGE Publications.

related to the different assistive technology frameworks, guides, and assessments) (Edyburn, 2001; Jones & Hinesman-Matthews, 2014).

UKAT Toolkit. The University of Kentucky Assistive Technology (UKAT) Toolkit provides forms to help guide assistive technology decision-making; the decision-making team, from the UKAT perspective, may or may not be the IEP team. The UKAT Toolkit includes downloadable forms (i.e., tools) that support decision-making teams in considering, selecting, assessing, and evaluating (see http://natri.uky.edu/assoc_projects/ukat2/at_intro/IntroToAT.pdf). UKAT recommends starting with the consideration tool, which specifies team members and identifies demands (i.e., tasks expected of the student) relative to seven functional areas (i.e., daily living; communication; body support, protection, and positioning; travel and mobility; environmental interaction; education and transition; and sports, fitness, and recreation). Next, is the preassessment profile tool, in which the team considers the individual student and his/her personal resources and external supports relative to behavior, communication, education foundations, academics, health/medical, physical, and sensory. In addition, a preassessment summary is written for each demand (i.e., task or function) that is a priority for the student (UKAT, 2002b).

The UKAT Assessment Planning and Data Collection tool guides decision-making teams through assistive technology assessment. Once completed, the decision-making team can use the Assessment Report Outline tool to guide their report writing; here the decision-making team can make recommendations for assistive technology. UKAT next recommends a trial implementation (see Trial Implementation tool) of the recommended assistive technology prior to a final recommendation. For the trial implementation, data should be collected to assess the implementation and provide feedback. Based on data collection, revised recommendations can be made. Finally, after the assistive technology is written into a student's IEP, the AT Implementation tool guides implementation. The tool provides a checklist for activities to be completed relative to the selected assistive technology (e.g., training), as well as space for monitoring the implemented technology (UKAT, 2002b). The UKAT Toolkit also includes a Knowledge and Skills Survey that is a self-rating tool for educators, parents, or students to assess one's expertise in different areas relative to assistive technology.

National Assistive Technology Research Institute, Assistive Technology Planner. The National Assistive Technology Research Institute (NATRI) produced an assistive technology planner (see http://natri.uky.edu) (Bausch, Ault, & Hasselbring, 2006). The purchased planner includes the implementation form as well as three booklets discussing assistive technology from IEP consideration to classroom implementation. One booklet is for teachers, one for administrators, and one for parents. The booklets describe each player's role in planning and implementing assistive technology as well as explaining assistive technology and how assistive technology devices and tools should be matched with each individual student. The teacher and administrator booklets also discuss developing the assistive technology implementation plan and then monitoring and evaluating the plan. The implementation plan form from NATRI can be used by IEP teams to record assistive technology devices and tools as well the training needed relative to these devices and how they will be implemented across different settings (i.e., school and home) (Bausch & Ault, 2008). The assistive technology planner can be purchased or the implementation form from the planner can be downloaded for free from the institute's website.

Chambers Consideration Model. The Chambers (1997) model of assistive technology consideration was produced on behalf of a joint effort of two Council for Exceptional Children (CEC) divisions: the Council of Administrators of Special Education (CASE) and Technology and Media Division (TAM). Chambers's model provides a flowchart for assistive technology consideration (see http://files.eric.ed.gov/fulltext/ED439561.pdf). The flowchart highlights questions decision-making teams need to answer as well as decisions that must be made. The Chambers' model advocated for the SETT Framework, which will be discussed later in the chapter.

Education Tech Points. Education Tech Points is an assistive technology decision-making framework by Bowser and Reed (1995). The Education Tech Points System is a series of questions that help decision-making teams understand when assistive technology should be addressed. The updated EdTech Points Manual (Bowser & Reed, 2012) guides decision-making teams through an assistive technology process; the process can be used with an individual child or as a whole-school approach. Decision-making teams answer questions and engage in discussions to determine if an assistive technology device or service is needed at seven points: consideration and referral, evaluation, trial period, plan development, implementation, periodic review, and transition for a student with a disability. Additional information on the EdTEch Points Approach can be found at its website (http://www.educationtechpoints.org/) or through its blog (http://www.educationtechpoints.org/manuals-materials).

Assistive Technology Assessments

In the assistive technology decision-making process, an IEP team needs to determine through an assistive technology assessment if a student would benefit from assistive technology. While assistive technology assessments may be typically conducted by an assistive technology specialist, as previously noted, access to these individuals may not always exist within a school or LEA.

Assistive technology assessments—like all assessments—should be multifaceted; one piece of data or information alone should not be used to base decisions. Assistive technology assessments include direct observations, interviews, and formal assessments. Direct observations include observing a student in his or her school settings. More than just one observation should be used, and the different observations should occur at different times and in different settings. Interviews can occur with students as well as parents or family members and the educators interacting with the student. A few formal assistive technology assessments do exist, such as the Functional Evaluation of Assistive Technology (FEAT; Raskind & Bryant, 2002).

Functional Evaluation for Assistive Technology. The formal assistive technology assessment Functional Evaluation for Assistive Technology (Raskind & Bryant, 2002) is an ecological assessment of a student's assistive technology needs. FEAT is five scales: Contextual Matching Inventory, Checklist of Strengths and Limitations, Checklist of Technology Experiences, Technology Characteristics Inventory, and Individual-Technology Evaluation Scale (Wissick & Gardner, 2008). FEAT focuses on an individual student, his/her tasks or functions, his/her contexts, and aspects of a device. FEAT is a for-purchase formal (i.e., validated, reliable, standardized) assessment.

Wisconsin Assistive Technology Initiative. The Wisconsin Assistive Technology Initiative (WATI) process for assistive technology assessment encompasses the SETT Framework (see http://www.wati.org/content/supports/ free/pdf/Ch1-ATAssessment.pdf) (Reed & Gierach, 2009). The WATI assistive technology assessment involves an in-depth exploration of a student's abilities and needs relative to WATI's 11 tasks: seating, positioning, and mobility; communication; computer access; motor aspects of writing; composition of written material; reading; mathematics; organization; recreation and leisure; vision; and hearing (Gierach, 2009). The assessment also guides decision-making teams to consider an individual student's abilities and difficulties within their environments and their tasks. The team then determines priority tasks (i.e., the most pressing or important areas to address) and generates solutions. The team selects a solution and develops an implementation plan. Once an implementation plan is developed, the selected solutions (i.e., assistive technology, ranging from no-tech to high-tech) are implemented on a trial basis, and those trials are reviewed to determine any necessary changes before a permanent plan is crafted (Gierach, 2009). When making assistive technology recommendations, the IEP team may consider using the Assistive Technology Checklist produced by WATI (see http://www.wati.org/content/supports/free/pdf/form/Checklist-Form.pdf). The checklist, although a bit outdated, suggests assistive technology devices and tools along the continuum of low tech to high tech (Gierach, 2009).

Assistive Technology Frameworks

Assistive technology frameworks, like guides, can assist IEP teams in the selection of assistive technology devices and services. In addition to frameworks, additional tools or resources exist and are also used to help educators consider different device and service options. It is important to note that often the frameworks do not start with a presumption of a particular technology but rather are meant to help teams understand different individual and environmental factors before determining assistive technology devices.

SETT. Although there are multiple decision-making guides or toolkits to assist with assistive technology decision-making, one of the most well known is the SETT Framework by Zabala (1995; 2005); SETT stands for students, environments, tasks, and tools. The SETT Framework focuses on assistive technology decision-making that considers not just the student but also his/her environment (i.e., setting) and tasks within that environment that s/he needs to perform. In other words, IEP teams using this framework consider the student's needs, strengths, challenges, and preferences. If a student does not prefer an assistive technology tool, s/he may not use it, and hence, assistive technology **abandonment** might occur. The student's environment must also be evaluated, with environment broadly defined as a student's classroom and all settings s/he might access throughout the day (e.g., cafeteria, community-based settings). The focus on the environment is not just the physical setting and its resources but also attitudes within that environment. An analysis of tasks is then what activities are occurring within the environments, as it is important for IEP teams to consider what the student is expected to do. The tasks should be concretely articulated so they are specific to the student in question and his/her environments. The last area of consideration when applying the SETT framework is the tools, or technology. Once an IEP team understands the student, his/her environment, and the tasks for that student, they are ready to consider what assistive technologies might be appropriate. On her website, Joy Zabala makes available different scaffolds, or forms, for helping IEP teams use the SETT Framework for considering assistive technology for students with disabilities as well as making assistive technology decisions.

Raymond is a seventh-grade student identified with a learning disability in mathematics and struggles with computation. He struggles to remember his basic facts as well as perform computations on demand. Raymond is in general education classes, except for a resource room period in which he receives assistance with mathematics, including preteaching, reteaching, or allowing extra time as needed. Raymond's seventh-grade mathematics class focuses on the application of mathematical ideas, especially as it relates to algebra and understanding proportions and linear equations. He is expected to compute his basic facts and to have the answers ready to apply to the more complicated mathematics the class is working on. Raymond is self-conscious about being in special education and does not want to stand out from his classmates.

At this IEP meeting, the IEP team, including Raymond, applies the SETT Framework to considering assistive technology. They consider his strengths (technology, reading, making friends) as well as his needs (support in computation and basic facts). They also consider his environments, especially relative to his mathematics class. The mathematics teacher does

iStock/monkeybusinessimages

not emphasize calculators, and they are frequently not available within the classroom. However, the school does have a policy that allows students to carry their phones with them in class. The IEP team also considers tasks that Raymond is often asked to do in his mathematics class, including reading problems, attending to the discussion, and independently calculating answers. And finally, they consider different technology that matches Raymond, his setting, and tasks.

During the meeting, the IEP team considers a scientific or graphing calculator, but Raymond expresses hesitation since other students do not actively use them. Given that the teacher and school allow cell phones, the IEP team explores different calculator-based apps that Raymond could use on his smartphone. The IEP team writes a calculator or calculator app into Raymond's IEP as an accommodation in mathematics and science classes. After the meeting, the special education teacher and Raymond install a few different calculator apps on his phone and allow him to try them out in his classes. After a week, Raymond and his special education teacher meet again and determine that the app to best meet his needs is the My Script Calculator app, which allows him to write the problem on his phone with his finger.

Matching Person and Technology Framework. The Matching Person and Technology (MPT) Framework is closely related to the SETT Framework for assistive technology decision-making (Scherer & Craddock, 2002), although it is used more for adults and by rehabilitation counselors than in preK–12 schools. The MPT focuses on matching the assistive technology device or tool with the individual, considering an individual's strengths or capabilities, needs or goals, preferences, psychosocial characteristics (e.g., self-esteem and self-determination), and expected benefits of the tool (Scherer & Craddock, 2002).

Adaptations Framework. Another framework for considering and selecting assistive technology is the Adaptations Framework proposed by Bryant and Bryant (1998). The framework involves examining setting-specific demands, student- or individual-specific demands, and then the technology itself. Under setting-specific demands, teams consider the specific settings a student may be in and then determine the tasks a student faces in those settings and skills needed to perform those tasks. For example, in an elementary school classroom, a task might be reading a textbook; the specific skills for reading include accessing the text, decoding, comprehending, and reading fluently (Bryant & Bryant, 2012). For student-specific demands, the student's functional capabilities and limitations are examined relative to the setting-specific demands of the tasks and requisite skills. For the above example, the student's cognitive (e.g., reading), sensory (e.g., visual), language (e.g., listening), and motor (e.g., fine) capabilities are determined. Likewise, the student's limitations in these same areas are examined relative to the tasks and requisite skills (Bryant & Bryant, 1998, 2012).

The decision-making team (i.e., the IEP team) then considers the technology that matches with the setting-specific and student-specific demands. Specifically, the team can consider the features of the technology as well as the attitudes and acceptance of the students of the particular technology (Bryant & Bryant, 2012). It is important the IEP teams consider the features of a particular device when making selections. For example, if a student frequently moves to different classrooms, the portability of the device is an important consideration. The features need to be ones that are accessible and usable by the student based on his/her functional capabilities. In addition, given that most assistive technology costs money, IEP teams will want to consider the reliability and durability of a particular device. A student must be willing to actually use the technology; hence, the student's attitude toward the technology is important to gauge. As previously stated, if a student is not willing to use a particular device, assistive technology abandonment can occur. Note that having students try out a device before it is finally selected is a good way for decision-making teams to determine if the features match a particular student and if the student is willing to use the particular technology. See Chapter 1 for information on state assistive technology lending programs.

Unifying Functional Model. The Unifying Functional Model (Melichar & Blackhurst, 1993) is another assistive technology decision-making framework; it is also referred to as the Human Function Model (UKAT, 2002a; Watts, O'Brian, & Wojcik, 2004). The Unifying Functional Model is a complex model that involves examining the interrelationships among a number of different elements (see the NATRI at http://natri.uky.edu/resources/reports/function. html for the schematic depicting the Unifying Functional Model). With this model, decision-making for assistive technology involves considering a student's environments and contexts and the demands placed on the student within those as well as external supports, personal resources, and personal supports (Wissick & Gardner, 2008). The Unifying Functional (or Human Function) Model is the framework that is underlying both the National Assistive Technology Research Institute's (2006) *Assistive Technology Planner: From IEP Consideration to Classroom Implementation* (see http://natri.uky.edu/atPlannermenu.html) as well as the University of Kentucky Assistive Technology Toolkit (see http://natri.uky .edu/assoc_projects/ukat2/at_intro/IntroToAT.pdf).

TPACK. While not an assistive technology framework, the Technological Pedagogical and Content Knowledge (TPACK) Framework can be applied to assistive technology decision-making. TPACK stems from Lee Shulman's (1986, 1987) original Pedagogical Content Knowledge (PCK), which suggested teachers need both pedagogy (how to teach) and content (what to teach) knowledge. Mishra and Koehler (2009) and Koehler and Mishra (2009) extended PCK to include technology, given the increasing role of technology in education. While

TPACK can be both a technology decision-making tool and a teacher preparation framework, in this book we are focused on the decision-making aspect. Within TPACK, technology is not an afterthought, nor is it where one starts when thinking about implementing technology. With TPACK, the team first needs to consider the pedagogical approach (P) to teaching and the content (C) teachers are delivering. Decisions about technology occur at the intersection of one's content and pedagogical approach for delivering that particular content (see Figure 2.1). In addition, critical for understanding TPACK and using TPACK to make technology decisions is understanding one's context; different contexts (e.g., two computer labs for an entire elementary school versus a one-to-one laptop program) mediate technology decisions (Koehler & Mishra, 2009; Mishra & Koehler, 2009).

While not to detract from the individualized nature of assistive technology considerations for students with disabilities, consistent with federal law

Figure 2.1 TPACK

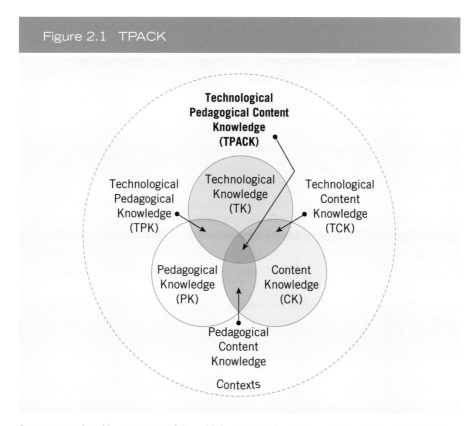

(i.e., IDEA, 2004), using the TPACK Framework supports assistive technology decision-making by encouraging team members to see the connection between technology and teaching and learning. In other words, using TPACK, IEP teams can consider what assistive technologies will help a student to access or learn the content as well as what works within a particular theoretical orientation of how a student learns. Viewed differently, the TPACK Framework can be applied to assistive technology decision-making by viewing the content as what an IEP team wants a student to be able to do and pedagogy as how they want the student do to it. In addition, with TPACK, IEP teams must understand the context that impacts technology implementation. While resources (i.e., what is available in the LEA [local education agency] or cost) cannot guide assistive technology decision-making, understanding context can help IEP teams consider and select devices and services. As discussed in the Adaptations Framework, the context may include different settings (e.g., classroom, lunchroom, community), and hence, for example portability, is important in an assistive technology device.

The TAPE Framework. From the TPACK Framework, educators are encouraged to adapt, reuse, and repurpose technology to be educational technology (Mishra & Koehler, 2009). The idea of repurposing—using a technology for its otherwise unintended purpose—can also be applied to assistive technology. Bouck and colleagues (Bouck, Flanagan, Miller, & Bassette, 2012; Bouck, Jasper, Bassette, Shurr, & Miller, 2013; Bouck, Shurr, et al., 2012) suggested taking everyday technology and using it as assistive technology. Repurposing common, socially desired technology as assistive technology can help combat the stigmatization, training, cost, and disconnect between the technology students with disabilities use outside of school and the technology they use in school. For example, an iPad can be repurposed as an augmentative and alternative communication device for students with complex communication needs; a Livescribe™ Smartpen can assist a student with note-taking by collecting audio as well as written notes; and clickers (i.e., student response systems) can be used for students to self-monitor their on-task behavior (Bouck, Flanagan, et al., 2012; Bouck et al., 2013; Bouck, Shurr, et al., 2012). Bouck and colleagues suggested the TAPE Framework for evaluating if a technology was a good candidate to be repurposed as assistive technology. The TAPE Framework stands for transportable, available, practical, and engaging (see Figure 2.2 for a think sheet for applying TAPE to everyday technology).

To use the TAPE Framework, an educator or IEP team would evaluate everyday technology based on its qualities relative to transportability, ease of access, practicality, and potential for engagement. For example, an audio recorder is a low-tech piece of everyday technology that can be repurposed to support students

Student support need: _____

TECHNOLOGY	Transportable					Accessible					Practical					Engaging				
	Can be used in different locations and for different purposes					Readily available online, in schools, or in stores					Easy to set up and use, realistic cost					Desirable, interactive, decreased stigma, socially acceptable				
	low		high			low		high			low		high			low		high		
1.)	1	2	3	4	5	1	2	3	4	5	1	2	3	4	5	1	2	3	4	5
notes																				
2.)	1	2	3	4	5	1	2	3	4	5	1	2	3	4	5	1	2	3	4	5
notes																				
3.)	1	2	3	4	5	1	2	3	4	5	1	2	3	4	5	1	2	3	4	5
notes																				
4.)	1	2	3	4	5	1	2	3	4	5	1	2	3	4	5	1	2	3	4	5
notes																				
5.)	1	2	3	4	5	1	2	3	4	5	1	2	3	4	5	1	2	3	4	5
notes																				

Final repurposed technology recommendation and why:

Source: Bouck, E. C., Jasper, A., Bassette, L., Shurr, J., & Miller, B. (2013). Applying TAPE: Rethinking assistive technology for students with physical disabilities, multiple disabilities, and other health impairment. Physical Disabilities Research & Practice, 32(1), 31–54. Reproduced with permission

with intellectual disability in acquiring independence in grocery shopping (Bouck, Satsangi, Bartlett, & Muhl, 2013; Bouck, Satsangi, Bartlett, & Weng, 2012). An audio recorder is highly transportable as it is small and is made to be portable (i.e., a rating of 5 under transportable in Figure 2.2). An audio recorder is also easy to access as one can purchase it online or from any major office supply store and at a low cost (i.e., a rating of 5 for accessible). The low cost and ease of training to use an audio recorder also supports its practical aspect (i.e., a rating of 5 for practical). Finally, while an audio recorder may not be as socially desirable compared to an smartphone or iPad, it is more socially desirable than using picture symbols to grocery shop for high school students and adults with intellectual disability. In addition, an audio recorder is small and hardly noticeable in school or community settings (i.e., a rating of 3 for engaging) (see Bouck, Jasper, et al., 2013, for the application of TAPE to other repurposed everyday technologies).

In applying the TAPE Framework to practice, Bouck and colleagues (Bouck, Satsangi, et al., 2012, 2013) used audio recorders to support high school students with intellectual disability in independent grocery shopping. Used in contrast to picture symbols or written grocery lists, Bouck, Satsangi, et al. (2012, 2013) found audio recorders were more effective for helping students identify items than written lists but slightly less effective than picture symbols. Students needed fewer prompts with the audio recorders and were more independent in the activity.

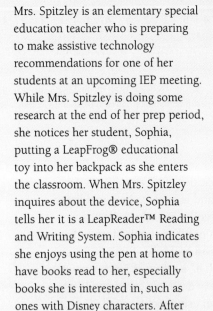

Case Study 2.2

Mrs. Spitzley is an elementary special education teacher who is preparing to make assistive technology recommendations for one of her students at an upcoming IEP meeting. While Mrs. Spitzley is doing some research at the end of her prep period, she notices her student, Sophia, putting a LeapFrog® educational toy into her backpack as she enters the classroom. When Mrs. Spitzley inquires about the device, Sophia tells her it is a LeapReader™ Reading and Writing System. Sophia indicates she enjoys using the pen at home to have books read to her, especially books she is interested in, such as ones with Disney characters. After school, Mrs. Spitzley investigated the LeapReader™ Reading and Writing System, finding out that it is a pen that reads specifically designed books from LeapFrog® and can support students by reading the text as a whole page, word by word, or letter by letter. The books, which all must be specifically purchased, focus on different skill areas (e.g., comprehension, long- and short-vowel words, vocabulary). The system is also designed for student progress and activities to be monitored. Mrs. Spitzley wonders if the LeapReader™ Reading and Writing System might support Sophia with her IEP goal of answering at least 80% of oral or written comprehension questions correctly when presented with a first-grade reading passage. Mrs. Spitzley decides to evaluate the LeapReader™ system using the TAPE Framework. Mrs. Spitzley determines that the

LeapReader™ is transportable. As is evident by Sophia bringing it to school to use on the bus, the tool can go from home to school and also between settings at school. The pen itself is small and the books, while hard cover, are standard book size. As for availability, Mrs. Spitzley's research indicates that she can order the LeapReader™ as well as books online from LeapFrog® or Amazon or purchase them in some stores. Mrs. Spitzley also feels that the device can be considered practical. While there is a cost associated, as one would need to purchase the pen and each book, it is relatively easy to learn to use as well as teach someone to learn to use, as Mrs. Spitzley found out when asking Sophia to teach her and then trying it herself. Finally, Mrs. Spitzley feels the tool is engaging. Sophia clearly enjoys using it as she elects to use it

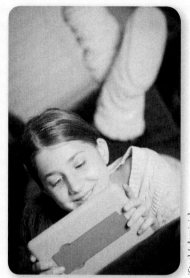

iStock/sdominick

during free time at home. Aside from the potential concern about the cost associated with purchasing each book, Mrs. Spitzley feels this tool could be discussed at Sophia's IEP meeting as an option for assistive technology.

Assistive Technology Selection Tools and Resources

In addition to the aforementioned guides, frameworks, and assessments, additional tools exist to help IEP teams identify and select different assistive technology devices and tools. The Technology and Media Division of the Council for Exceptional Children produced the Assistive Technology Consideration Quick Wheel (TAM, 2004). The Quick Wheel provides the definitions of assistive technology devices and services as well as resources for an IEP team. The Quick Wheel provides actual assistive technology devices and tools for the WATI categories of assistive technology (e.g., mobility, math, communication, and vision). TAM also sells products known as TAM Technology Fans, including fans (i.e., 2" x 7" colored paper clipped on one end that can spread out like a fan) that describe supports for young children (Mistrett et al., 2006), considerations for academic success (Jeffs, Reed, & Warger, 2007), Web 2.0 (Carling & Thompson, 2011), and Universal Design for Learning (Castellani, 2010). These fans provide assistive technology tool and device suggestions.

In addition to products produced by TAM, IEP teams can consider other reliable and trusted sources. For example, the QIAT Consortium, discussed in Chapter 1, provides resources on its website (see http://www.qiat.org/resource-bank.html). The resources are quite diverse, but some include reviews of different assistive technology products, which may be helpful to IEP teams in considering and selecting assistive technology devices and tools. The WATI Assistive Technology Assessment Technology Checklist, discussed earlier, can also provide options for assistive technology consideration and selection for IEP teams. Finally, the NATRI provides videos on different assistive technology tools and devices IEP teams may want to consult (see http://natri.uky.edu/assoc_projects/viewer/index.html).

Assistive Technology and the IEP

As previously discussed, IEP teams need to consider assistive technology for *all* students with disabilities. When an IEP team decides assistive technology would benefit a student with a disability, the device and/or service is written into the IEP. Assistive technology can be written into an IEP as a goal, a related service, a supplementary aid and service, or as an accommodation (Reed & Bowser, 2005; The QIAT Leadership Team, 2012). When an assistive technology device or service is written into the IEP, it is provided to the student at no cost; the assistive technology device or service contributes to securing a free, appropriate public education (FAPE) for the student with a disability. Note, the exception to schools paying for assistive technology written into an IEP is surgically implanted assistive technology (Individuals with Disabilities Education Improvement Act, 2004). According to the law, the cost of an assistive technology device cannot be a factor in assistive technology decision-making. Schools may use their public education funds, Medicaid, or community means in securing the assistive technology (Chambers, 1997; Golinker, 2009).

During the IEP process relative to assistive technology, family and cultural considerations are important to take into consideration (Jones & Hinesman-Matthews, 2014). In other words, an assistive technology device or service needs to be consistent with a family's values or their cultural values. It is insufficient to focus on what the school or educators want; a plan for assistive technology must include a family's perspectives (Coleman, 2011). When deciding upon a particular assistive technology device and/or service, the attitudes of the family as well as those of the student and educators should be considered by the IEP team (Coleman, 2011).

Once an assistive technology device is written into an IEP, the team must consider assistive technology service to support the implementation of the device or tool. As discussed in Chapter 1, assistive technology services can include conducting the assistive technology assessment or evaluation, securing devices for trial implementation, determining IEP goals relative to assistive technology, acquiring a selected device or tool (e.g., purchasing, making), monitoring the implementation of the device or tool, maintaining the device or tool, and training (IDEA Improvement Act, 2004). Some of the previously mentioned decision-making resources include support for monitoring assistive technology implementation, such as the UKAT Toolkit, the NATRI Planner, and the WATI materials. In addition, as discussed in Chapter 1, IEP teams should use the Quality Indicator for Assistive Technology (QIAT) to ensure the assistive technology services provided to students with disabilities are high quality (see http://www.qiat.org/indicators.html). The Quality Indicators of Assistive Technology (QIAT; please refer back to Chapter 1 for a more detailed discussion of QIAT) include five quality indicators relative to assistive technology in the IEP (see Table 2.2)

While all assistive technology services are important, it is important for IEP teams to note that devices and tools require training, even low-tech assistive technology. When planning training for an assistive technology device, IEP teams should remember that training should involve not just the student but also the educators

Table 2.2   Quality Indicators of Assistive Technology

Quality Indicators of Assistive Technology in the IEP
"The education agency has guidelines for documenting assistive technology needs in the IEP and requires their consistent application."
"All services that the IEP team determines are needed to support the selection, acquisition, and use of assistive technology devices are designated in the IEP."
"The IEP illustrates that assistive technology is a tool to support achievement of goals and progress in the general curriculum by establishing a clear relationship between student needs, assistive technology devices and services, and the student's goals and objectives."

(Continued)

Table 2.2   (Continued)

"IEP content regarding assistive technology is written in language that describes how assistive technology contributes to achievement of measurable and observable outcomes."

"Assistive technology is included in the IEP in a manner that provides a clear and complete description of the devices and services to be provided and used to address student needs and achieve expected results."

Source: The QIAT Community (Retrieved February 26, 2015 from http://www.qiat.org/documents

who will be working with the student using the assistive technology (e.g., special education teacher, general education teacher, paraprofessional) and parents and/or family members (Coleman, 2011). Training for educators and family members should not only focus on how to use the device or tool but how to meaningfully integrate the tool into the student's learning and/or facets of daily living.

Web 2.0 Resources and Apps

Educators may want to use apps or Web 2.0 technologies relative to assistive technology decision-making, IEP meetings, or UDL. Apps and Web 2.0 technologies relative to UDL were discussed in Chapter 1 (please see Table 1.6). While not directly related to assistive technology decision-making, there are a few apps educators may want to consider regarding IEPs. For example the IEP Goals, & Objectives with Common Core State Standards app (National Association of Special Education Teachers [NASET], 2014) is available from the iTunes store for purchase. Developed by the NASET, this iPhone and iPad app allows educators to select and build IEP annual goals and short-term objectives for their students.

To help with scheduling of IEP meetings, educators can use the free website Doodle (http://doodle.com/), which allows a variety of meeting times (dates and times) to be proposed, and then, all participating parties can select when they are available. The person responsible for scheduling then selects a time representing everyone's availability. Similar to Doodle, Schedule Once (http://www.scheduleonce.com/) can also be used for meeting participants to respond to different times, indicating their availability so a common time can be found without multiple reply all e-mail exchanges. The free website SignUp Genius (http://www.signupgenius.com/) also allows potential IEP participants to select available times to convene and then be sent reminders for the meeting. Finally, IEP teams may want to consider Web 2.0 technologies to involve parents in meetings when they cannot be there in person, in accordance with IDEA 2004 (Yell, 2012). Beyond the phone, websites and apps like Google Hangout (http://www.google.com/hangouts/) and Skype (http://www.skype.com/) allow participants to participate via video on a computer or mobile device for free.

KEY TERMS

assistive technology
   specialists, p. 28

individualized education
   program, p. 27

EXTENSION ACTIVITIES

- Watch an interview with Joy Zabala (https://www.youtube.com/watch?v=NkpmJqZswvc). Engage in a discussion regarding the role of technology in the education of students with disabilities as well as the changes—or lack thereof—in assistive technology for students with disabilities across the years.

- Watch "Disability-led innovation for the masses: Chris Bugaj at TEDxAshburn" (https://www.youtube.com/watch?v=D-hPct3oIow). Consider how technology originally designed as assistive technology for students with disabilities is now widely popular among mainstream technologies.

APPLICATION ACTIVITIES

- If students are in a practicum setting or field experience (or if students have access to a special education classroom, setting, or students through other means, such as teaching or volunteering) during this course, have students work with an assistive technology specialist, special education teacher, speech-and-language therapist, or occupational therapist to participate in an assistive technology assessment. In addition to reflecting on the experience, consider the assessment protocols or resources used. If allowed, have participating students conduct some aspects of the assessment relative to the example assessments presented in this chapter (refer to Table 2.1).

- If access to a special education setting or student is not possible, have students consider the following scenario and brainstorm the decision-making process to address assistive technology consideration:

  ○ Luke is a third-grade student identified with a learning disability; his learning disability involves both reading and writing. He spends his time in the general education classroom but receives support from a resource room for about one hour a day. Luke is expected to participate in his state's general large-scale assessment with accommodations as well as expected to follow his state's grade level standards, including in the areas of reading, writing, and mathematics. Luke's struggle with reading occurs with comprehending what he is writing, and his struggles with reading occur more with production than the mechanics of writing. Luke loves to play video games and sports and spending time with his friends. He does not like to stand out from his peers, and he has increasingly become self-conscious about going to the resource room for assistance.

- Have students download the QIAT indicators matrices (http://www.qiat.org/indicators.html). In small groups, instruct students to go through the matrices and understand what makes a school's process relative to assistive technology unacceptable versus following best practices.

- Have students in small groups brainstorm a list of possible everyday technologies that could be repurposed to be assistive technology. Each group should apply the TAPE Framework to their list of potential repurposed assistive technology (see Figure 2.2).

DISCUSSION QUESTIONS

1. What are some of the roles or tasks of an assistive technology specialist?

2. Where can assistive technology be included on an IEP? When might it be appropriate to list assistive technology in the different places?

3. How can the SETT Framework guide an IEP team in assistive technology decision-making? The Adaptations Framework? The TPACK Framework?

RESOURCES/ADDITIONAL INFORMATION

- The Technology and Media Division of the Council for Exceptional Children sells a variety of products relative to assistive technology decision-making as well as Universal Design for Learning. Interested individuals can explore TAM's Assistive and Instructional Technology Planning Tools (http://www.tamcec.org/publications/

planning-tools/) as well as their TAM Technology Fans (http://www.tamcec.org/publications/technology-fans/).

- The Practitioner's Guide to TPACK includes text- and video-based case studies (see http://tpackcases.org/).

- Assistive Technology Tip of the Day online calendar (see http://lcps.org/Page/109652)

SUGGESTED ENRICHMENT READINGS

- Petcu, S. D., Yell, M., & Fletcher, T. (2014). Assistive technology: Legislation and legal issues. *Exceptionality, 22*(4), 226–236. doi:10.1080/09362835.2013.865538

- Naraian, S., & Surabian, M. (2014). New literacy studies: An alternative frame for preparing teachers to use assistive technology. *Teacher Education and Special Education, 37*(4), 330–346.

CHAPTER 3

Assistive Technology for Communication

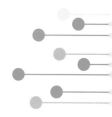

Chapter 3 discusses one specific type of assistive technology: assistive technology for communication, known as augmentative and alternative communication (AAC). The chapter explains AAC and the primary categorization of AAC devices: unaided, nonelectronic aided, and electronic AAC. In addition, the chapter provides examples of the different types of AAC devices, including dedicated devices and apps for mobile devices, and considerations IEP teams make when selecting the appropriate AAC for a particular student.

"Communication is the exchange of ideas, information, thoughts, and feelings" (Gargiulo, 2015, p. 365). Communication is not just verbal or spoken communication but can also include nonverbal communication like body language and gestures. Communication is social, as communication typically involves at least two individuals—a sender and a receiver (i.e., communication partners). And for successful communication, the receiver needs to understand the sender's mode of communication. Communication is considered a basic human right, and regardless of one's struggles, everyone has a right to make a request, give or refuse his or her consent, provide preferences, and attempt to solicit another individual's attention (National Joint Committee for the Communicative Needs of Persons with Severe Disabilities, 1992). In other words, everyone should have the right—through speech, signs, behaviors, or technology—to engage in communication.

If an individual struggles with verbal communication, assistive technology options exist. One category of assistive technology—as identified in Chapter 1—is

Chapter Objectives

After reading the chapter, the reader will be able to do the following:

1. Discuss communication and its role in daily lives

2. Explain the different categorizations of AAC

3. Provide clear examples of devices or tools that fit within each AAC categorization

4. Identify features decision-making teams consider when recommending an AAC device

Technology Mindset

Before we get into Chapter 3, where we define and describe augmentative and alternative communication, let's first take a step back and think about how you communicate and what you communicate throughout the day. Communication—the sharing of messages—most often occurs between two people (i.e., communication partners): a sender and a receiver. For communication to be effective, the receiver needs to understand the sender. Has there ever been a time or situation in which you tried to communicate and someone did not understand you or your message? What did you do? What mode of communication were you trying that was ineffective? Did you try a different mode of communication? How did it feel when someone could not understand the message you were trying to communicate? Please consider responding to each of the questions individually and then sharing with a small group or in a large-group discussion.

specifically focused on communication: **augmentative and alternative communication**. AAC is a specific type of assistive technology to support students with complex communication needs, including students with severe **speech and language impairments**, **autism spectrum disorders**, **cerebral palsy**, or **intellectual disability**, among others. AAC "includes all forms of communication (other than oral speech) that are used to express thoughts, needs, wants, and ideas" (American Speech-Language-Hearing Association [ASHA], n.d.a). AAC tools or devices can be systems that support or supplement a student's current abilities or that serve as their primary means of communication. In other words, AAC augments (i.e., enhances) one's communication or serves as an alternative (Hanline, Nunes, & Worthy, 2007).

AAC Categorization

AAC devices themselves are a heterogeneous category of assistive technology. Like all assistive technology, AAC can include no-tech, low-tech, mid-tech, and high-tech options. Recently, AAC options have also been viewed as dedicated devices (i.e., technology specifically developed to be a stand-alone AAC device) and nondedicated devices. Nondedicated devices involve repurposing technology, such as an iPad, to serve as an AAC device through an app. AAC, unlike other categories of assistive technology, is also often commonly categorized into two groups: unaided and aided AAC.

Unaided Communication

An **unaided communication** system is communication that is not external to an individual. In other words, an unaided communication system involves communication an individual can do with his/her body (e.g., face, hands; ASHA, n.d.c; Beukelman & Mirenda, 2013). The most common unaided communication system that may come to mind is **sign language**. However, unaided AAC also includes gestures and body language.

While one might presume that sign language is only for individuals who are deaf, this is not true. Individuals with complex communication needs—individuals who might have a severe speech and language impairment and/or struggle with verbal communication—also use sign language. The most common sign language in the United States is American Sign Language (ASL). The National Institute on Deafness and Other Communication Disorders (NIDCD, 2014) defined American Sign Language as "a complete, complex language that employs signs made by moving the hands combined with facial expressions and postures of the body" (n.p.) (see Figure 3.1 for common phrases in ASL). ASL is common in the United States, but in other countries (e.g., England, France) other sign

Figure 3.1   Simple ASL Phrases

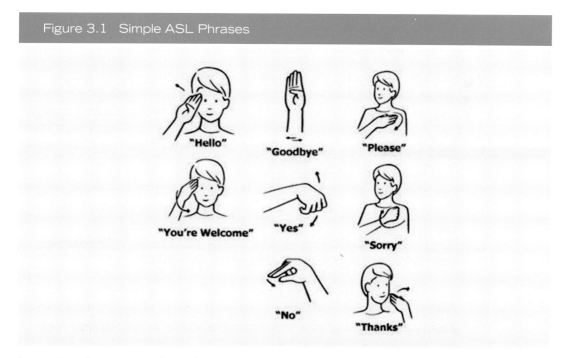

Source: National Institute on Deafness and Other Communication Disorders (NIDCD). See http://www.nidcd.nih.gov/

languages are used. ASL is distinct from English as it is its own language; ASL contains its own rules for grammar as well as word order. Like other languages, ASL has its own variations or accents based on regions (NIDCD, 2014).

Case Study 3.1

Max is an eight-year-old boy with moderate intellectual disability and is considered to have complex communication needs. Max does not communicate verbally but uses sign language as one of his means of communication. Max can use sign language to initiate communication, including spontaneously signing cookie when he wants a cookie. He has also dedicated signs to special individuals in his life, such as his teacher and parents.

iStock/Lokibaho

Finger spelling can be used to supplement ASL. Finger spelling involves the spelling of words using the individual sign associated with each of the 26 alphabetical letters. Users often use finger spelling to spell words for which a sign does not exist or which they do not know the sign. However, it is not commonly used in place of sign language given the impracticality (e.g., time) of individually spelling each word.

In addition to ASL, other sign languages or manually coded English systems exist, the most common being Signing Exact English (SEE). According to the SEE Center (see http://www.seecenter.org/), Signing Exact English is a sign language, but in contrast to ASL, it uses the same syntax as English. In other words, Signing Exact English provides a literal interpretation of English. Signing Exact English can be used to supplement ASL, as desired.

Aided Communication

Aided communication refers to communication systems that require a device or tool external to the individual; in other words, the individual uses something other than his or her body to communicate (Beukelman & Mirenda, 2013).

Aided communication systems include low-tech, mid-tech, and high-tech options. Each level of technology option typically involves some form of symbol, such as a photograph, picture/photo, or line drawing, to represent words or phrases by selecting the symbol an individual is communicating.

Multiple options exist for symbols, and one is not limited to purchasing symbols but can make their own, such as through pictures or photos. However, one of the most well-known symbol programs is Boardmaker by Mayer-Johnson (2014) (see Figure 3.2 for sample symbols from Boardmaker). Boardmaker is actually a software program that allows individuals to print symbols or communication boards; the symbols are known as Picture Communication Symbols (PCS™).

Aided communication systems involve different means of selection, such as direct selection or scanning. As a selection technique, direct selection involves

Figure 3.2   Sample Boardmaker Symbols

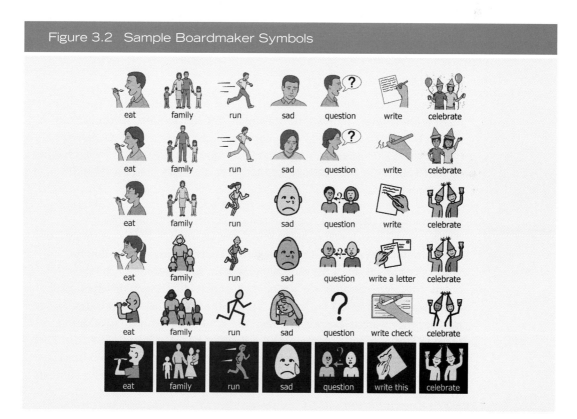

an individual selecting a symbol. The individual can directly select with his/her finger or via another body part (e.g., toe, elbow, via eye gaze) (ASHA, n.d.b). Scanning involves students selecting their choice (i.e., symbol) when choices are presented. With scanning, an individual is still making a selection but chooses from symbols presented one at a time (ASHA, n.d.b). Both direct selection and scanning are used with electronic (e.g., Proloquo2Go® for the iPad or iPod) and nonelectronic (e.g., Picture Exchange Communication System) aided AAC. Direct selection is often considered easier, results in the least amount of fatigue, and may be the access mode or selection technique first used by individuals. Scanning is typically considered to require more cognitive ability. A third, less common selection technique is encoding. Encoding involves codes assigned to different messages, and the individual selects a code or combines codes to communicate (ASHA, n.d.b). Recent advancements in technology allow individuals with complex communication needs who experience physical challenges, such as physical disabilities, to use eye tracking to control an AAC device (Fager, Bardach, Russell, & Higginbotham, 2012). However, additional research is needed on this approach of access.

Nonelectronic Aided AAC

As with assistive technology in general, nonelectronic aided AAC (i.e., low-tech) is often where individuals in need of AAC devices begin. Similar to low-tech assistive technology in general, nonelectronic aided AAC devices are typically less expensive. Common nonelectronic aided AAC, or low-tech AAC, include communication boards, communication books, and eye gaze displays (or e-Tran boards).

Communication boards or communication books are similar. Both involve displaying symbols for students to select (see Figure 3.3). For a communication board, multiple symbols are presented on a board via rows and columns. Students can then select the message they want to communicate via the board. Communication books are books that actually contain multiple small communication boards. Students first select the board that contains the message they want to express and then the symbol or symbols. In addition to the standard or typical communication book or board, variations do exist. For example, students can use communication purses or communication bracelets. These devices work under the same premise of displaying symbols for students to select.

Figure 3.3 Communication Board/Book

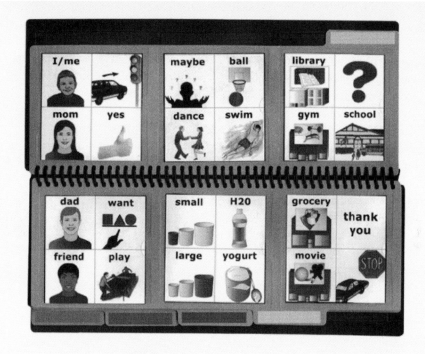

Source: Attainment Company. Used with permission.

Although labeled as an AAC intervention package, a Picture Exchange Communication System is another means to provide students, especially students with autism spectrum disorder, with nonelectronic AAC (see http://www.pecsusa.com/). PECS involves a student giving a picture to a communication partner (Bondy & Frost, 1994, 2001). PECS involves six phases: (1) how to exchange (i.e., communicate), (2) communicating in different places and with different people, (3) selecting from multiple pictures (i.e., discrimination), (4) creating a sentence structure with "I want," (5) expanding vocabulary with other parts of speech (e.g., adjectives, verbs), and (6) answering questions. A review of the existing research on PECS indicated the benefit of PECS in terms of improved communication, especially in young children with autism spectrum disorder (Sulzer-Azaroff, Hoffman, Horton, Bondy, & Frost, 2009).

Sofi is a 10-year-old girl diagnosed with autism spectrum disorder. Sofi attends a special self-contained classroom at her school for elementary students with autism spectrum disorder during the academic year, and her parents enroll her in an inclusive day camp program during the summer. The day camp partners with an organization to provide one-on-one inclusion counselors for students with disabilities to be included into the typical day camp experience (e.g., crafts, swimming, exploring). During the day camp, Sofi continues to receive her therapy, such as from a speech-language pathologist (SLP). Her SLP typically works with Sofi in the pool, which is Sofi's favorite activity. Sofi has limited verbal communication. She says, "Coke," when she wants to drink Coke, and her one-on-one inclusion counselor is working with her to say, "More Coke," before giving her the beverage, in addition to her therapy from the SLP. Beyond using behavior and gestures to communicate, those working with Sofi are also trying to get her to use a communication book. The communication book, which includes

iStock/ktayorg

icons or photographs of different objects, allows Sofi to make choices. For example, at lunch time, Sofi's one-on-one inclusion counselor can ask Sofi what she would like to eat first and provide her with the icons or pictures for her to make a selection (e.g., sandwich or pretzels). Sofi's inclusion counselor can also use the icons or photographs to present a picture schedule to Sofi so she knows what activities will occur throughout the day and in what order (e.g., horseback riding, archery).

In contrast to communication boards, books, and similar products that tend to be small and portable for individual users to select symbols for communication, eye gaze displays, or eTran boards or frames, are larger boards typically constructed from Plexiglas, thick transparency material, or similar materials (see Figure 3.4). Eye gaze

Ganz, Davis, Lund, Goodwyn, and Simpson (2012) asserted that PECS was one of the most widely used picture-based AAC systems. In conducting a meta-analysis (i.e., an approach to synthesizing the research literature involving effect sizes, which represent the magnitude of an intervention; Hattie, Rogers, & Swaminathan, 2010), Ganz et al. (2012) found students with autism spectrum disorders improved in their functional communication (e.g., initiating interactions) by using PECS. The researchers also found PECS to be more beneficial with younger students, such as preschool age.

displays can include letters, numbers, or symbols, and these can be permanently printed, attached with Velcro, or attached with a tacky tape. To use the eye gaze display, typically a communication receiver holds the eye gaze display, and the sender gazes at the message (i.e., symbol, letter) she or he wants to communicate.

Figure 3.4   Eye Gaze Display

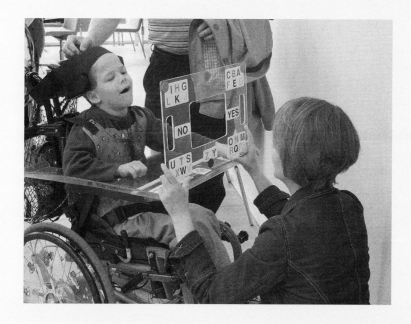

Source: COGAIN. Reproduced with permission.

Electronic Aided AAC

Electronic aided AAC devices include both mid-tech and high-tech options and are sometimes referred to as voice output communication aids (VOCAs) or speech-generating devices (SGD; see Table 3.1). Multiple and varied options exist for electronic aided AAC devices. Electronic aided AAC devices include those that play a single message that an individual records (e.g., GoTalk Button from Attainment Company and QuickTalker 1 from AbleNet). Electronic AAC devices also include options in which an individual records the messages, and more messages can be stored (e.g., four, 20) in multiple-level devices (e.g., GoTalk 9+ from Attainment Company and SuperTalker Progressive from AbleNet; see Figures 3.5 and 3.6). The devices in which an individual records

Table 3.1 Electronic Aided AAC Examples

Device	Description
Go Talk (see Figure 3.5)	• Produced by the Attainment Company (http://www.attainmentcompany.com/) • Records own messages and can print own symbols • Multiple options exist, including Go Talk Button (one message), Go Talk 4+ (22 messages), Go Talk Express 32 (plays sequence of messages)
QuickTalker Family	• Produced by AbleNet (http://www.ablenetinc.com/) • Family of communication devices, ranging from single message (QuickTalker 1) to 23 messages (QuickTalker 23) • Record own messages
DynaVox®T10 & DynaVox®T15	• Produced by DynaVox (http://www.dynavoxtech.com/) • Recorded symbols in natural sounding male and female voices, available in different languages • Tablet that generates speech; T15 is bigger than the T10
DynaWrite™2.0	• Produced by DynaVox (http://www.dynavoxtech.com/) • Users type messages on a QWERTY keyboard, which appear on a screen and output via natural sounding voices • Users can store messages with their own voices
Accent series (see Figure 3.7)	• Produced by Prentke Romich Company (http://www.prentrom.com/) • Four different options offering different sizes and features • The two biggest contain an advanced eye gaze system • Touch screen display of symbols

Figure 3.5 Multiple Level Voice Output System: GoTalk 20+

Source: Attainment Company. Used with permission.

Figure 3.6 SuperTalker Progressive Communicator

Source: AbleNet. Used with permission.

messages use **digital speech**; digital speech is in contrast to **synthesized speech**, which is computer-generated speech (Brownlee, 2014). While digital speech typically sounds more natural, it does have to be recorded by another individual, and a user of this AAC option is restricted to only the prerecorded messages rather than spontaneous expression (York & Fabrikant, 2011). Electronic AAC devices also include more sophisticated technology in which a natural sounding synthesized voice voices the message a user selects, typically from a touch screen display (e.g., Maestro from DynaVox and Accent Series from Prentke Romich Company; see Figure 3.7).

Many different options for aided electronic AAC devices exist—too many to exhaustively list in this textbook. In addition to the samples provided in Table 3.1, readers are encouraged to peruse the websites of companies focused on AAC devices, such as Attainment Company (http://www.attainmentcompany.com/product-categories/assistive-technology/communication-aids), DynaVox (http://www.dynavoxtech.com/products/), and Prentke Romich Company (http://www.prentrom.com/). Readers can also examine different charts that compare devices, such as one

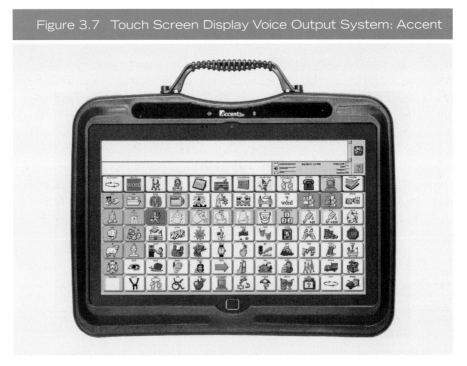

Figure 3.7   Touch Screen Display Voice Output System: Accent

Source: Accent™ 1200, Prentke Romich Company. Reproduced with permission.

In a TED (Technology, Education, and Design) Talk in 2013, Dr. Rupal Patel discussed creating customized crafted voices for individuals who are nonverbal. Dr. Patel feels a voice should be unique to an individual and represent their age, gender, ethnicity, accent, and other features. However, the current options for synthesized speech, which speech-generating AAC devices use, do not differentiate. In other words, many individuals who use AAC devices use the same voice. Dr. Patel's work involves creating a customized, unique voice by using surrogate voices (see VocaliD, 2014). Those interested in learning more should see Dr. Patel's website and VocaliD (see http://www.vocalid.co/) as well as watch Dr. Patel's TED Talk (https://www.ted.com/talks/rupal_patel_synthetic_voices_as_unique_as_fingerprints).

created by Enabling Devices (see http://enablingdevices.com/files/content/ComparisonChart.pdf), which presents information on features and cost. AAC TechConnect also offers individuals an opportunity to purchase their AAC Device Assistant, which provides research, features, and manufacturer information on different AAC devices (see http://www.aactechconnect.com/wp-content/uploads/2011/03/example10.17.13.pdf for an example).

In addition to stand-alone electronic aided AAC devices, increasingly popular are AAC apps for iOS (e.g., iPad) or Android devices. These apps, which range from free to hundreds of dollars worth, operate similar to the stand-alone electronic aided AAC products but can be used on multipurpose devices (e.g., the iPad). AAC apps, like stand-alone, dedicated AAC devices, range in the type of display (i.e., grid display of symbols versus use of a photograph or image to express language) (Gevarter et al., 2014). In addition, the apps can vary in use of digital and synthesized speech, use of premade symbols or pictures versus taking one's own, the amount of vocabulary, and use of symbols versus typing or spelling (AAC TechConnect, 2014). The aforementioned are just examples of the ways in which AAC apps can differ.

The reader is invited to review some examples of AAC in Table 3.2 as well as to visit the website Jane Farrall Consulting (http://www.janefarrall.com/aac-apps-lists/) for AAC lists by type as well as reviews for the different apps. In addition, given the volume of apps developed related to AAC (i.e., over 300 in 2014), Spectronics created an app to simply find AAC apps with the features one is seeking called AAC Ferret. AAC Ferret is available for purchase from the iTunes store.

Table 3.2 Example AAC Apps

App	Device	Description
Proloquo2Go® (AssistiveWare, 2013) (see Figure 3.8)	iPad, iPhone (iTunes)	• Voice output symbol-based app • Multiple natural sounding English-speaking voices • Customizable, including creating own buttons • For purchase
SoundingBoard™ (AbleNet)	iPhone, iPhone, iPod Touch (iTunes)	• Create own boards—including with own photos or preloaded symbols—and record messages • Available in English • Free but within-app purchases
Alexicom AAC (Alexicom Tech LLC)	iPad, iPhone (iTunes) Android phone or tablet (Google Play)	• Voice output symbol-based app • Can edit existing pages and includes adjustable voices • 36 pages free but can purchase additional premade pages and symbols/photos
Flip Writer AAC (Navanit Arakeri)	iPad (iTunes)	• Type message on a two-way keyboard that sender and receiver can both see; typed selection can also be presented via speech • Free
Sono Flex (Tobii Technology)	iPad, iPhone, iPod (iTunes)	• Voice output symbol-based app • Uses SymbolStix® symbols • Five English voices, including children • For purchase
Speak For Yourself (Speak For Yourself, LCC)	iPad (iTunes)	• Designed by speech-language pathologists who specialize in AAC • Includes symbols and words • Can search for vocabulary • For purchase
GoTalk Now (Attainment Company, 2014) (see Figure 3.9)	iPad (iTunes)	• Modeled after Attainment's dedicated GoTalk devices • Customizable app (i.e., choose layout) and can use symbols or insert own images • For purchase (free lite version)

Figure 3.8   Image of the iPad App Proloquo2Go

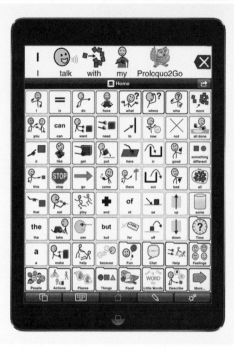

Source: Proloquo2Go® is an AssistiveWare® product. Used with permission.

Figure 3.9   GoTalk Now for the iPad

Source: Attainment Company. Used with permission.

Case Study 3.3

Damon is an 11th-grade student identified with moderate intellectual disability and a speech and language disorder. Damon communicates verbally, but others are often unable to understand what Damon is saying. This is due to the fact that Damon speaks softly and many of his words are unable to be discerned. Damon uses the stand-alone AAC device Dynavox Maestro™ but his parents recently requested an IEP meeting to revisit the AAC selected. Although Damon is supposed to use his AAC in school, at home, and in the community, more often than not, Damon is not using the device. His parents are requesting the IEP

iStock/karelnoppe

team, led by the speech-language pathologist, consider AAC apps for an iPad because Damon enjoys interacting with the iPad. Damon's parents feel that he would be more willing to use AAC if it was on the iPad. They also feel the iPad is multifunctional in that it can support Damon in other aspects as well as it is socially acceptable.

In addition to AAC apps that are structured similarly to dedicated AAC devices (i.e., speech-generating devices with a grid format for symbol presentation), there are apps that use visual scene display (Tuthill, 2014). Visual scene display (VSD) is not only an app-based AAC option but can exist on dedicated devices as well. VSD involves language embedded into photographs or images (i.e., scanned or graphically designed) (Wilkinson & Light, 2011). The VSD is in opposition to the typical grid display of the AAC option, in which symbols are selected (Ganz, 2014, refer back to Figures 3.5-3.9). VSD involves the selection of language from naturalistic settings. Wilkinson and Light (2011) found better results with VSDs when humans were presented within the scenes. Some VSD apps include Scene Speak for the iPad, Scene and Heard for all iOS devices, and AutisMate for iOS and Android devices (Sutton, 2013; Tuthill, 2014) (see Figure 3.10). Light and McNaughton (2012) argued VSDs benefit students as they focused on contexts in which communication is used and present language in familiar or lived experiences.

Figure 3.10   Visual Scene Display App: Scene Speak

Source: Good Karma Applications. Used with permission.

In addition to specifically dedicated AAC apps (e.g., Proloquo2Go, Sono Flex), apps can be repurposed to be AAC. (Please refer to the discussion of repurposing technology and the TAPE framework in Chapter 2.) Gosnell (2011) discussed how doodle or sketch-based apps (e.g., Doodle Buddy) could be repurposed to serve as AAC for expressive and receptive language. In other words, a student draws or writes on a doodle or sketch app to demonstrate their expressive (e.g., "Hello," or draw a smiley face) or receptive (e.g., draw a picture of swimming in response to a question of what someone did last night) language.

AAC Decision-Making

AAC decision-making is a team process, much like decision-making for assistive technology in general and all other facets of a student's Individualized Education Program (IEP). Consistent with the IEP, the special education teacher, general education teacher, parents, LEA representative, and someone to interpret any evaluation results are critical members to the IEP team (Yell, 2012). For AAC specifically, the speech-language pathologist (therapist) is also an essential team member (Beukelman & Mirenda, 2013). In fact, "developing, selecting, and prescribing multimodal augmentative and alternative communication systems, including unaided strategies (e.g., manual signs, gestures) and aided strategies (e.g., speech generating devices, manual communication boards, picture schedules)" are the responsibility of the speech-language pathologist (ASHA, 2007, p. 7). In addition, the speech-language pathologist is also likely to provide speech and language services to students using an AAC device (ASHA, 2007). As important as speech-language pathologists and special education teachers are to the decision-making regarding AAC, IEP teams must value and respect parent/family participation and insights. In other words, IEP teams should adopt family-centered practices and address issues of family and culture during AAC decision-making (Parette, Huer, & Brotherson, 2001).

role of speech-language pathologist

Considerations for Selecting AAC

Selecting an AAC device for a student requires many considerations. Like selecting assistive technology in general, understanding the student as well as for what purpose and where the student will be expected to use or need the AAC device are important. IEP teams need to determine the student's current communication skills as well as physical or motor, cognitive, and sensory abilities. In addition, consideration of an individual's preference is important; researchers suggest individuals with complex communication needs vary in their preferred AAC (Lorah et al., 2013; van der Meer, Sigafoos, O'Reilly, & Lancioni, 2011). IEP teams do not start by selecting the technology first but rather by understanding the student and considering his/her wants and needs (Light & McNaughton, 2013).

In considering and selecting the AAC, IEP teams must remember not to focus on the latest or most sophisticated technology. While apps and mobile devices provide AAC to individuals with complex communication needs and often at a lower price and with greater acceptance, AAC apps are not always the most appropriate choice (McNaughton & Light, 2013). Despite the allure of AAC apps and the latest technology, older technologies as well as unaided AAC and aided nonelectronic AAC should not be discarded (Light & McNaughton, 2013). Ultimately, AAC decision-making, like all assistive technology decision-making, should apply a framework. Central to the different frameworks are both (a) that technology decisions come after understanding other factors (e.g., settings, tasks) and (b) the need to focus on each individual student. (Refer to Chapter 2 for a discussion on assistive technology frameworks and decision-making.)

When comparing different AAC device options—unaided AAC versus low-tech aided AAC versus high-tech AAC versus an AAC app—decision-making teams needs to consider a number of factors. One factor in AAC decision-making is with whom the individual wishes to or will communicate. As previously stated, communication requires a sender and a receiver, but effective communication necessitates the receiver understand the sender. It can be problematic if a student uses sign language, but no one understands the language. Likewise, if a student uses a communication board but a receiver does not understand the student is communicating, the exchange can be impaired. Hence, there is a need to consider if potential communication partners can understand the sender's language. That being said, all AAC—regardless of type—requires training and not just for the user (i.e., sender) but also for potential communication partners. Communication partners could include parents, teachers, other service providers, and peers, as appropriate. The needs and preferences of the student are paramount, but communication partners should also be a consideration.

What about public situations?

Selecting an appropriate AAC requires matching the type of AAC (i.e., unaided AAC, aided nonelectronic AAC, electronic AAC) to the individual student and his/her skills, preferences, contexts, tasks, and other factors. When selecting within the different categories, such as aided electronic AAC, the particular features of the tool are important to consider. Decision-making teams need to evaluate a number of factors, including direct selection versus scanning, type of voice output, voice quality, and memory size of device. Decision-making teams may also evaluate the portability, type of symbols, and construction of message (AAC TechConnect, 2013).

As stated earlier in the chapter, students can access AAC through direct selection or scanning, which can involve a switch or eye gaze, for example. IEP teams need to determine which method of access will work best for each particular student. Next, with electronic aided AAC devices, selection involves considerations of the voice output, as in digitized (i.e., human recorded) or synthesized (i.e., electronically produced). The type of voice output can impact the quality of the voice. Digitized speech can be impaired in the recording but is completely natural sounding (i.e., is a human voice so it sounds like the human who recorded it, whether an adult or child). Older versions of synthesized speech sound less human, but technology is improving, and increasingly, synthesized voices sound natural. Many devices offer users the option of different languages as well as child versus adult and male and female voices. It should also be noted that devices can also vary greatly in the amount of messages (i.e., vocabulary). As stated, an electronic aided AAC device can consist of a single message or possess the vocabulary of 14,000 symbols. Last, AAC decision-making can involve consideration of different types of symbols (e.g., letters/words versus icons versus digital photos), how the

Although many different AAC apps exist for mobile devices, most of the research is limited to one app: Proloquo2Go (Kagohara et al., 2013; Xin & Leonard, 2014). In their systematic review of the literature, Kagohara et al. (2013) found eight published studies to date on using an iOS device (e.g., iPod) to teach communication skills to students with autism spectrum disorder; seven of the studies used the app Proloquo2Go. Most of the existing research was focused on students requesting a preferred stimuli (e.g., snack, toy), rather than other communication purposes. In a recent meta-analysis, Alzrayer, Banda, and Koul (2014) expanded their review of AAC apps for just iOS devices to include students with other developmental disabilities in addition to students with autism spectrum disorder. Alzrayer et al. (2014) concluded AAC iOS apps were effective for improving communication skills. Additional research is needed for other apps, other communication purposes, and just use of an iPad or other mobile device as a speech-generating device.

message is displayed (e.g., icons versus words), as well as portability and age appropriateness of different devices.

A final—but not legal—decision-making factor involves cost. While IEP teams cannot legally consider cost when making assistive technology decisions (Yell, 2012), a range of costs exist for AAC devices. On one side are free AAC apps, and on the other side are devices costing thousands of dollars. While cost is often predictive of features and options, a higher cost, especially for apps, is not always correlated with a better product. To that end, decision makers should be cognizant of cost but recognize that cost does not mandate decisions. Decision-making teams should perform trials with an AAC device before making a formal decision, utilizing state lending libraries or other organizations or agencies (refer to Chapter 2).

While on the subject of cost, a tricky question relative to AAC can be who pays for such devices. A school may pay for an AAC device as part of its requirement to provide a free appropriate public education (FAPE) to all students with disabilities (Golinker, 2011; Yell, 2012). Medicaid, Medicare, private health insurance, or even vocational rehabilitation may also be used to pay for the AAC (Golinker, 2011). Schools are allowed to legally use other means, such as Medicaid or private health insurance, to pay for AAC, although they cannot force parents to do so. New laws - that went into effect in late 2014 - are changing the status of speech generating devices covered through Medicare (Kander &

Satterfield, 2014). To pay for an SGD through Medicare, an individual will need to see a physician as well as a speech-language pathologist. In addition, if an app-based SGD is selected, Medicare will not pay for the mobile tablet (e.g., iPad) but may cover some apps if purchased through an approved provider (Kander & Satterfield, 2014). Medicare will not pay for a device that can also operate as a computer (Bardach, 2014; ASHA Leader, 2014). For SGDs covered by Medicaid, IEP teams should consult their state as Medicaid varies by state, including coverage of AAC apps. Likewise, private insurance provider policies should be individually examined (Kander, 2013).

Case Study 3.4

Pei is an AAC consultant for an intermediate school district (ISD), serving the schools and school districts in the county where she works. Pei is a licensed speech-language pathologist and received additional training regarding AAC. For Pei's job, she works with students who are in need of AAC devices, per their IEP. She not only assists with the evaluations, she also makes device recommendations and helps to procure the devices. Pei takes advantage of the ISD's AAC lab to try out different devices with students, ranging from low-tech (e.g., communication books) to high-tech (e.g., DynaVox Xpress™). If

iStock/lisafx

the ISD lab does not have a device Pei wants to use for an evaluation or trial, she works with the lending library in the state. In addition to working directly with students to support their acquisition, use, and maintenance of AAC, she also consults with teachers regarding implementation and training.

Resources for AAC Consideration

While the tools, resources, and frameworks discussed in Chapter 2 apply to considering, selecting, and implementing AAC devices—just as they apply to all assistive technology—decision-making teams for AAC may also consider additional resources specifically targeting technology for communication. For example, AAC TechConnect (see http://www.aactechconnect.com/) is a company focused on providing resources regarding AAC. Their different tools and resources include, for example, an AAC device features form (see Figure 3.11) to assist teams in evaluating AAC features that an individual user may need and an AAC decision-making form. Likewise, the app evaluation rubrics discussed in Chapter 1 can be applied to AAC apps. In addition, Fonner and Marfilius (2011) developed a specific apps evaluation tool for AAC apps focused on determining the various features of individual apps to help guide decision-making (see http://www.spectronics.com.au/conference/2012/pdfs/handouts/kelly-fonner/Feature_Match_Checklists_JAN2012.pdf).

Figure 3.11 AAC Apps/Devices Features to Consider

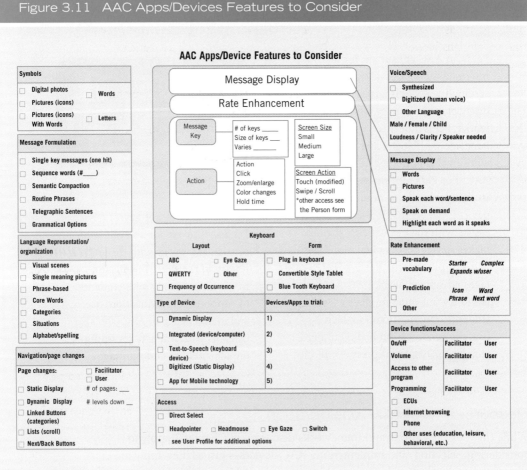

Source: Debby McBride (2014). Retrieved from AAC TechConnect.

Research on AAC

There is a lot of existing research on AAC. In fact, there is a journal devoted to AAC: *Augmentative and Alternative Communication* published by the International Society for Augmentative and Alternative Communication (ISAAC; see https://www.isaac-online.org/english/publications/aac/). In addition, the American Speech-Language-Hearing Association (ASHA) also publishes journals that include research relevant to AAC, such as the *Journal of Speech, Language, and Hearing Research* and *Language, Speech, and Hearing Services in Schools*.

Current research on AAC devices supports their use. Current research also suggests that use of AAC devices does not negatively impact speech development (Millar, Light, & Schlosser, 2006; Schlosser & Wendt, 2009). Some parents or families might worry that use of AAC will decrease speech production or reduce emphasis on verbal communication. However, existing research suggests that speech production is not negatively affected, and in fact, many students experience gains in speech when using AAC (Millar et al., 2006).

Recent research also exists to compare the effectiveness of different AAC options, particularly comparing previous models, such as nonelectronic aided AAC, with the current, sophisticated technology of AAC apps. In a study comparing picture symbols created by BoardMaker™ presented on a Velcro strip with an iPad app called Pick a Word by PUSH Design Inc., Flores et al. (2012) found the participating students increased their communication or stayed the same using the iPad-based system as compared to their traditional picture- or symbol-based system.

Web 2.0 Resources and Apps

In addition to the AAC apps presented throughout this chapter, Web 2.0 and other app technologies may also be used in ways to assist the participation of individuals with complex communication needs. For example, if students possess fine-motor skills, teachers may want to consider using Plickers (see https://www.plickers.com/ or download the app from the App Store on iTunes or Google Play). Plickers is a play on clickers, or student response systems. Students are given cards that the teacher can print with possible answers of A, B, C, and D represented by different orientations

(Continued)

(Continued)

of a square figure with varying spaces cut out. Students, each using a specifically numbered card, hold up their answers to a multiple choice or true/false prompt, and the teacher scan student responses using his or her tablet or smartphone. The answers can appear in a live feed or be archived for later teacher viewing. This allows for formative assessment data to be collected by the teacher and for students with complex communication needs to engage, as their participation is not based on verbal responses.

Concluding Considerations

AAC devices and options augment (i.e., enhance) one's communication or serve as an alternative. They allow students with disabilities to communicate and to communicate more independently, which creates opportunities for individuals with complex communication needs (e.g., communicating their idea, involvement in postsecondary education or employment). AAC options support individuals across a lifespan. Options for AAC run the spectrum from low-tech (e.g., picture symbols) to high-tech (e.g., app on an iPad) and everything in between. However, AAC is more than just a device; AAC involves making sure that the student as well as his/her communication partners (e.g., teachers, parents, other service providers) are trained to use the device for communication (Light & McNaughton, 2013).

[handwritten margin note: Was not discussed.]

[handwritten margin note: How do these work for people w/ dis. outside of school / community trained in their use?]

KEY TERMS

Aided communication, p. 52

augmentative and alternative communication, p. 50

autism spectrum disorders, p. 50

cerebral palsy, p. 50

digital speech, p. 60

intellectual disability, p. 50

sign language, p. 51

speech and language impairments, p. 50

synthesized speech, p. 60

unaided communication, p. 51

EXTENSION ACTIVITIES

- Show the National Center for Technology Innovation's "I Can Soar: Angie" video (see http://www.nationaltechcenter.org/index.php/2007/03/04/vid-195/) in class or have students watch individually. Engage in a discussion regarding how students would classify the AAC devices in the video and discuss some of their features (e.g., direct selection versus scanning, digitized versus synthesized speech).

- Show the Family Center on Technology and Disability's "Meet Elle" video (see http://bit.ly/1HGX4vm) in class or have students watch individually. Engage in a discussion regarding the different aspects of AAC devices presented as well as AAC decision-making raised in the video.

- Show Dr. Rupal Patel's TED Talk (https://www.ted.com/talks/rupal_patel_synthetic_voices_as_unique_as_fingerprints) in class or have students watch individually. Engage in a discussion regarding the limitations of synthesized voices in current AAC devices and the potential for customized voices as suggested by Dr. Patel.

APPLICATION ACTIVITIES

- Download a free AAC app (see sample, nonexhaustive list below). (Students are invited to find their own app as well as purchase one if desired.) Complete the "Sorting Through AAC Apps" form by Fonner and Marfilius (2011). Engage with the app, and form your own impression of its benefits and its limitations. Write down if you would recommend this app and, if so, for whom and, if not, why not. Then compare your assessment of the AAC apps with the perceptions of AAC professionals. (Purchase access to the AAC Apps Assistant at http://www.aactechconnect.com/?page_id=555 or scroll through the free evaluation by Jane Farrall at http://www.janefarrall.com/aac-apps-lists/)

  o GoTalk Now Free
  o iComm
  o Tap to Talk
  o Verbally

- Consider the following scenarios below. Based on the information presented in this chapter and previous chapters, present the type of AAC you would recommend for additional investigation/trial and why. Please note that there is not one correct answer; important to this activity is the thought process and consideration as to when and why different options of AAC might be preferred or offer benefits.

  o Jeni is a five-year-old child identified with autism spectrum disorder. Jeni does not spontaneously produce much speech, but she expresses interest in wanting to communicate her needs and interests (e.g., without AAC she expresses herself more physically or with behaviors). Jeni attends school and is educated in both a general education kindergarten class as well as a special education classroom. She needs AAC for both at school and at home. Her parents are willing and interested in learning new things to assist Jeni.

o Jake is a high school student identified with a moderate intellectual disability. He produces verbal speech but it is not always understandable to new communication partners, and at times, his consistent communication partners need him to repeat what he says a few times to fully comprehend his message. Jake enjoys using technology, such as playing games on the computer or tablet, as reinforcement for positive behaviors and during free time. Jake does not want to use technology that will make him look different from his peers.

- Using a computer, download the 30-day trial of Boardmaker by Mayer-Johnson (see http://www.mayer-johnson.com/downloads/trials/). Explore Boardmaker. Take an opportunity to consider how you might construct a communication book or a picture schedule using Boardmaker.

- Ask to meet with or speak with a speech-language pathologist at a local school. Discuss with the speech-language pathologist how s/he participates in the decision-making regarding AAC for students. Also ask him/her about what are the common AAC devices or tools s/he is seeing in schools with students with disabilities of all ages.

DISCUSSION QUESTIONS

1. What are the different categorizations of AAC? Provide a concrete example of a device for each different AAC categorization.

2. Who uses AAC devices? How does a student benefit from using an AAC device?

3. What are some of the considerations IEP teams make when selecting a particular AAC device for a student with a disability?

4. Why might students use an AAC app on a tablet or smartphone versus a dedicated device?

RESOURCES/ADDITIONAL INFORMATION

- The Company DynaVox has its own YouTube channel (see https://www.youtube.com/user/DynaVoxVideos/). Students can view different videos to gain additional exposure to AAC and how AAC benefits individuals with disabilities.

- Pyramid Educational Consultants, the developers of PECS, has its own YouTube channel (http://bit.ly/1KdwXQ2). Readers can explore the different videos on the channel to learn more about PECS.

- The International Society for Augmentative and Alternative Communication (see https://www.isaac-online.org/english/home/)

- PrAACtical AAC (http://praacticalaac.org/)

- The Division for Communicative Disabilities and Deafness of the Council for Exceptional Children (http://community.cec.sped.org/DCDD/home)

- The American Speech-Language-Hearing Association (http://www.asha.org/)

SUGGESTED ENRICHMENT READINGS

- Light, J., & McNaughton, D. (2014). Communicative competence for individuals who require augmentative and alternative communication: A new definition for a new era of communication? *Augmentative and Alternative Communication*, 30(1), 1–8. doi:10.3109/07434618.2014.885080

- Ganz, J. B. (2014). Aided augmentative and alternative communication: An overview. In J. B. Ganz (Ed.), *Aided augmentative communication for individuals with autism spectrum disorders* (pp. 13–30). New York, NY: Springer.

- Chung, Y. C., & Douglas, K. H. (2014). Communicative competence inventory for students who use augmentative and alternative communication: A team approach. *TEACHING Exceptional Children*, 47(1), 56–68. doi:10.1177/0040059914534620

CHAPTER 4

Assistive Technology for Mobility and Positioning

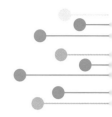

Chapter 4 presents assistive technology for both mobility and positioning. The chapter will familiarize the reader with assistive technology considerations for mobility, with large attention to wheelchairs and wheelchair decision-making. Other mobility assistive technology options will also be discussed (e.g., gait trainers, mobile standers). Chapter 4 will also discuss and provide options for assistive technology for positioning, including for students with mobility considerations as well as students with attention or behavioral challenges, such as the use of seat cushions or stability balls.

Mobility and **positioning** are important aspects of an individual's daily life and independence. As suggested, many of us take our independent mobility and comfortable positioning for granted. While many might presume that assistive technology for mobility and positioning are for students with orthopedic impairments, students with other disabilities can also benefit from assistive technology in these areas (e.g., students with ADHD, emotional-behavior disorders, or visual impairment). See also Perspective 4.1.

Chapter Objectives

After reading the chapter, the reader will be able to do the following:

1. Provide clear examples of assistive technology for mobility

2. Consider the complex decision-making process involving wheelchairs

3. Provide clear examples of assistive technology for positioning

Assistive Technology for Mobility

Assistive technology for mobility involves tools and devices that support the movement of students within a classroom, school, and community. While assistive technology itself, related to mobility, involves the devices

Technology Mindset

Many of us often take for granted the fact that we can move easily anywhere we want and that we are usually properly positioned and do not need specific devices to assist us. However, if you think about it, you can probably come up with instances in which you were not in a good sitting or standing position. How did that feel? What effects did that poor positioning have on you? Examine your own experiences with positioning while you were sitting, standing, or lying down. Find an instance in which you were not comfortable. Carefully consider the effects of this poor positioning on you as you answer the following questions:

- What position (or positions) did you think of? Please describe the situation.

- What effects did this poor position have on you, such as on your attention, comfort, or productivity?

to support such movement, features of an environment are essential to support unrestricted movement. With the Americans with Disabilities Act (ADA) of 1990 and Section 504 of the Rehabilitation Act of 1973 (Yell, 2012), classrooms, schools (public and private), and public places within the community (e.g., restaurants, stores, zoos, golf courses) need to conform to supporting unrestricted movement for individuals with disabilities. While full discussions of Section 504 and ADA are outside of the focus of this chapter, with respect to mobility, ADA and Section 504 ensure that facilities, such as a classroom and school, are physically accessible and reasonable accommodations are provided to individuals with disabilities (Yell, 2012). These laws seek to remove barriers for individuals with disabilities, including the provision of the universal design architectural aspect from which Universal Design for Learning (UDL) was built (refer back to Chapter 1).

Physical access to a classroom or school involves removing any architectural barriers. This can involve such things as a ramp, rearranging furniture, installing accessible doors, and installing accessible restroom facilities (Yell, 2012). Teachers and other educators will want to consider if clear pathways exist for students with mobility issues, including students with orthopedic impairments as well as students who are blind, to ensure students can maneuver around classrooms and the school. Educators should also ensure materials are accessible to all students within the classroom regardless of their height.

Figure 4.1   Accessible Folding Desk

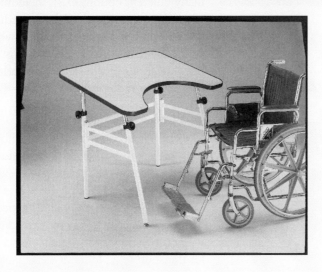

Source: Lesro Industries, Inc. Reproduced with permission.

Low-tech options also exist to make the classroom more accessible. Tools and devices to help ensure physical access for easier mobility and participation within the classroom include adjustable height desks and tables, including lab tables and computer desks. Desks are also made to accommodate a wheelchair (see Figure 4.1). Technology such as this can also aid in positioning, which will be discussed later in the chapter.

Wheelchairs

The most commonly associated assistive technology for mobility is a wheelchair. While not the only mobility-focused assistive technology, wheelchairs are perhaps the most well known. The wheelchair has a long history, with claims of conceptual development dating back to the sixth century (WheelchairNet, 2006). In the United States, a patent for a manual wheelchair was issued in 1894, and in the mid-20th century, the power wheelchair was developed (Bourgeois-Doyle, 2004; WheelchairNet, 2006). Wheelchairs have continued to advance since their development (Karp, 2008), and the extent of the options and considerations of wheelchairs may be surprising.

Figure 4.2   Pediatric Manual
              Wheelchair: Zippie® 2

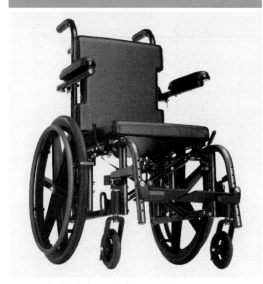

Source: Sunrise Medical (U.S.) LLC. Reproduced with permission. See http://www.sunrisemedical.com/company-information/presscentre.aspx

Wheelchairs are not a homogenous collection of choices. All wheelchairs are not the same, and many different options exist, including manual wheelchairs, power wheelchairs, pediatric (i.e., children's) wheelchairs, sport wheelchairs, and racing wheelchairs. The two big categorizations of wheelchairs include manual wheelchairs and power wheelchairs (Carroll, 2014; Srinivasan & Lloyd, 2011).

Manual Wheelchairs. Manual wheelchairs are wheelchairs without a power source; they are propelled by the user or another individual, such as a caregiver (see Figure 4.2). Manual wheelchairs themselves, including pediatric manual wheelchairs, vary in their features, including their weight, weight capacity, features for transport (e.g., folds vs. detachable seat), and, of course, cost (see http://www.spinlife.com/critpath/match.cfm?categoryID=304 for different pediatric manual wheelchairs). Manual wheelchairs are typically lightweight and lower in cost than power wheelchairs.

Power Wheelchairs. Power—or electric or motorized—wheelchairs are wheelchairs powered by an external source (i.e., battery; see Figure 4.3). Power wheelchairs are generally more expensive than manual wheelchairs as well as heavier because of the motor equipment (Karp, 2008). Power wheelchairs offer options, including front-wheel drive and rear-wheel drive. A user typically operates a power wheelchair via a joystick, push button, or switch.

Wheelchair Decision-Making. Important to determining the appropriate wheelchair is understanding the student, his or her abilities and preferences, and the tasks and settings in which the student will use the wheelchair. In other words, when making a decision about wheelchairs, one should consider following a decision-making framework as discussed in Chapter 2. However, it should be noted that most wheelchair decision-making is often outside the purview of an Individualized Education Program (IEP) team. Individuals with expertise in mobility and technology, such as occupational therapists and physical therapists, are often involved in wheelchair decision-making; wheelchair suppliers can also assist with wheelchair selection (Minkel, 2011). Wheelchairs can be paid for through private medical insurance, Medicare/Medicaid, or from the pocket of an individual or family. There are also organizations that assist with donations or funds.

When making decisions about wheelchairs, individuals, their family members, and/or therapists (e.g., occupational and/or physical therapists) consider the individual student, including the student's cognitive and physical abilities as well as his or her age. The student's context at school and home (e.g., accessibility, transportation options within the family) should also be evaluated (Carroll, 2014). Decision-making teams also consider the many components of a wheelchair, which are, nonexhaustively, the chair (i.e., manual versus power), cushion, seat, seat back, tires, and armrest. These decisions are interrelated, as a cushion or chair decision impacts the options for the others (Karp, 2008). In other words, if a particular chair is selected, one's cushion options may be limited and vice versa.

Chairs. The chair portion of a wheelchair can be manual or power, as previously discussed. The decision regarding a manual or power wheelchair is generally made by determining the physical abilities of an individual, such as dexterity, strength, and balance (Karp, 2008). Individuals without the strength or energy to use a manual chair typically use a power wheelchair. Both manual and power wheelchairs offer different advantages (see Table 4.1 for some positive aspects for each type of wheelchair).

Given the variety of different types of wheelchairs that exist within both the manual and power options, additional considerations must be made in selecting the best option. For manual wheelchairs, consideration is also given to a rigid frame (i.e., ones that does not fold) versus a folding frame. While rigid frames tend to be lighter and the seat can be adjustable, folding chairs can—as their name implies—be folded and placed into almost any car (Karp, 2008; Srinivasan & Lloyd, 2011). Different weights for manual chairs also exist; lighter

Figure 4.3 Pediatric Power Wheelchair: Skippi

Source: Ottobock. Reproduced with permission.

A special education teacher will not be expected to select or maintain a student's wheelchair (Carroll, 2014). However, a special education teacher does still play an important role in supporting students with disabilities who use a wheelchair for mobility. A special education teacher can help identify issues or challenges a student may be experiencing with the wheelchair (or other mobility-based technology) on a daily basis within the school environment and report it to other service providers (e.g., physical therapist). A special educator should also ensure the school environment is accessible to students who use wheelchairs, including physical accessibility in and around classrooms and the school (e.g., ramps, adjustable height tables) as well as that materials and resources a student needs within a class are accessible to the student. Teachers also collaborate with other service providers (e.g., physical therapists) and can help parents in being active members of the collaboration regarding educational decisions for his/her child (Carroll, 2014).

Table 4.1 Comparison of the Advantages of Manual Versus Power Wheelchairs	
Manual Wheelchair	**Power Wheelchair**
• Less expensive (i.e., purchase and maintenance) • Easier to transport • Lighter weight • Do not need to be recharged • Provide additional features for reclining and tilting	• Conserve energy • Provide greater independence • Provide additional features for positioning, including reclining, tilting, and standing

Source: Cook & Polgar (2015); Karp (2008).

weight chairs may be easier for an individual to move. Different features on a wheelchair, such as the type of spokes, can add weight, yet efforts to lighten a wheelchair can also make the product more expensive (Karp, 2008).

Other choices or selections for a manual wheelchair that are made include the size of the wheel (i.e., typically 24 in.), placement of the wheel axle, angle of the wheels (i.e., greater angle is used for sports wheelchairs), and, as stated, type of wheel spokes (i.e., different spokes can make a wheel lighter) (Karp, 2008). Wheelchairs can also involve additional options, including wheels that incorporate gears to move instead of one's hands, handrims for grasping and braking, and hand brakes or wheel locks (Karp, 2008).

Power wheelchairs involve different considerations, such as the drive wheel type, control system, battery power, and safety, including speed (Karp, 2008). Drive wheel type options include front, rear, or mid-wheel. In other words, drive wheel type refers to the placement of the drive wheel relative to the chair. Each drive wheel placement comes with different advantages and disadvantages (see Karp for an in-depth discussion regarding the different options). In terms of control systems, joysticks are the most common, although other options exist (e.g., sip and puff switches or controls operated by the chin or head) (Karp, 2008; Srinivasan & Lloyd, 2011) (see Chapter 5 for information on switches).

Case Study 4.1

Brendan is a high school student who receives special education services under the IDEA category of multiple disabilities. Specifically, Brendan was diagnosed with muscular dystrophy as a young child and mild intellectual disability (Full Scale IQ of 66). In addition to attending a life skills classroom for a significant portion of his school day, Brendan also receives occupational-therapy and physical-therapy services. Brendan uses a power wheelchair for mobility and independence throughout the school, his home environments, and the community. At school, each classroom Brendan attends is equipped with a wheelchair-accessible desk.

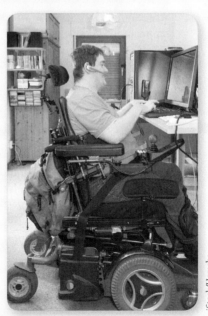

iStock/Horsche

Cushions

Options for cushions exist, and as previously noted, decisions regarding one aspect of a wheelchair, such as the cushion, influence other decisions (e.g., chair, seats, armrests) (Karp, 2008). Cushions need to provide postural stability as well as prevent pressure sores; pressure sores (i.e., bed sores or pressure ulcers) are places on a body where skin tissue has died because of a lack of blood supply caused by the area of the body being pressed against a surface, such as a part of a wheelchair (U.S. National Library of Medicine, 2014). Cushion choices can include foam, gel, air or dry floatation, urethane honeycomb, and alternating pressure (Karp, 2008; Srinivasan & Lloyd, 2011). Each different cushion option presents its own advantages (e.g., lower cost, washable, comfort) and disadvantages (e.g., additional weight, greater susceptibility to breaking or leaking).

Seats and Backs

Decision for seats, backs, and cushions are connected. Considerations for seats include width, depth, height, angle, back support, and back height (Karp, 2008). The goal with seat and back decisions is postural stability and the prevention of health problems, such as pressure sores or issues with the spinal cord. Ideally the seat should be narrow but not so much that it creates issues (e.g., sores) or prevents an individual from wearing a coat in colder weather. Decisions of seats and backs affect the weight of the wheelchair. Personal preferences should be taken into consideration for decisions of these elements (e.g., angle, height) (Karp, 2008; Srinivasan & Lloyd, 2011).

Armrests and Footrests

Armrests and footrests are additional wheelchair features. Users can generally remove armrests, as these can be purchased separately. Armrests provide benefits (e.g., weight bearing, assist in transferring in and out of the chair) as well as limitations (e.g., prevent an individual from going under a table and add weight). Armrest options include sculpted, flip-ups, swingaways, and desk style (Karp, 2008; Srinivasan & Lloyd, 2011). Users also have options for footrests—support for one's feet. A footrest can be fixed or swingaway. Footrests can be placed at different angles or put in different positions on the chair (Karp, 2008).

Tires and Casters

As with other components of a wheelchair, tires and casters are a consideration and selection, with options offering advantages and disadvantages. Options for tires can include pneumatic tires, solid rubber tires, and rubber insert tires (Karp,

2008; Srinivasan & Lloyd, 2011). Likewise, the selection of casters—smaller wheels—can impact mobility and aesthetics. Typically, casters are solid rubber or plastic, although larger pneumatic casters exist. Casters are typically in the front, but depending on the chair, casters may be in other locations (e.g., back) (Karp, 2008).

Mounting Systems and Attachments

Individuals can also purchase mounting systems to attach to a wheelchair. These mounting systems can support and provide stability for augmentative and alternative communication (AAC) devices and iPads, among other options (Carrington, Hurst, & Kane, 2013) (see Figure 4.4). When mounting an AAC or another device (e.g., mobile tablet), educators need to consider the shock absorption of the technology (Abbott & McBride, 2014). Another type of attachment for a wheelchair can be a removable tray or a laptop desk.

Figure 4.4   AbleNet's Mobile Mount for the iPad on Ottobock's Skippi

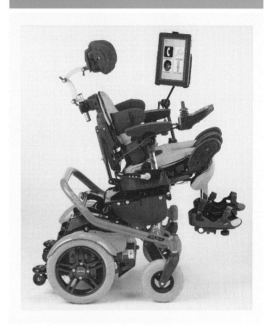

Source: AbleNet. Reproduced with permission.

Sports Wheelchairs

Sports wheelchairs are wheelchairs specifically designed for playing sports. Sports wheelchairs are designed to be very stable yet very lightweight (1-800-WHEELCHAIR.com, n.d.; Srinivasan & Lloyd, 2011). Within sports wheelchairs, options exist, including specialized chairs for tennis, racing, and extreme sports, for example. Sports wheelchairs or other mobility assistive technology options can be used for a variety of sports or adaptive sports, including, for example, soccer, tennis, football, basketball, and sled hockey.

Scooters

Scooters, or carts, are motorized mobility systems. Scooters are different from power wheelchairs and are typically less expensive than power wheelchairs (Stindt, Reed, & Obukowicz, 2009). Scooters are also steered by a steering wheel, in opposition to a joystick. Use of one's arms is generally required to use a scooter (Srinivasan & Lloyd, 2011; Stindt et al., 2009).

Gait Trainers

A gait trainer is a device with wheels that provides support for children and adults with walking (see Figure 4.5). A gait trainer offers mobility and balance. A gait trainer is different from a walker; walkers are typically used for support with an individual who bears his/her own weight. A gait trainer is designed to help a child learn to walk and develop a good gait and provides more support and stability (Bundonis, 2009). Gait trainers are used before an individual possesses weight-bearing strength (Noble, 2011). Gait trainers support or enhance a student's participation in activities (Paleg & Livingstone, 2015).

Although gait trainers are reported to be widely used, Paleg and Livingstone (2015) suggest little research exists as to the benefits for students with disabilities, such as cerebral palsy. Within the limited descriptive research on gait trainers, researchers found gait trainers can increase the number of steps students take as well as the distance they move (Lancioni et al., 2013; Willoughby, Dodd, Shields, & Foley, 2010).

Figure 4.5   Gait Trainer Example: Rifton Pacer

Source: Photo © 2014 by Rifton Equipment. Used with permission.

Case Study 4.2

Brittany is a 9-year-old girl diagnosed with cerebral palsy. Brittany uses a wheelchair for mobility. Her wheelchair also includes a mounting device to secure her augmentative and alternative communication device. In addition to using a power wheelchair, Brittany enjoys mobility-based assistive technologies that get her out of her wheelchair. Her favorite technology is her gait trainer, which allows her to move more independently and also allows her to be at the same height as her peers. Brittany was especially excited that her gait trainer was purple, her favorite color. In addition to her mobility-based assistive technology, Brittany uses other seating- or positioning-

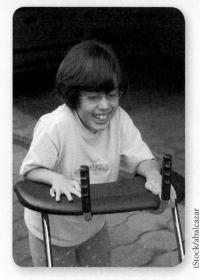

iStock/abalcazar

based assistive technologies at home, including shower chairs and adaptive seat options for mealtime.

Standing Devices

Standing devices provide support for children and adults to stand upright (see Figure 4.6). Standing devices can be used for individuals who cannot bear their own weight. Through pads and supports, individuals can stand up to engage in activities or conversations with peers and adults. There are multiple types of standing devices, including sit-to-stand standers, prone or supine standers, mobile standers, and active standers (Walker, 2007). Professionals, such as physical therapists, assist with the selection of the most appropriate stander given each individual student; students may want to try out different options if available (Low, Westcott, Beling, & Adams, 2011; Walker, 2007).

Sit-to-stand standers represent two different options: a device that can take an individual from a seating position to a standing position (and vice versa) and a device that uses straps to lift an individual out of a wheelchair (Krueger & Sullivan

Source: Photo © 2014 by Rifton Equipment. Used with permission.

Coleman, 2010; Walker, 2007). Prone and supine standers are similar; a prone stander supports an individual on his/her stomach and a supine on his/her back. There are standers that can be switched between the two options, often referred to as multiposition standers (Walker, 2007). Mobile standers are on wheels to provide mobility, which allows students to more freely and independently participate with their peers in activities while also strengthening their own motor skills (Rifton Equipment, 2015). Active standers involve a glider attachment so an individual moves him or herself (Walker, 2007).

Standing devices are also commonly used for students with physical disabilities. However, little research exists on their use as an evidence-based practice (Paleg, Smith, & Glickman, 2013). Existing evidence suggests use of standing devices can benefit individuals in terms of bone mineral density, increasing range of motion, and bowel function (Glickman, Geigle, & Paleg, 2010). Although more research is needed, Paleg et al. (2013) recommend use of mobile standers as part of the daily program for students.

Equipment, like gait trainers and standing devices, is likely to be shared among students at a school. Hence, such equipment is often adjustable and includes different attachments and options (Low et al., 2011).

Adaptive Strollers

For a child with a disability, an adaptive stroller may also be a consideration for mobility. For parents of children with disabilities that impact mobility, an adaptive stroller can also be very helpful. Adaptive strollers vary in design and features. Some features for adaptive strollers include increased weight capacity (e.g., up to 250 lbs), five-point harness systems, reclining seats, and safety wrist

In the mid 1980s, a curriculum was developed to focus on improving the functional mobility of individuals with severe multiple disabilities, the Mobility Opportunities Via Education (MOVE®) Curriculum. The MOVE Curriculum focuses on enhancing the movement of students and adults within natural contexts (Barnes & Whinnery, 2002; Whinnery & Whinnery, 2011). Specifically, MOVE helps individuals sit, stand, transition, and walk to enable greater participation. While mobility-based assistive technology (e.g., a gait trainer or mobile stander) may be used, therapists and educators implementing MOVE may seek to phase out such technology (MOVE International, n.d.). For more information on the MOVE Curriculum, one can visit their website, MOVE International (see http://www.move-international.org/). The MOVE Curriculum is credited with increasing the use of technology aside from wheelchairs in schools for students with physical disabilities (Low et al., 2011).

straps (see http://www.1800wheelchair.com/category/special-needs-strollers/ for sample adaptive stroller options).

Belts

Belts, such as gait belts or walking belts, can support students with disabilities who struggle with mobility and/or balance. Gait or walking belts, held by an adult, can support students, preventing falling during movement and/or providing stable movement.

Canes

For individuals who are blind, a cane can be a beneficial low-tech mobility tool. Canes help a student who is blind to independently navigate his/her environment (Loeding, 2011). Multiple cane options exist, including the traditional white cane, collapsible canes, laser canes, and sonar canes (Loeding, 2011). Additional technologies to support students who are blind are discussed in Chapter 6.

Assistive Technology for Positioning and Seating

Assistive technology to support positioning and seating is important for individuals who use a wheelchair for mobility as well as other individuals with

Ms. Croel is a special education teacher who works at an intermediate school district special school in a program for elementary students with physical disabilities and intellectual disability. The school that Ms. Croel works at uses the MOVE Curriculum. With the MOVE Curriculum, Ms. Croel and her paraprofessionals work to get the students out of their wheelchairs when they arrive in the classroom and into other mobility as well as seating assistive technology, including gait trainers, standing devices, and adaptive seats. When participating in different activities, students are learning movement, as appropriate, including transitioning from sitting to standing and standing to sitting. Ms. Croel feels that by using mobility assistive technology other than wheelchairs allows students to increase their independence and more actively participate in a variety of classroom activities.

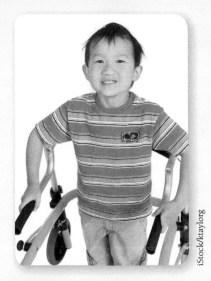

iStock/ktaylorg

disabilities. Positioning is an individual's postural alignment; assistive technology to support positioning is devices and tools to support such alignment (Srinivasan, & Lloyd, 2011). While assistive technology for positioning might be commonly thought of for individuals with physical disabilities, assistive technology for positioning can also be used to support other students, such as students with ADHD or emotional-behavior disorders. In addition, technology for positioning can be implemented as part of a Universal Design for Learning (UDL) approach within a classroom (refer to Chapter 1 for an in-depth discussion of UDL).

Seating Options

Assistive technology for positioning and seating, outside of a wheelchair, can include different options for seats. Traditional classroom seats can be replaced with seats specifically designed to support children and achieve good positioning (see eSpecialNeeds® Adaptive Seating at http://www.especialneeds .com/seating-positioning-adaptive-seating.html for examples). For example, one specific type of adaptive seat for positioning is the corner chair, which provides children with supports on three sides and is adjustable (AbleData, 2014) (see Figure 4.7). Another type of specific adaptive seat for positioning is a hi–low chair. A hi–low chair has adjustable height and provides more positioning support than traditional chairs. A final example of a specific adaptive chair to help students with positioning is the Kaye Kinder (see Kaye Products), which is also adjustable, works at standard tables, and has accessories that can be purchased for support (e.g., casters for movement). Special seats also exist for sitting on the floor, such as during circle or calendar time in a young elementary or early-childhood classroom.

Traditional seats can also be enhanced through the use of a cushion. Seat cushions can be round or square and can be filled with, for example, air, gel, beads, or foam (see Figure 4.8). Cushions can simply be placed on the seat or secured, such as the special tomato soft-touch liner by eSpecialNeeds®, which has straps that are clipped around the back and bottom of a standard chair. Some cushions simply provide secure positioning, and others also provide sensory integration. The cushions can offer students additional stimulation, which may be beneficial to students with ADHD, students with emotional-behavior disorders, students with autism spectrum disorder (ASD), or other students who benefit from movement when sitting. Researchers and practitioners suggest some students benefit from adding a cushion to their seats, including reducing off-task

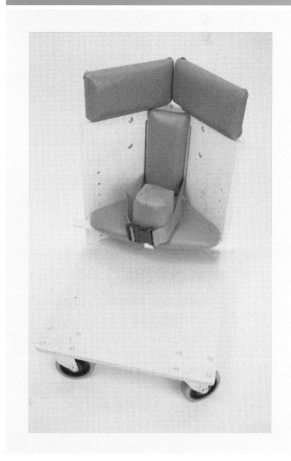

Figure 4.7   Kaye Products Corner Chair

Source: Kaye Products. Reproduced with permission.

Figure 4.8   Seat Cushion

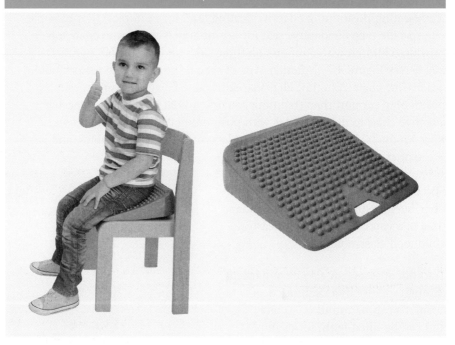

Source: Gymnic. Reproduced with permission.

behavior for preschool-aged children (Merritt, 2014). However, a small research study on two students with autism spectrum disorders found little impact from use of cushions (Umeda & Deitz, 2011).

Outside of specifically designed cushions for positioning and/or sensory integration, other seating alternatives can be repurposed as assistive technology for positioning (Bouck et al., 2012). A common repurposed objective for positioning is an exercise ball, also known as a stability or therapy ball. Instead of a traditional chair, students can use a large stability ball filled with air. The use of stability balls as seating can be implemented in a UDL fashion in which each child can select his/her seating preference— traditional chair or stability ball; seat cushions can be also be used in this manner. Students can select each day as well as change what they prefer throughout the day.

mixed results in effectiveness of ball.

Research on the use of exercise or stability balls for students with disabilities is somewhat mixed (Barton et al., 2015). Fedewa and Erwin (2011) found increased attention and time on task, with decreased hyperactivity in

What is sensory integration? Sensory integration involves providing sensory experiences (e.g., tactile, auditory) to students who may benefit (e.g., students with ADHD, students with ASD, and students with sensory integration disorder) (Barton, Reichow, Schnitz, Smith, & Sherlock, 2015; Zimmer & Desch, 2012). Technologies to provide sensory experiences can include such low-tech options as seat cushions or therapy seats, weighted vests, brushes, silly putty, and Koosh balls (Barton et al., 2015). It is important to note that in a recent meta-analysis of research on sensory-integration therapy, Leong, Carter, and Stephenson (2014) concluded the evidence for use of such intervention was weak for individuals with disabilities. A more detailed discussion of sensory-based assistive technology relative to behavior, inclusive of self-regulation, occurs in Chapter 7.

---

elementary-aged students with attention and/or hyperactivity concerns through use of a stability ball. However, Bagatell, Mirigliani, Patterson, Reyes, and Test (2010) did not find positive impacts (i.e., levels of engagement) when using a stability ball for the students with autism spectrum disorders. It is recommended that one consider student preference in seating, especially when alternatives (e.g., cushion or stability ball) are offered.

Another option for positioning assistive technology is a standing desk, or even allowing students to stand at their own traditional desks. Desks exist that are able to convert from a sitting desk to a standing desk. Recent attention has been given in the media to individuals in general about the negative health impacts of sitting, as opposed to standing (Park, 2014). The benefits of standing extend to students in schools, including sustaining attention (Bright, n.d.; Deardorff, 2012). In other words, fidgeting and movement are positive for learning. And like the stability ball, desks that convert from sitting to standing or desks that are tall enough to use stools or to be used when standing can be implemented in a UDL fashion to provide students with choices (Bright, n.d.; Deardroff, 2012).

Tools to Support Positioning in Seats

In contrast to alternative seats, devices can be included on seats, such as a footstool, or desks can be modified to serve as positioning assistive technology. A range of footstools for purchase exists, and one can make his or her own from a stack of books or a sturdy box. An example of a specifically marketed

Ms. Beard and Mrs. Fish co-teach a third-grade class of 28 students, including students identified with autism spectrum disorder, emotional-behavior disorders, and learning disabilities. Ms. Beard, the general education teacher, and Mrs. Fish, the special education teacher, actively plan lessons together. They also met over the summer to engage in frank conversations regarding the structure of their classroom and considerations for teaching together. Both teachers agreed they wanted to try to implement practices related to Universal Design for Learning as well as focus on issues of seating and positioning. They decided to focus on seating and positioning because of their awareness of the needs of a few students in their classroom as well as research they read regarding the

negative implications of just sitting. In their classroom, Ms. Beard and Mrs. Fish allow students to select which type of seat they want: traditional seat, traditional seat with seat cushion, or therapy/exercise ball seat. Students are not committed to a seat for the whole year or even an entire day but can switch when desired at appropriate times (i.e., transition times). They also allow students to stand as needed for a few minutes and build in time to move around throughout the day.

type of footstool is the FootFidget® Foot Rest (see Figure 4.9). Other low-tech tools to support the positioning of students with disabilities in seats can include belts or harnesses.

Tools for Positioning Outside of Seats

Aside from a stability ball, other everyday items can be repurposed for positioning assistive technology. For example, a beanbag chair without a zipper that can open could be repurposed to assist students. Likewise, a rolled towel, pillows, and a wedge—even one made from foam and covered in material—can serve as positioning assistive technology. Of course, specially designed wedges and therapy roll options do exist that can be purchased to support the positioning of students with disabilities, such as Tumble Form 2®. Some for-purchase wedges even come with straps to provide stability.

Other positioning system options exist, including ones that involve a student laying on his/her front (i.e., prone, face down), back (i.e., supine, face up), or side. While repurposing everyday items like pillows and towels can be cost-effective and readily available, for-purchase positioning systems might prove more sanitary, such as the Tumble Forms 2® Universal Grasshopper® System, the Tumble Forms 2® Deluxe Square Module Positioning System, or the Tumble Forms 2® Universal Side Layer (see http://www.tumbleforms.com). Such specifically designed positioning technology exists for children from ages zero through adult.

Figure 4.9   FootFidget® Foot Rest

Source: Classroom Seating Solutions. Reproduced with permission.
See http://www.classroomseatingsolutions.com/concept_solution.html

Web 2.0 Resources and Apps

One way apps can be used in support of mobility is to measure activity or to serve as activity trackers. Different apps and devices (e.g., FitBit) exist to measure steps or movement; these apps or devices may be used to measure activity or movement for individuals who use mobility-based assistive technology, including a wheelchair or gait trainer. Examples of apps to measure movement are Moves (ProtoGeo, 2015) and Steps Pedometer & Step Counter Activity Tracker by Supercritical Flow (2015).

Concluding Considerations

Many different options exist for assistive technology for mobility, positioning, and seating. And assistive technology considerations for mobility and positioning are not limited to individuals with physical disabilities or orthopedic impairments. For students with considerations of assistive technology for mobility and positioning, physical and occupational therapists should be important members of the IEP team (Gierach, 2009). **Occupational therapists** provide occupational therapy, which involves assisting students with disabilities to participate in school and school activities (i.e., their everyday activities in school). Occupational therapists can work with children as well as adults; occupational therapy can exist across a lifespan (American Occupational Therapy Association, 2014). Similarly, **physical therapists** provide physical therapy across the lifespan and in different settings. In school settings, physical therapists work with students with disabilities around issues of mobility (American Physical Therapy Association, 2014).

KEY TERMS

mobility, p. 77

occupational therapists, p. 96

physical therapists, p. 96

positioning, p. 77

EXTENSION ACTIVITIES

- Show "Meet Ryan and His Family" from Ottobock USA (see https://www.youtube.com/watch?v=qkWph1Qbm1Q) and/or "A Day in the Life: Jacqueline" from Ottobock USA (see https://www.youtube.com/watch?v=KGDNeidrjq0) in class or have students watch individually. Engage in a discussion regarding wheelchairs for children, including the benefits provided to the student as well as any accessories or features of the wheelchairs that benefit the student.

- Show the National Center for Technology Integration's "I Can Soar" video on Aaron (see http://www.nationaltechcenter.org/index.php/2007/03/04/vid-aaron/) in class or have students watch individually. Engage in a discussion regarding the assistive technology—with special emphasis on the mobility or positioning assistive technology-Aaron uses in the video.

- Show "Moving Forward—Woodland's Journey with MOVE" (see https://www.youtube.com/watch?v=rkXoZq3HTBQ), which highlights the MOVE® Curriculum, in class or have students watch individually. Engage in a discussion regarding the mobility, positioning, and seating assistive technology showcased in the video. Also engage in a discussion regarding the benefits of the MOVE Curriculum.

APPLICATION ACTIVITIES

- Try an alternative positioning assistive technology for yourself. For example, find a stability or exercise ball and try it as an alternative seat. Or try a standing desk or a footrest while you are sitting. What do you notice regarding the effects of these tools on you and your productivity, attention, or on-task behavior?

- Consider how you might use children's books to help explain the use of wheelchairs or other mobility-based assistive technology to children. Please consider a few suggestions below or find your own.

*Heelan, J. R. (2000). *Rolling along: The story of Taylor and his wheelchair*. Atlanta, GA: Peachtree Publishers.

*Berenstain, S., & Berenstain, J. (1993). *The Berenstain Bears and the wheelchair commando*. New York, NY: Random House.

*Kats, J. (2011). *Cinderella's magical wheelchair: An empowering fairy tale*. Ann Arbor, MI: Loving Healing Press.

DISCUSSION QUESTIONS

1. Why might an individual, parent, or team consider a manual wheelchair versus a power wheelchair?

2. When and why might different assistive technology for mobility options (e.g., wheelchair, gait trainer, mobile stander) be used for a student with a disability?

3. What are benefits associated with proper positioning or seating?

4. What everyday items can be repurposed as assistive technology for positioning for individuals with disabilities?

RESOURCES/ADDITIONAL INFORMATION

- The Division for Physical, Health, and Multiple Disabilities of the Council for Exceptional Children (http://community.cec.sped.org/DPHMD/home/)

- 1-800-WHEELCHAIR.com (http://www.1800wheelchair.com/)

- A YouTube video about some wheelchair features, specifically positioning equipment, at https://www.youtube.com/watch?v=JImfAMxiZTI

SUGGESTED ENRICHMENT READINGS

- Livingstone, R., & Field, D. (2015). The child and family experience of power mobility: A qualitative synthesis. *Developmental Medicine and Child Neurology*, 57(4), 317–327. doi:10.111/dcmcn.12633

- Livingstone, R., & Paleg, G. (2014). Practice considerations for the introduction and use of power mobility for children. *Developmental Medicine and Child Neurology*, 56(3), 210–222. doi:10.111/dcmcn.12245

CHAPTER 5

Assistive Technology for Computer Access

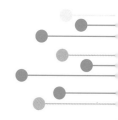

Chapter 5 discusses assistive technology for computer access. The chapter will familiarize the reader with standard and alternative access options for computers, including alternate keyboards, voice recognition, and switches. Chapter 5 will present options and considerations for access to Windows-based (i.e., PC) and OS X–based (i.e., Mac) desktop and laptop computers as well as computer-like devices, such as an iPad. The chapter will also present some app considerations for supporting students who might need alternative access to computers and computer-like devices.

Computers and computer-like mobile devices (e.g., tablets, smartphones) are increasingly being used by school-aged students out of school as well as in school. Recent statistics indicate the majority of teenagers in the United States report access to a computer at home (Madden, Lenhart, Duggan, Cortesi, & Gasser, 2013), and over 90% report daily computer use out of school (Herrick, Fakhouri, Carlson, & Fulton, 2014). While the mode for the number of hours of computer use outside of school for 12- to 15-year-olds was less than 1, over 40% reported using a computer daily for 2 or more hrs (Herrick et al., 2014). From a survey of parents with children in preschool through 12th grade, children have access to technology at home, and children of all ages are accessing such technology (e.g., computer, tablet, smartphone) daily or weekly (Grunwald Associates, 2013).

Access to a computer or mobile device is no doubt becoming increasingly important. However, not everyone accesses a computer or a mobile device in the same manner. Beyond the standard options of keyboards,

Chapter Objectives

After reading the chapter, the reader will be able to do the following:

1. Provide clear examples of assistive technology for computer access as alternatives to keyboards and mice

2. Evaluate when and why different alternative access options for computers might be used by students

3. Provide clear examples of different types of switches

4. Consider built-in, standard accessibility features on the operating systems of computers and mobile devices as assistive technology

Technology Mindset

Reflect—or keep data for a day—on the number of times you use or access your computer or a computer-like device, such as a smartphone or mobile tablet (e.g., iPad). How do you access these devices? What if your standard or typical means of accessing your computer was not available? How could you use your computer or computer-like device? What alternative means would you try and why?

trackpads, and a mouse, other options exist for individuals for whom standard options are not possible or who would benefit from alternative means. Examples of alternative methods of accessing and using a computer that are discussed in this chapter include voice or speech recognition, alternative keyboards, and switches. In addition, this chapter will discuss access and alternatives to computers, such as tablets, and assistive technology to support such access.

Assistive Technology for Computer Access

The common means for accessing a computer—desktop or laptop—are the standard keyboard and a mouse or trackpad (or touch pad); a mouse is more typical with a desktop and a trackpad with a laptop (see Perspective 5.2). However, these ways are not universally accessible to all individuals. Modifications to existing products and alternative means of accessing a computer—for both Windows (i.e., PC) and OS X (i.e., Mac) operating systems—along with built-in accessibility features for computers will be discussed in this chapter.

Keyboards

A keyboard is a basic computer input tool (Shih, 2014). The standard keyboard format—whether built in (i.e., laptop) or stand-alone (i.e., desktop)—is the QWERTY, whose name comes from reading the first six keys appearing on the top left letter row and reading from left to right; the exact reason for the QWERTY layout from the 1800s is not known although different theories exist (Noyes, 1983). However, a standard keyboard is not accessible to all students. Keyboard options also exist (see Table 5.1), including variations on layouts, alternative devices, and adaptations to standard keyboards.

Desktop vs. Laptop vs. Tablet

Here are a few examples of the ways in which desktops, laptops, and tablet devices differ when considering which might be the most appropriate for a student with a disability.

Desktop	Laptop	Tablet
• Larger monitor and keyboard • Can now include built-in touch screen	• Smaller monitor and keyboard • Can now include built-in touch screen • Portable	• Smaller screen; external or on-screen keyboard • Built-in touch screen • Portable • Weighs less than a laptop

Source: Green (2014).

Table 5.1   Example Keyboard Options and Alternatives

Types	Information
Adaptations	
Large keys	• Supports young children as well as those with cognitive challenges or those with fine motor challenges
Color coding	• More typical with young children or students with intellectual challenges
Alternative layout	
Alphabetical	• Supports students unfamiliar with QWERTY or who struggle with that format
Dvorak	• Reduces strain or movement as most used keys in the homeroom
Maltron	• Helps to reduce strain or movement
Alternative devices	
Ergonomic	• Decreases strain and discomfort
One-handed	• Benefits students with amputation or who use one hand
Intellikeys	• Supports students with fine-motor challenges, including young children, or cognitive challenges • Overlay options provide for flexibility

(Continued)

Table 5.1 (Continued)

Types	Information
Onscreen	• Supports students who use a mouse or a head stick or mouth stick with a computer
Wireless	• Supports students who want or need flexibility in keyboard location
Mini or contracted	• Benefits students with limited space or for use on a wheelchair • Benefits students who have fine-motor skills but limited range of motion • Creates difficulty for students with fine-motor challenges
Mouth and head stick compatible	• Supports students who use a head stick or mouth stick with a computer

Source: Burgstahler (2012); Cook and Polgar (2015); Dell, Newton, and Petroff (2012); Shih (2014); York and Fabrikant (2011).

Keyboard Options: Alternatives and Adaptations. Keyboards can be modified in a variety of ways, including making changes to a standard keyboard and providing an alternative keyboard. Modifications to a standard keyboard include enlarging the letters on the keys and/or adding color to different types of keys, such as color-coding vowels and consonants and as well as numbers and keys such as shift.

An increasingly common alternative to a standard keyboard is a wireless keyboard; individuals use a wireless keyboard with both desktop and laptop computers. With a wireless keyboard, an individual can move the keyboard to his/her desired location and still access the computer. A user is then not restricted to using the keyboard at a cord's length away from the computer. A wireless keyboard is a relatively minor adaptation as it maintains the same basic structure and format as a traditional keyboard. Likewise, ergonomic keyboards—keyboards intended to increase comfort and decrease strains or injuries—are also adaptations. A variety of ergonomic keyboards exist. Some examples of ergonomic keyboards include ones raised in the middle and sloping down on either side as well as keyboards that disconnect in the middle so users can adjust the space between the sides for their right and left hands.

Other options for alternative keyboards include mini keyboards, one-handed keyboards, and IntelliKeys®. Mini keyboards are keyboards that are smaller than standard keyboards, however, their layouts can vary. Mini keyboards can work when students have limited space, such as on a wheelchair tray or table.

Google Chromebooks

One special type of laptop is a Google Chromebook (Green, 2014). Google Chromebooks are becoming a poplar option in schools because of their low cost, versatility, and standard features (i.e., they come with a physical keyboard) (Herold, 2014; Hoffman, 2014). Chromebooks are considered easier to manage than other portable options, especially if Google Apps for Education is already being used by a school. In addition, students can share Chromebooks through individual logins (Hoffman, 2014). Chromebooks can support schools with 1:1 initiatives (i.e., one computer device per child) as well as schools who use classroom computer carts (i.e., mobile computers that are shared among classrooms) or computer labs. One consideration of Chromebooks, however, is that schools need strong Internet access as applications and data are stored in the cloud. Also, Chromebooks use the Google Chrome operating system (Herold, 2014).

*Google Apps for Education is a free set of tools that educators can use. Google Apps for Education include Classroom, Gmail, Drive, Calendar, Docs, Sheets, Slides, and Site (see https://www.google.com/edu/products/productivity-tools/).

One-handed keyboards are designed for individuals who have use of one hand. One-handed keyboards can also be produced with the QWERTY layout but truncated so keys share letters (i.e., just the letter keys are represented) as well as with the Maltron layout. Another alternative keyboard is IntelliKeys (York & Fabrikant, 2011) (see Figure 5.1). IntelliKeys is a flat, touch-based keyboard. When one purchases IntelliKeys, the tool comes with multiple keyboard overlay options, including, but not limited to, QWERTY, alphabetical, and mathematics (Parette, Blum, & Quesenberry, 2013). The IntelliKeys keyboard can function as both a keyboard and a mouse. Additional features can be added to IntelliKeys, including keyguards that help isolate separate keys and help guide one's fingers.

An additional alternative type of keyboard is a laser-projected keyboard. A laser-projected keyboard works via Bluetooth technology. It allows flexibility for laptop computers or mobile devices as the keyboard can be projected on a surface and a user just needs to bring the projection device, which is battery powered. The user then types via selecting the projected keys. Laser-projected keyboards, such as the Epic by Celluon, also provide mouse features.

Other alternative keyboards involve changing the layout of the keys. Alphabetical keyboards are keyboards in which the order of the keys is alphabetical as

Picabay/Cianna

Mr. Ward glances at his schedule for the day and then prepares to gather the assistive technology equipment he will need for the day from his lab at the intermediate school district (ISD). Mr. Ward is an assistive technology specialist and serves students and teachers in the ISD's school district. When Mr. Ward reviews his schedule, he notes that a lot of his day will be spent working with students who, for various reasons, need alternative access to a computer or computer-like device, such as a tablet. First on his schedule is to visit with Tyrian, a second-grade student with low vision whose general education class is increasingly going to start using the school's computer lab. The standard keyboard is not working for Tyrian, and Mr. Ward wants Tyrian to try a keyboard with enlarged letters that is also color-coded. Mr. Ward meets with Tyrian during his morning independent work time and shows him how to use the keyboard. Mr. Ward also works with the media specialist to make sure she knows how to install the keyboard and support Tyrian. Since Tyrian's teacher is engaged, Mr. Ward makes a note to stop in on her planning time the next time he

is in the building to make sure she is comfortable with the keyboard and supporting Tyrian. Next, Mr. Ward is going to visit Naomi and her teacher. Naomi is a fifth grader with cerebral palsy. Given Naomi's fine-motor challenges, Mr. Ward is going to have Naomi's special education teacher try Intellikeys® with her. Mr. Ward sets up the Intellikeys on the classroom computer in the special education room and then trains the special education teacher, Naomi, and Naomi's paraprofessional. The paraprofessional and the special education teacher are going to record data about Naomi's success with the technology, and Mr. Ward also schedules a time to return and observe Naomi with the technology before the IEP team makes a final decision regarding assistive technology to support Naomi in terms of accessing a computer.

Figure 5.1 IntelliKeys®

Source: AbleNet. Reproduced with permission.

opposed to QWERTY. Alphabetical keyboards also exist in which both formats are available; the alphabetical layout is dominant, but QWERTY is still an option. With such keyboards, users can switch between the layouts by pressing a button (e.g., Fast Finger Keyboards, see http://www.fastfingerkeyboards.com/). Another alternative keyboard layout is Dvorak, which arranges keys by frequency of use and to more evenly share the work between the fingers. With Dvorak, the home row contains vowels on the left side and the most commonly used consonants on the right (A O E U I D H T N S and then hypen or dash key [Cassingham, 2012]; see the Dvorak keyboard at http://www.dvorak-keyboard.com/). With the Dvorak layout, a user does not need to purchase a separate keyboard. Standard keyboards can be converted to Dvorak keyboards by changing the settings within the computer's operating system and printing a diagram or relabeling keys. A Maltron layout keyboard represents another alternative. The Maltron layout is based on frequency of letter use and places the most used letters and functions where the fingers and thumbs may easily and comfortably reach them (A N I S F D T H O R) (PCD Maltron, 2014).

A final alternative keyboard option discussed is on-screen keyboards or keyboard emulators (Lancioni, Sigafoos, O'Reilly, & Singh, 2013). On-screen keyboards are, like their name implies, virtual keyboards on one's computer screen. With on-screen keyboards, keys are selected, just as with a typical keyboard, but selection can be completed via touching (if a touch screen is on a computer), with the click of a mouse (or alternative), or via scanning and use of switches (Holland Bloorview Kids Rehabilitation Hospital, 2010). A common on-screen keyboard used in research is that of WiViK (see http://www.nanopac.com/Wivik.htm) (Holland Bloorview Kids Rehabilitation Hospital, 2010).

Keyboard Accessories. Beyond alternative keyboards, additional options or accessories for individuals with disabilities exist for the different keyboards. For example, keyguards are plates—plastic or metal—that sit on a keyboard to help an individual better select keys (Drescher, 2009; Fentek, 2014; Summers, Ruggiero, & Quist, 2011). Keyguards help to prevent a user from accidentally selecting an incorrect key. Keyguards are available for different types of keyboards as well as mobile devices. Different keyguards can even be purchased to specifically work with particular apps for mobile devices. Another adaptation for keyboards is a moisture guard. A moisture guard goes over a keyboard to protect it from moisture, such as drool or something spilt on the keyboard (Drescher, 2009; see Figure 5.2). Instead of a moisture guard, another way to prevent moisture is to purchase a water-submersive keyboard or a water-resistant keyboard; the latter is typically flexible.

Figure 5.2   Enlarged Keys Keyboard with Moisture Guard

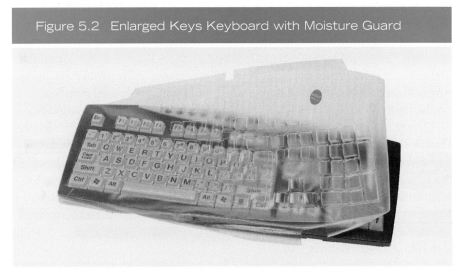

Source: AbleNet. Used with permission.

Head sticks (or head pointers), mouth sticks (or wands), and hand pointers also serve as keyboard accessories (WebAIM, 2012). A mouth stick is a plastic or rubber tool that an individual holds in his/her mouth and uses its pointy end to type. A head wand is similar, but instead of holding something in one's mouth, a stick or wand is placed on one's head, often strapped on (Cook & Polgar, 2015). While these tools can be used with a variety of keyboard options, specially designed keyboards for use with mouth sticks or head wands are produced to minimize movement, such as the Maltron head or mouth stick keyboard (see Maltron head or mouth stick keyboard at http://www.maltron.com/component/k2/item/465-head-or-mouth-stick-keyboard). A typing aid (e.g., hand pointer) can be secured via a strap onto a student's hand to aid in typing and accessing a keyboard (Cook & Polgar, 2015).

[handwritten margin note: Is this the most dignified option for students with limited hand movement???]

[handwritten margin note: Limits verbal communication.]

Mouse Options

Along with a keyboard, a mouse is a common input tool to access a computer. A mouse allows a user to move around a computer and to make selections, often by clicking. A variety of different types of mice are available, including, but not limited to, a wireless mouse, a left-handed mouse, a one-button mouse, and an optical mouse. However, use of a mouse does require hand control (Green, 2014). Of course, with a laptop computer, one can elect to use a mouse or the built-in trackpad or touchpad that operates like a mouse (Drescher, 2009; Summers et al., 2011). Users can now purchase trackpads to be connected to a desktop computer if they are more comfortable with operating the trackpad as opposed to a mouse. While the variety of mouse options provides users with choice and flexibility, alternative options may better support some individuals with disabilities.

Mouse options exist that are designed to serve as assistive technology for individuals who may struggle with using their fingers or hands. For example, there exists a mouse that can be controlled by one's foot, such as the NoHands Foot Mouse, which involves foot pedals, as well as the Footime™ Mouse (see Fentek Industries' ergonomic computer mouse products at http://www.fentek-ind.com/ergmouse.htm#.VDwg0ucfs70) (Cook & Polgar, 2015; Drescher, 2009; York & Fabrikant, 2011). Other hands-free mouse options include the head mouse, which tracks one's head movement (e.g., Smartnav 4 EG Hands Free Mouse, CameraMouse).

Eye Gaze. An alternative type of mouse is one that moves a cursor and makes selections based on eye movement or eye dwelling or blinking, which is often referred to as eye gaze or eye track technology (e.g., EyeTech EyeOn Hands Free

Mouse Alternative, Eyegaze Edge, Tobii PCEye Go) (Cook & Polgar, 2015). Alternatives to a traditional mouse, like eye gaze systems, work with on-screen keyboards for typing . Eye gaze systems are appropriate for individuals with no hand movement but who can reliably move their eyes and hold their heads still (Dell et al., 2012). Note, eye gaze is also a means in which students with complex communication needs can interact with augmentative and alternative communication (AAC) devices to communicate (see Chapter 3 for a discussion of AAC) (Shane, Blackstone, Vanderheiden, Williams, & DeRuyter, 2012).

Joysticks and Trackballs. Both joysticks—common with older video games—and trackballs serve as alternatives to a mouse. Commonly referred to as an upside down mouse, a trackball is a large ball that rolls (i.e., moves the cursor) and with buttons for clicking (see Figure 5.3). Trackballs can represent an option for students with fine-motor issues, including coordination challenges (Green, 2014). Trackballs are considered a durable device. Multiple trackball options exist, including standard as well as larger or mini-size trackballs (Dell et al., 2012). Joysticks are sticks that can also move the cursor in various directions and make selections (Fulk, Watts, & Bakken, 2011). Students may use standard or adapted joysticks.

Figure 5.3 BIGTrack™ Trackball

Source: AbleNet. Used with permission.

Touch Screen

Touch screens also enable alternative access to a computer (York & Fabrikant, 2011). With a touch screen, a user can navigate a computer and make selections by just touching the screen. In the past, touch screens were retroactively added to computer monitors (i.e., they were secured on top of an existing monitor), such as Magic Touch by KEYTEC, Inc. Nowadays, however, students are likely to be more familiar with touch screens as smartphones, mobile tablets (e.g., iPad), and some computers operate via a touch screen. Regardless of the device, touch screens operate in the same manner: The user can simply access and interact with the device via his/her fingers.

Voice Recognition

Along similar lines of being hands-free, as discussed earlier, voice recognition—sometimes referred to as speech recognition—provides an alternative option to using a mouse (York & Fabrikant, 2011). Voice recognition involves performing operations on a computer via one's voice, from opening an application to searching in Google and even dictating a paper in Microsoft Word. The program recognizes one's voice commands and performs the operations verbalized. The latest Windows operating systems, including Vista, 7, and 8.1, allow users to control their computers via speaking commands (see Windows' "What can I do with Speech Recognition?" at http://windows.microsoft.com/en-us/windows/what-can-do-speech-recognition#1TC=windows-7). The same is true for Mac operating systems, such as OS X Mountain Lion (see "OS X Mountain Lion: Use spoken commands to control your Mac" at http://support.apple.com/kb/PH11258) and OS X Mavericks.

Another application of voice recognition is speech-to-text, which takes one's spoken words and translates them into documents or e-mails. Speech-to-text is the technology that allows individuals allows individuals to speak a message rather than typing (also known as voice to text) on their iOS devices. Currently, speech-to-text uses what is known as continuous speech, in which a user fluently dictates text with pauses between sentences (SNOW, 2013). Older technology, which is not used much now, is discrete speech. In discrete speech, a user had to pause between each word when dictating (SNOW, 2013). For-purchase speech-to-text programs exist (e.g., Dragon Dictate from Nuance), however, both Windows and OS X operating systems come with a built-in speech recognition program for controlling one's computer as well as translating spoken words to text documents. Speech-to-text capabilities will be discussed in more detail in Chapter 8.

Keyboard Shortcuts, Mouse Keys, and Sticky Keys

Three other alternatives to a mouse, built into both Windows and Mac OS X operating systems, are keyboards shortcuts, mouse keys, and sticky keys. Keyboard shortcuts involve the user pressing a combination of keys to complete a task (Microsoft, 2014). Common examples of keyboard shortcuts are Control-C for copy on a Windows machine; for a Mac, the shortcut is Command-C. These keyboard shortcuts can save time for everyone, in addition to replacing a mouse. See "Keyboard shortcuts for Windows" (http://support.microsoft.com/kb/126449) for an expanded list of keyboard shortcuts for a Windows machine and "Mac keyboard shortcuts" (http://support.apple.com/kb/ht1343) for keyboard shortcuts for a Mac.

Although keyboard shortcuts can be used automatically, one needs to turn on mouse keys. Mouse keys involve moving the cursor and making selections with specific keys from the keyboard (Apple, 2014; Wendt & Weed, 2011). Using a numbers keyboard or specific keys on a standard keyboard, the cursor moves in different directions as well as makes selections (see Windows' "Use Mouse Keys to move the mouse pointer" at http://windows.microsoft.com/en-us/windows7/use-mouse-keys-to-move-the-mouse-pointer for a Windows computer and "OS X Mavericks: Control the pointer using Mouse Keys" at http://support.apple.com/kb/PH14235 for a Mac computer).

Sticky keys, like mouse keys, also need to be turned on. Sticky keys, which work with Windows or OS X computers, prevent an individual from having to use two hands or having to press two keys simultaneously. When sticky keys are turned on, an individual can press two keys (such as capitalizing a letter [shift and letter] or using Control-C to copy) sequentially rather than simultaneously (Douglas, Courtad, Mustian, & Parette, 2013).

Switches

Although switches can exist as alternatives to a mouse, they are multifunctional stand-alone technology. As discussed in Chapter 10, switches can operate battery-powered toys. They can also operate AAC devices as well as a powered wheelchair or control appliances or light switches in one's environment (i.e., environment control units) (Assistive Technology Training Online Project, n.d.; York & Fabrikant, 2011). (Note, environment control units will be discussed in greater detail in Chapter 9.) Switches can be used for direct selection (i.e., activate a switch and a selection, or input, is made) or scanning, which involves the different options being highlighted, with the user again activating the switch to make a particular selection. Drescher (2009) advised

When considering assistive technology to support computer access, one must also consider positioning to access a computer (Sadao & Robinson, 2010) (please see Chapter 4 for additional information on positioning assistive technology). To effectively use a computer, students need to be positioned to reach the devices they will use, including the computer (i.e., touch screen), keyboard, and mouse. The devices, including a table, being at the correct height and distance are important considerations. Computers placed on adjustable-height desks can support students, as can trays that tilt a keyboard (DO-IT, 2012). A student will also need proper support for his/her head, trunk, and wrists (Sadao & Robinson, 2010). One example of low-tech options to provide support to students to engage with a computer is pads for keyboards or mice. Gel or foam rests or pads exist to support one's wrists.

that switch access be the last consideration given the demands—cognitively and with regards to patience—placed on an individual using a switch. Yet switches offer an option to individuals as they can be operated with multiple body parts (e.g., hands, head, foot, elbow), thus creating opportunities for individuals with limited use of their hands (Green, 2014).

A variety of different types of switches exist. Switches vary by how a user engages with the switch, such as movement of a part of one's body, respiration (e.g., puffing), or sound or voice (Cook & Polgar, 2015). Switches also vary in terms of the feedback a user receives after activating or deactivating the switch, such as auditory or tactile. Other aspects of switches include their size and the amount of force or effort to activate or deactivate (Cook & Polgar, 2015). There can also be single switches or multiswitches (see the switch selection guide by AbleNet, available from http://www.ablenetinc.com/Portals/0/KnowledgeBase/Selection_Grids/Switch_Selection_Grid.pdf).

Switches activated by movement involve movement of any part of one's body, including hands, feet, elbow, and head. The movement can both involve physically touching (e.g., pressing to activate) or without contact (i.e., activated via proximity). Switches that respond via movement include ones characterized as mechanical (i.e., apply force, such as with hand or head), electromagnetic (i.e., involves radio or light waves), electrical (i.e., electrical signals), and proximity (i.e., part of the body comes close to the switch but does not need to contact) (Cook & Polgar, 2015; York & Fabrikant, 2011).

Mechanical switches can also be activated differently, such as by touch or pushing; by moving a lever; by grasping, pulling, or gripping; and by sipping and puffing (Drescher, 2009). Mechanical switches can be wired or wireless. With wireless switches, one will need a receiver, as typically a switch is plugged into the device it is operating. The most common type of mechanical switch is a push switch, also called a touch or button switch (Bornman, 2011; Drescher, 2009). An example of a wireless push switch is the Big Beamer by AbleNet (see Table 5.2). As stated, push switches operate by pushing or touching the switch, such as with one's hand or any other body part that can apply pressure (e.g., head, foot). There are also lever switches, which involve moving a lever in a particular direction, and wobble switches, which are activated by moving in any direction. Other motor movement–based switches involve activating via grasping

Table 5.2 Examples of Switches

Switch Type	Image	Considerations for Whom It May Be Appropriate
Movement: Mechanical		
Push switch (e.g., Big Bed or Jelly Bean)		• Students who can move their hand, foot, elbow, head, or other body part to press. Supports students who need tactile and/or auditory feedback.
Pillow switch		• Students with limited movements of head or limbs, who may activate via head or face (e.g., cheek). Supports students who need tactile and/or auditory feedback.
Lever switch (e.g., Flex)		• Students who require a mounted switch and can move the end in any direction. Supports students who need tactile feedback.
Grasp switch (e.g., Grasp)		• Students who can grasp and release within a short duration of time.

Switch Type	Image	Considerations for Whom It May Be Appropriate
Chin switch		• Students who can move their head/neck but may have limited limb movement. Supports students who need tactile and/or auditory feedback.
Ribbon switch		• Students who can move the switch in any direction with a body part, such as head or hand.
Leaf switch		• Students who can press against the switch in one direction.
Paddle switch (e.g., Rocker switch)		• Students who need multi or dual switches and can press down on switch. Supports students who need tactile and/or auditory feedback.
String switch		• Students with limited strength; can move hand or finger. Supports students who need tactile and/or auditory feedback.

Source: AbleNet. Photos reproduced with permission.

(e.g., grasp switch), gripping, pulling (e.g., string switch), bending (e.g., ribbon switch) or pinching (AbleNet, 2014; Assistive Technology Training Online Project, n.d.; Bornman, 2011; Drescher, 2009).

Other movement-based switches involve proximity and electromagnetics. Switches like the Candy Corn™ proximity sensor work when a user moves a body part close to the switch. Infrared switches can be controlled with many body parts (e.g., eyebrow, finger, blinking eye) and work by "detecting a beam of reflected pulsed infrared light" (Bornman, 2011; Cook & Polgar, 2015; Drescher, 2009, p. 19) (see Table 5.3).

Table 5.3 Examples of Switches

Switch Type	Image	Considerations for Whom It May Be Appropriate
Movement: Proximity		
Proximity (e.g., Candy Corn™)		• Student who can move a body part but physically touching a switch is challenging. Supports students who need auditory or visual feedback.
Movement: Electromagnetic		
Infrared (e.g., SCATIR)		• Students who can move, for example, their eyes (i.e., blink), eyebrows (e.g., raise), or lips. Students who need auditory feedback.

Source: AbleNet. Photos reproduced with permission.

Non–movement-based switches involve those activated by respiration, such as pneumatic switches, often from puffing (or blowing) or sipping (Bornman, 2011; Cook & Polgar, 2015) (see Table 5.4).

Table 5.4 Examples of Switches

Switch Type	Image	Considerations for Whom It May Be Appropriate
Respiration		
Pneumatic switch (e.g., Imperium Sip and Puff)		• Students with limited movement, can sip or puff with mouth.

Source: AbleNet. Photos reproduced with permission.

Using a switch involves more than just the switch. For wireless switches, one needs a wireless receiver. And switches do not just plug into a piece of technology, such as a computer or a mobile tablet (Cook & Polgar, 2015; Drescher, 2009). Switches are plugged into a switch interface, which is then plugged into the technology. In addition, some switches will need to be mounted, such as onto a wheelchair, table, or even a body part (e.g., arm or leg) (Cook & Polgar, 2015). A mounting system can range from hundreds of dollars to the cost of securing Velcro to the switch and a table (Drescher, 2009).

Selecting a switch involves many considerations. Like other assistive technology, it is important to use an assistive technology decision-making framework, as discussed in Chapter 2, to make switch selections. When considering a switch, IEP team members want to ensure that a student will actually use the device and that it will work for the individual student (e.g., s/he can activate the switch with his/her abilities). Additional considerations for a switch might also include the force needed to activate the switch, the body part one can move to activate the switch (i.e., the positioning of the switch), durability, portability, and feedback (i.e., all switches provide feedback, such as auditory or visual) (Assistive Technology Training Online Project, n.d.; Bornman, 2011).

Case Study 5.2

Humberto is a 17-year-old high school student with multiple disabilities: physical disabilities and intellectual disability. Humberto uses a power wheelchair, which he controls with a joystick using his right hand. Humberto enjoys playing games on a computer or a tablet and uses a switch (e.g., Jelly Bean switch by AbleNet or Blue2 Bluetooth switch by AbleNet) to interact with the devices using his right

iStock/mtreasure

hand. He also uses a push switch to activate his AAC device.

Assistive Technology for Mobile Devices

Technology has become faster, smaller, and more personal (Thomas & McGee, 2012). Mobile technology today is not a portable laptop but mobile, handheld devices, such as a tablet (e.g., iPad) or smartphone (Edyburn, 2013). A benefit to using mobile technologies for students with disabilities is the similarity to what peers are using as well as the built-in or obtainable accessibility features and tools.

Mobile devices, including tablets and smartphones, come standard with built-in accessibility, as do computers. (Please see the next section on built-in accessibility for additional information.) For mobile devices, one of the main accessibility features is the touch screen and the affordances that it can create (Trewin, Swart, & Pettick, 2013). Yet touch screens are not universally accessible, and some users still struggle with using such technology. However, stand-alone assistive technology devices can also be used with mobile devices. For example, iOS devices come with a built-in accessibility feature called AssistiveTouch, which allows users to interact with the device via a compatible accessory (e.g., joystick) (Apple, 2015c; Morris & Mueller, 2014). Mobile devices can also be switch compatible. For example, the New Blue2™ switch by AbleNet is compatible with iOS and Android mobile devices as well as computers operating OS X and Windows. In addition, many users without disabilities elect to use a separate keyboard when using a tablet rather than relying on a mobile device's on-screen keyboards.

Accessories

Accessories are pretty standard for mobile devices (e.g., OtterBox protective cases for smartphones and tablets). In terms of accessibility accessories, multiple options exist. One area of accessibility is cases. While many individuals may use a case, such as OtterBox, to protect their mobile tablet, cases are also marketed for individuals with disabilities. These specially designed cases can go beyond durability protection to include options for easier grasping or holding, for mounting on a wheelchair or table, or to be water resistant. For example, the Rugged iPad case by AbleNet is not only water and dust resistant and also can be mounted, but an attachable shoulder strap can also be used for transporting the device. Another product by AbleNet—Connect—supports an iPad while allowing switch access and scanning capabilities as well as works for mounting (see Figure 5.4). It is notable that Apple explicitly states that Connect from AbleNet can be used with the iOS AssistiveTouch.

Figure 5.4   Connect by AbleNet

Source: AbleNet. Reproduced with permission.

Styluses can also support accessibility to mobile devices for students with disabilities. Rather than using one's fingers on the mobile device touch screen, one can use a stylus to interact, such as Pogo™ stylus. A variety of styluses exist, including ones that look like pens or pencils. One can purchase a mouth stick or a head stick stylus for touch screen interaction. For students with gripping challenges, one can support their use of a stylus with low-tech assistive technology, such as by putting a tennis ball or similar material around the stylus (Parette & Blum, 2015). Of course, for-purchase stylus grip tools also exist, in which the stylus is secured via Velcro around one's wrist or hand.

As indicated, some users of mobile devices elect to use a separate keyboard. Separate keyboards can be purchased as part of a case for a mobile device, although others can be detached from the case and operate via Bluetooth technology. While the keyboards are generally smaller than desktop and laptop keyboards, additional supportive features do exist, such as color-coded keys. Laser-projected keyboards that operate via Bluetooth technology, such as Epic by Celluon, can be especially useful with mobile devices given the small size and portability of the device. Similarly, as previously indicated, individuals can use switches with mobile devices as well joysticks, such as the J-Pad Bluetooth Joystick for iOS devices. (See Figure 5.5 for an example of a switch compatible with a mobile device. Blue2™ switch from AbleNet is a Bluetooth switch that works with iOS and Android devices as well as Windows and Apple operating systems.)

Mounting systems are also accessories that can benefit students with disabilities who make use of mobile devices. Such mounting systems can include options for mounting to a wheelchair or a table as well as mounting to a part of one's body, such as leg or arm. These mounting systems can incorporate low-tech solutions, such as suctions (i.e., for tabletop mounting) and adjustable straps for arm and leg mounting. Beyond mounting, some mobile-device users may prefer stands, such as for use on solid surfaces. These stands can support a tablet or smartphone upright and at an angle.

Built-In Accessibility

Computers and computer-like devices (i.e., mobile tablets and smartphones) come with built-in accessibility features. As discussed earlier in this chapter, both Windows and Mac operating systems come equipped with speech recognition programs in which an individual can operate his or her computer

Figure 5.5   Blue2™ Bluetooth from AbleNet

Source: AbleNet. Reproduced with permission.

with his or her voice, from opening applications to creating Word documents. Also discussed were the keyboard shortcuts and mouse keys with both Windows and Mac operating systems to also create accessibility for users. Mobile devices—both Apple and Android—offer standard accessibility features, including connections to braille displays, magnifications or screen enlargers, and screen readers. (See Table 5.5 for sample accessibility features built into

Table 5.5 Sample Accessibility Features from Apple OS X and iOS, Windows, and Android Devices			
Apple OS X (Mac)	**Apple iOS (iPhone, iPad)**	**Windows 7 or 8**	**Android Devices**
• Voice over (reads computer screen); text-to-speech (reads any highlighted text) • Zoom (magnifies screen) • Dictation (speech recognition to navigate or compose text) • Contrast options (change screen and text color) • Cursor size (change size of cursor) • Screen flash (screen flashes as an alert) • Switch control (allows navigation by a switch) • Sticky keys (press keys consecutively instead of simultaneously to perform task) • Word completion (word prediction in certain apps)	• Font adjustments (makes size of font in iOS apps bigger) • Made for iPhone Hearing Aids (manage hearing aids from iPhones) • AssistiveTouch (change gestures required for interacting with device and apps) • Switch control (use of Bluetooth-enabled switch to use device) • Keyboard shortcuts (create customized text shortcuts/ abbreviations) • Guided Access (disables Home button so one cannot exit app or can limit time allowed on an app) • Safari reader (provides just the content of articles on Safari)	• Speech Recognition (operate computer via speech or dictate documents/e-mails) • Magnifier (magnifies the entire screen or particular parts of a screen) • On-screen keyboards (on-screen keyboard with choice of selection mode) • Narrator (provides audio description of all actions on a computer) • High contrast (increases color contrast of text and screen) • Visual notifications (notifications presented visually and not aurally) • Mouse keys (operate mouse functions with arrow keys)	• TalkBack (screen reader to provide auditory information and feedback as one uses the device) • Captions (turn on closed captioning) • Large text (increase the text size) • BrailleBack (connects to refreshable braille display)

Source: Apple (2015a, 2015b); Google (2015); Microsoft (2015).

Windows and Apple products, including computers and mobile devices. Please note the table is not exhaustive of all built-in accessibility features and that features are updated with the release of new or updated products.) Before for-purchase options or additional technologies are selected, individuals making the assistive technology decisions should explore the capabilities of built-in accessibility features. While built-in accessibility features may not work for all students (i.e., lacking critical features), built-in features are cost-effective (i.e., free) and should be at least considered.

Web 2.0 Resources and Apps

For students for whom the typical means of accessing a computer—keyboard and mouse—are not feasible or easy to use, alternate means of access exist. As discussed in this chapter, alternative means can include alternative keyboards, voice recognition or speech-to-text, and switches, to name a few. While the chapter was focused more on alternative means for computers, these products can also be used with mobile devices, such as iPads, through apps. In addition to utilizing existing keyboard options, such as QWERTY, AZERTY, and QWERTZ keyboards with iOS 8 for the iPad, as well as word prediction, third-party apps are available. For example, one can select for purchase or free Dvorak apps for both Apple and Android devices (see the Application Activities at the end of the chapter). Other app-based alternative keyboards also exist, such as SwiftKey (http://swiftkey.com/en/), Swype (http://www.swype.com/), and Fleksy (http://fleksy.com/). Note, SwiftKey recently received

attention with its integration into the Assistive Context Aware Toolkit (ACAT) from Intel, an open-source system created for Dr. Stephen Hawking (Collins, 2014).

In addition to the options discussed in this chapter, educators may also want to consider Web 2.0 or apps to support students who benefit from alternative means of accessing and using a computer or computer-like device. For example, VoiceThread (see https://voicethread.com/) is an app for Apple products available from iTunes in which a user can record him or herself. Users can take a picture and voice a response. Students with manual dexterity can also animate or draw on the photo as they are talking. As an alternative to just voice, a video can also be made of the user that allows for overlays on the image. This can be used for students for whom typing or printing is challenging to voice their responses to different prompts or questions. The products can then be shared, such as via e-mail, with a teacher. There are a variety of apps that operate similar to VoiceThread that are free or low cost (e.g., Educreations and ShowMe Interactive). For example, with Educreations, students who struggle with holding a pencil can draw or write with their fingers on the tablet's touch screen. Educators and students should conduct trials to determine the app that works best for each individual and his/her device.

Case Study 5.3

Ms. Fisher is a high school special education teacher in a self-contained program supporting students with multiple disabilities, including intellectual disability and physical disabilities. In Ms. Fisher's classroom, there are a lot of assistive technology options, both designed for the whole class as well as individual options.

© vtsaran

For example, Ms. Fisher has a variety of different keyboards for her three classroom computers that can be interchanged to support her students with different needs. These include a standard keyboard with a keyguard as well as a compact keyboard that works well with a mouth guard. She also has multiple mouse options, including a joystick and trackball, again to be changed to meet each of her students' individual needs. Finally, her individual students use switches throughout the day. Not only do they use switches to interact with computers and tablets but also their AAC devices and environmental control units to prepare to be as independent as possible in their daily lives. Ms. Fisher's students use push-button switches, some of which they activate with their hands and others with their heads. Increasingly, her students are using wireless push-button switches, such as the Big Beamer™ from AbleNet. Within her class, a student uses a pillow switch with his cheek, another a wobble switch that she moves with her hand, and a third a pneumatic switch, which the student operates via puffing.

Perspective 5.5

Future Trends

Technology for the future includes wearables, including in everyday life and possibly classrooms and schools through bring your own device (BYOD) initiatives. Individuals might be aware of wearables now, such as the Apple Watch or Android-based watches or even previously as Google Glass. However, the potential for wearables is much greater, beyond what is currently available in commercial markets. To learn more about the potential of wearables, consider watching *Make It Wearable* from Intel UK, which includes five episodes that explore wearables (see, for example, *Make It Wearable*, "Episode 4: Becoming Superhuman UB" at https://www.youtube.com/watch?v=x6dwYKfoEG0).

Concluding Considerations

Computer and computer-like devices (i.e., mobile tablets and smartphones) are increasingly being used by all individuals, including students with disabilities. While different computer operating systems and mobile-device operating systems come standard with built-in accessibility features (refer to Table 5.5), stand-alone assistive technology devices can also support access to such tools. For computers, students with disabilities may use a standard keyboard or an alternative keyboard, including ones with different layouts. Students with disabilities may also use a standard mouse or an alternative, such as a trackball or joystick. Switches also provide accessibility for students with disabilities to independently use computers and mobile technologies. While this chapter provided examples of currently existing assistive technology options and standard accessibility features for computing, technology is rapidly changing. And that is especially true for computers and mobile devices. Technological advances increasingly provide built-in accessibility to students with disabilities to access and independently use computers and mobile technologies.

EXTENSION ACTIVITIES

- Show the National Center for Technology Innovation's "I Can Soar" video on Aaron (http://www.nationaltechcenter.org/index.php/2007/03/04/vid-aaron/) in class or have students watch individually. Engage in a discussion regarding the assistive technology that Aaron uses, with special emphasis on accessing a computer.

- Show "Assistive Technology in Action: Meet Jared" (https://www.youtube.com/watch?v=bYKUxOdUAao) in class or have students watch individually. Engage in a discussion regarding the switch Jared uses in the video.

- Show "Computers" from Christopher Reeve's website (http://bit.ly/1Dsyf4w), which discusses the iPad and iPad accessories, in class or have students watch individually. Engage in a discussion regarding how Christina uses accessories with the iPad to support her access.

- Show "How Intel Keeps Stephen Hawking Talking" (https://www.youtube.com/watch?v=uXIG0sqQItA) in class or have students watch individually to provide an example of how an infrared switch mounted to Dr. Hawking's eyeglasses and cheek sensor allow Dr. Hawking to communicate; technology from SwiftKey is also highlighted as it enables better word and character predictions. Engage in a discussion regarding the benefits of switch technology for individuals with disabilities.

APPLICATION ACTIVITIES

- Try an alternative keyboard. For example, one can convert his/her computer to the Dvorak keyboard. One can also use a Dvorak keyboard app on an iOS device, such as the free iPad or iPhone app Dvorak from iTunes (Mao, 2014) or the Alphabetical Keyboard (Rayamangalam, 2013) for Android devices available through Google Play. Experiment with the alternative keyboard and decide for oneself the benefits and limitations of QWERTY versus another layout or alternative keyboard.

- Try using other alternative app-based keyboards for mobile devices, such as SwiftKey (http://swiftkey.com/en/), Swype (http://www.swype.com/), and Fleksy (http://fleksy.com/).

- Try using a Windows or a Mac computer with their built-in speech recognition systems (see http://windows.microsoft.com/en-us/windows/what-can-do-speech-recognition#1TC=windows-7 or http://support.apple.com/kb/PH14232 and http://support.apple.com/kb/PH11258). Experiment with accessing and using one's

computer via voice commands. Consider the benefits as well as any limitations.

- If you have access to a switch, download a switch-accessible app (see Jane Farrall and Alex Dunn's "Switch Accessible Apps for iPad/iPhone" at http://www.janefarrall.com/html/resources/Switch_Accessible_Apps_for_iPad.pdf for a list of some iPad apps that are switch accessible). Consider how the app works via a switch.

- Explore the switch examples from Tables 5.2, 5.3, and 5.4. Describe what body parts and actions could activate the switch. Also, describe one potential application of the switch. In other words, what task can the switch help an individual with a disability perform?

- Explore the accessibility features on either a Windows or Mac operating system computer. Try some of the different accessibility features (see https://www.apple.com/accessibility/osx/ for Mac and http://www.microsoft.com/enable/products/windows8/ for Windows).

DISCUSSION QUESTIONS

1. What adaptations can be made to keyboards to benefit students with disabilities? When and why would one use such an adaptation with students?

2. What alternative options to keyboards exist for students with disabilities? When and why might a student use an alternative option?

3. What alternative options to a mouse exist for students with disabilities, and why might a student use an alternative option?

4. What considerations are needed when selecting switches for students with disabilities?

5. Consider the standard, built-in accessibility features on a computer or mobile device. When might a student benefit from a separate device or technology as opposed to using the standard accessibility features? How do the built-in accessibility features work in conjunction with other pieces of assistive technology?

RESOURCES/ADDITIONAL INFORMATION

- The Division for Physical, Health, and Multiple Disabilities of the Council for Exceptional Children (http://community.cec.sped.org/DPHMD/home/)

- YouTube video on how to use IntelliKeys (http://www.youtube.com/watch?v=FRVLirkVhXY)

- AbleNet's YouTube Channel (https://www.youtube.com/channel/UC2sMiMtHWfIGHRxXYmhwDuA)

SUGGESTED ENRICHMENT READINGS

- Cihak, D. F., McMahon, D., Smith, C. C., Wright, R., & Gibbons, M. M. (2014). Teaching individuals with intellectual disability to email across multiple device platforms. *Research in Developmental Disabilities, 36,* 645–656. doi:10.1016/j.ridd.2014.10.044

- Manresa-Yee, C., Ponsa, P., Salinas, I., Perales, F. J., Negre, R., & Varona, J. (2014). Observing the use of an input device for rehabilitation purposes. *Behaviour & Information Technology, 33*(3), 271–282. doi:10.1080/0144929X.2013.795606

CHAPTER 6

Assistive Technology for Vision and Hearing

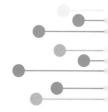

Chapter 6 presents assistive technology considerations for students with sensory disabilities (i.e., students with visual impairments, hearing impairments, or who are deaf-blind). In other words, it is focused on technology to support vision and hearing. Chapter 6 discusses options to support students in terms of vision and hearing with regard to academics, communication, and daily living. Specific examples of different technology will be provided that can support independence and access.

Chapter 6 is focused on assistive technology for vision and hearing. The reader should note that this chapter is primarily focused on technology to support students in terms of vision and hearing with regard to academics, communication, and daily living; assistive technology to support computer access, including for students with visual impairments and hearing impairments, is predominantly discussed in Chapter 5. Although the assistive technologies discussed in this chapter can apply to a range of different disabilities (e.g., text-to-speech and FM systems), Chapter 6 is primarily focused on students with **visual impairments**, including blindness; students with **hearing impairments** (i.e., hard of hearing), including deafness; and, briefly, students who are **deaf-blind**. The Individuals with Disabilities Education Act (IDEA, 2004) includes the following sensory disability classifications under which a student can receive special education services: visual impairment (including blindness), hearing impairment, deaf, and deaf-blind. Under IDEA, the visual impairment and hearing impairment must not adversely affect a student's educational obtainment.

Chapter Objectives

After reading the chapter, the reader will be able to do the following:

1. Consider technology options to support access to printed text

2. Evaluate technology that supports content area learning for students with visual impairments

3. Provide examples of assistive technology to support daily living for students with different sensory disabilities

4. Consider communication-based technology options for students who are deaf or hard of hearing

Case Study 6.1

Mr. Green is a secondary mathematics teacher at a state school for the blind and visually impaired. In Mr. Green's algebra class, there are eight students: four who are braille proficient and use braille textbooks, one who uses a large-print textbook, one who accesses the textbook via a closed-circuit television (CCTV), and one who elects to use small print with a magnifying glass because the answers to the odds are in the back of the small-print book but not the large-print version, and he can sit wherever he wants when he does not use the CCTV. The students who read braille appreciate the tactile graphics but do not enjoy transporting the number of braille books needed to study for a chapter test; they also note

the errors that arise in the translation into braille. The student who uses the CCTV wants a portable magnifying system that creates more flexibility. While Mr. Green's students are already using a variety and range of assistive technology, what other assistive technologies also can support their access, participation, independence, and success in mathematics?

Assistive Technology for Vision

Assistive technology for vision can include the spectrum of low-tech to high-tech options and support students with low vision and blindness. The chapter focuses on tools to assist students with visual impairment in academics (e.g., literacy and mathematics) as well as everyday living. Within these categories, low-tech, mid-tech, and high-tech options will be presented to support students with visual impairments.

Reading

Despite the increased use and reliance on computers and computer-like devices (e.g., smartphones), there is still a great deal of traditional printed text in the world. And, as we all know, text appears on computers and computer-like

Consider the mathematical equation $12 = \frac{10+x}{2}$. If you were blind and taking algebra, how might you access the equation to solve the problem? In other words, if you cannot read printed mathematical text, what are other ways to access the information?

Tough!

devices, which students with visual impairments can find inaccessible. Tools can support students with visual impairments by providing ease of access to printed text and text appearing on computer screens.

Braille. **Braille** is an alternative text option; it can be read and produced. According to the American Foundation for the Blind (AFB, 2014b), "braille is a series of raised dots that can be read with the fingers of people who are blind or whose eyesight is not sufficient for reading printed material" (n.p.). There are different types of braille: Grade 1 braille is less common, as it involves the expression of every letter of every word in braille; Grade 2 braille involves contractions and short-form words and is the typical mode of books; and Grade 3 is an individual's shorthand (i.e., their own style). With Grade 1, if a person wants to use the word *you*, he or she would express the *y*, *o*, and *u* in braille, but in Grade 2 braille, it would just be presented by the letter *y* (AFB, 2014b; Mulloy, Gevarter, Hopkins, Sutherland, & Ramdoss, 2014). Braille also exists for mathematics and science symbols and notations, called the Nemeth Code (Loeding, 2011).

Despite the significance of braille and its extensive history (such as Louis Braille publishing the braille code in 1834) (Blackhurst, 2005), a decline is occurring in individuals who use braille (Brittain, 2007; National Federation of the Blind, 2009; Wiazowski, 2013). Much of the decline in braille literacy is attributed to the increase in sophisticated technology to support individuals with visual impairments, including speech output (Danielson, 2013). However, additional factors may also contribute to the decline in braille literacy, and subsequent braille instruction, including a decrease in educators who are braille proficient (Bell, 2010; National Federation of the Blind, 2009).

Students can also read braille from a computer using a refreshable braille display. A refreshable braille display provides braille characters that students can read based on information available on a computer. In other words, a refreshable braille display allows students to read in braille what a screen reader (i.e., software programs that read information on a computer screen) is reading on a computer (Mulloy et al., 2014). Some refreshable braille displays, such as Braille Note by Humanware, allow students to input braille as well as read braille as output (Mulloy et al., 2014). Refreshable braille displays are also produced to not just connect to a computer but also smartphones and mobile tablets, such as iPads (Freedom Scientific, 2015) (see Figure 6.1 for an image of a refreshable braille display). Bickford and Falco (2012) found no differences in the reading and writing performance of students who were blind when using traditional braille as compared to a refreshable braille display, although students were more motivated with the more sophisticated technology.

Enlarged print. Some students with low vision benefit from enlarged print. This can occur both in textbooks (i.e., large-print textbooks) as well as enlarging the font size for a document a teacher uses (i.e., 18-point font or 24-point font); large print is typically an 18-point font size or larger (American Foundation for the Blind, 2013; Kitchel, n.d.). For published materials, educators may need to enlarge them on a copier machine; Willings (2014) suggested a 16-point type is produced by enlarging print on a copy at 129%. Willings noted that enlarging print on a copy machine can result in blurry products. While large-print books provide a common and effective means of access, Bouck, Meyer, Joshi, and Schleppenbach (2013) found students with

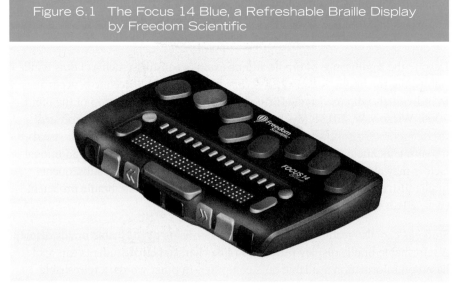

Figure 6.1 The Focus 14 Blue, a Refreshable Braille Display by Freedom Scientific

Source: Freedom Scientific. Reproduced with permission. Retrieved from http://freedomscientific.com/About/MediaCenter#FocusBlue

visual impairments reported problems with large-print textbooks, including a lack of color in older versions, sometimes an increased number of volumes as compared to traditional small-print textbooks, and no answers in the back of a mathematics textbook, which are often included in standard small-print textbooks.

Magnification. Aside from adjusting the size of printed text, other text-based technology solutions exist. For example, some students with low vision use a low-tech magnifying glass to enlarge the printed text. Others use more sophisticated mid- to high-tech technology, such as electronic vision enhancement systems (EVES) or **closed-circuit televisions** (see Figure 6.2). CCTVs can project enlarged versions of text and can range from desktop versions to hand-held, portable versions (e.g., the Ruby® handheld video magnifier from Freedom Scientific that is portable, has freeze frame, and can store images) (Mulloy et al., 2014). A variety of CCTV options exist. The American Foundation for the Blind provides a nonexhaustive list of CCTVs—both desktop and portable—along with

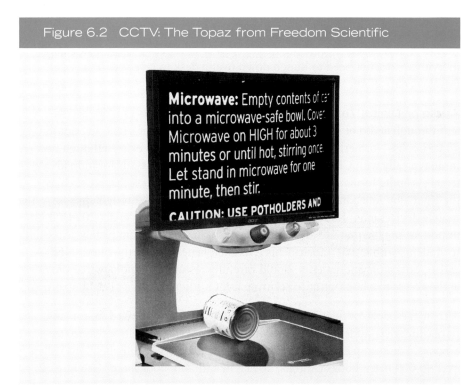

Figure 6.2   CCTV: The Topaz from Freedom Scientific

Source: Freedom Scientific. Reproduced with permission. Retrieved from http://www.freedomscientific.com/Products/LowVision/TopazProductFamily

brief descriptions (see http://www.afb.org/ProdBrowseCatResults.asp?CatID=53). Challenges with viewing text on CCTV are navigating within the document or book being magnified as well as ensuring students can read all the text, as the words might be magnified so that one or two sentences, or even words, appear at a time. Although a range of different magnification options exist, Lusk's (2012) research indicated the optimal magnification device is an individual decision based on one's needs and preferences.

Enlargement can also occur with text on a computer screen through use of a screen magnification program. Individuals can use the built-in screen magnification accessibility feature with Mac (i.e., Zoom) or Windows-based (i.e., Magnifier) computers (Ahrens, 2011). With both operating systems, the magnification feature allows users to magnify the whole screen or a portion of the screen. For-purchase products also exist for screen magnification, such as MAGic® by Freedom Scientific and ZoomText by Ai Squared. Also, a larger monitor can be effective for some students with low vision.

Book Stands. Students with low vision who like to have a book close to them may benefit from a book stand; book stands can be purchased or made. A book stand supports a book so it can be closer to an individual's eyes. A book stand also minimizes the stress on one's back or other parts of the body, as the individual does not need to hunch down over a desk to be close to the book (Mulloy et al., 2014; Willings, 2014).

Audio or Digital Text. Students with visual impairments can also access text through audio or digital versions, including e-books or eText. In addition, audio books—formerly referred to as books on tape—still exist, although now more typically with CDs. However, more common nowadays is for individuals to access audio formats of books through a dedicated e-book device, such as the Kindle by Amazon, the Nook by Barnes and Noble, or through apps for mobile devices (e.g., Kobu, Nook, Blio, and iBooks) (Mulloy et al., 2014). It is important to note that not all dedicated e-book readers are completely accessible to students with visual impairments (National Federation of the Blind [NFB], 2014). Educators and parents should carefully research technology that provides audio access to a book prior to securing it for a student with a visual impairment.

Although e-books or digital books can be purchased or borrowed from many public libraries, students with visual impairments can also gain access to free e-books. For example, Project Gutenberg (see https://www.gutenberg.org/) offers over 46,000 free e-books (Ahrens, 2011). In addition, Bookshare® (see https://www.bookshare.org/cms) exists, which provides accessible e-books to individuals with **print disabilities**; print disabilities is typically inclusive of students with

Recall in Chapter 1 we discussed the National Instructional Materials Accessibility Standard (NIMAS) that was included in the 2004 reauthorization of IDEA. NIMAS mandates students with **print disabilities** be provided accessible instructional materials through such option as large print, braille, audio, and digital text (National Center on Accessible Instructional Materials, 2014). Under NIMAS, students with visual impairments are to receive textbooks and other school materials in a format they can access (e.g., braille, large, print, digital or eText) (Loeding, 2011).

---

visual impairments, learning disabilities, and physical disabilities that make access to traditional printed text challenging. Bookshare is free to students in the United States and offers, to date, over 300,000 titles to access. With Bookshare, students can elect how they read their accessible text (Bookshare, n.d.b). These options include on a computer, with Bookshare's own web readers (e.g., Bookshare Web Reader or Read: Outloud—Bookshare Edition 6), or via a different free or for-purchase reader an individual might elect to use (e.g., Kurzweil 3000-firefly, Read&Write Gold, or ReadHear) (Bookshare n.d.a). Other options include reading on a smartphone or mobile tablet, using such options as Bookshare's Android app (Go Read) or their iOS app (Read2Go) (Bookshare, n.d.b; Preece & Burton, 2012). Individuals can use other apps to read books from Bookshare, but not all features of Bookshare's apps may be available (Bookshare n.d.a). Finally, an individual can read a book from Bookshare on a different hardware technology, such as braille notetakers or DAISY audio players (Bookshare n.d.a).

Outside of specific e-books or digital books, other assistive technology can support students with visual impairments in reading electronic material, such as text-to-speech. Text-to-speech reads text on a computer, such as a Word document, PDF, and e-mail. Both free and for-purchase text-to-speech readers exist. However, as with e-readers, not all free options are accessible to students with visual impairments. An example of a for-purchase text-to-speech option that can support students who are blind or with low vision is the Kurzweil 1000 Windows Version 14. The reader can refer to Chapter 8 for additional information on text-to-speech in general.

Screen readers can help students with visual impairments access text on a computer screen. Screen readers are software programs that read information on a computer screen (AFB, 2014a). For a student with a visual impairment,

Example E-Reader Apps for Students with Visual Impairments

E-Reader App	Brief Information
KNFB Reader (iOS) (for purchase)	• Reads almost any type of printed text (e.g., mail, receipts, or instructional handouts) • Includes speech or braille output • Highlights text as reading • See http://www.knfbreader.com/
Blio (iOS) (free, with in-app purchases)	• Reads variety of purchased or free e-books • Within in-app purchases provides text-to-speech • Compatible with VoiceOver within iOS devices • Allows notes and highlights to be added to pages • See https://www.blio.com/ for library
Read2Go (iOS) (for purchase)	• Reads e-books, including textbooks • Provides speech or braille output • Allows font size adjustments • See http://read2go.org/

the information can be presented aurally or via a refreshable braille display, which was previously discussed. A screen reader not only can read text from a document or e-mail but can also present information about menu choices or applications on a desktop. A variety of different screen readers exist, including for-purchase as well as free options (see American Foundation for the Blind screen reader at http://www.afb.org/prodBrowseCatResults.asp?CatID=49 for a chart of different options). Free screen readers include those that come already installed on a computer's operating system, such as Narrator for computers with a Windows operating system and VoiceOver for Mac computers (see Chapter 5 for additional information about standard accessibility features on computers) (Mulloy et al., 2014). For-purchase screen readers also exist, such as JAWS by Freedom Scientific (note, JAWS is only compatible with a PC computer) and Zoom Text Magnifier/Reader by Ai Squared.

more versatile than text-to-speech

Abby is a 19-year-old student enrolled at a state school for the blind. She is legally blind and uses a cane and guide dog but is not braille proficient. Abby accesses her course subjects via a computer and uses the screen reader JAWS to navigate as well as provide text-to-speech for her documents. JAWS also has a built in DAISY Player, and, hence, she can use JAWS as a means of providing speech output for her textbooks obtained through NIMAS.

iStock/BONNINSTUDIO

Tactile Graphics. A final text-based reading technology is tactile graphics. Tactile graphics are a means of presenting information interpreted by touching. Tactile graphics are most commonly used with mathematics, science, and social studies (i.e., geography) to provide information such as graphs or maps (Smith & Smothers, 2012). Smith and Smothers (2012) indicated there were a variety of different ways to produce tactile graphics, each with its own advantages and disadvantages. They also acknowledged that tactile graphics vary across materials, given the lack of any certification for tactile graphics transcribers, unlike with braille transcribing, which must follow specific regulations.

Writing

Students with visual impairments are also expected to produce text. While students can use traditional means of paper and pencil, some students with visual impairments may need enhancements to traditional lined paper or pencils. Students with visual impairment may benefit from black-lined paper, in contrast to blue-lined paper or lined paper with bolded lines (AFB, 2014c; Mulloy et al., 2014). These students may also benefit from writing with a tool that produces darker ink, such as a felt tip marker, in contrast to a pencil or pen (Mulloy et al., 2014).

Students with visual impairments can also produce text via braille. One such technology is braille printers, known as embossers. Of course, earlier means of producing braille were even more low tech, including the slate and stylus, in which an individual embossed braille by pressing the stylus onto the slate via paper (see the American Federation for the Blind Assistive Technology videos to get a clear example of a slate and stylus and how they may be used at http://www.afb.org/media/AT_videos/Quicktime/06_Braille_Writing_Devices-Slate_and_Stylus.mov). Computers can also be equipped with software that converts alphabetical characters in a document (e.g., Microsoft Word) and translates it to braille for printing. One of the more common software programs is called Duxbury Braille Translator (Mulloy et al., 2014). In addition, students can use a braille typewriter (e.g., Perkins Brailler), refreshable braille display, or braille notetaker to type notes or work (Mulloy et al., 2014). Kamei-Hannan and Lawson (2012) found students with visual impairments wrote longer and higher quality pieces when they used a braille notetaker versus a traditional Perkins Braille Writer. They also found students took advantage of the features on the more sophisticated technology, including checking spelling and copying and pasting text.

Beyond physically writing or typing, students with visual impairment can construct text with their voices. In other words, students can use speech-to-text or voice recognition software to dictate and create text (Mulloy et al., 2014). Speech-to-text programs take one's spoken words and convert them into text on a computer in such applications as Word documents and e-mails. As noted in Chapter 5, students can purchase speech-to-text products (e.g., Dragon Dictate), or they can use the free speech-to-text programs that come as accessibility features on both Windows and Mac operating-system computers. (Please refer to Chapter 5 for additional information about standard accessibility features on computers, including speech-to-text.)

Mathematics

Students with visual impairments benefit from technology to support their access and success in mathematics. Common mathematics-based assistive technology devices include tools for calculation (e.g., talking calculator or abacus), special eText players to read mathematic language, and then the aforementioned technologies to support reading and writing (e.g., tactile graphics and adapted graph paper) (Mulloy et al., 2014; Smith & Smothers, 2012). While students with visual impairments can use standard calculators (e.g., four-function, scientific, and graphing), they may benefit from talking calculators that provide aural feedback on numbers entered as well as the answer to the operation inputted (Bouck, Flanagan, Joshi, Sheikh, & Schleppenbach, 2011). Traditionally, talking calculators were restricted to more basic calculators, however, now talking graphing calculators exist, supporting students with visual impairments in more advanced mathematics classes (American Printing House for the Blind, 2014). Calculators can be adapted in other ways for students with visual impairments as well, including high-contrast screens, larger keys, and braille input/output (Center for Assistive Technology and Environmental Access, 2009). Beyond calculators, an abacus is still used in mathematics for students with visual impairments (Amato, Hong, & Rosenblum, 2013). An **abacus** can support students with visual impairments in the basic operations of mathematics (i.e., addition, subtraction, multiplication, and division) as well as more advanced skills, such as fractions (Mulloy et al., 2014).

In mathematics, digital or eText can support the access of students with visual impairments to mathematics, particularly higher level mathematics, such as algebra. Digital textbooks can circumvent challenges with getting braille or large-print books in a timely fashion, which is often reported as a problem, and avoiding errors in translation (Bouck et al., 2013; Toussaint & Tiger, 2010). Yet even traditional text-to-speech players are limited with regard to aurally producing algebraic expressions and equations (Alajarmeh & Pontelli, 2012; Archambault, Caprotti, Ranti, & Saludes, 2012; Power & Jürgensen, 2010). Digital mathematics textbooks for students with visual impairments can be marked up with a specific input code (e.g., MathML) that results in the algebraic expressions and equations being read correctly.

Let's return to the perspective that started Chapter 6 and the mathematical equation $12 = \frac{10 + x}{2}$. With a traditional text-to-speech device, the algebraic equation is likely to be read to the student as "12 equals 10 plus x over 2." This reading actually yields two possible equations: $12 = \frac{10 + x}{2}$ and $12 = 10 + \frac{x}{2}$. By using technology that supports the MathML input language and the

MathSpeak output language, for example, students will receive an accurate oral representation of an equation: "12 equals open fraction 10 plus x over 2 close fraction" (gh, 2006; Steinman, Kimbrough, Johnson, & LeJeune, 2004). MathSpeak is a standard for producing output based on the Nemeth Braille Code for Mathematics and Science Notation; it offers precise and consistent readings of mathematics, especially algebraic expressions and equations. One technology that provides access to advanced mathematics in this manner is Read Hear™ by gh (Bouck & Meyer, 2012).

[handwritten margin note: "10 plus x all over 2"]

The students in Mr. Green's algebra class can use a variety of different assistive technology to support their access, participation, independence, and success in mathematics. One such technology includes ReadHear™ by gh (see https://www.gh-accessibility.com/software). ReadHear is a Section 508–compliant software player for Windows or OS X computers that can read NIMAS files—Digital Accessible Information System (DAISY) books and other digital formats (ePub and HTML). ReadHear includes a variety of accessible features, including color tracking; panning; contrast; choice in background and text colors; and selection of voice, rate, and volume for the speech input. In addition, for students in Mr. Green's class who are braille proficient, ReadHear provides braille output through a refreshable display. Through MathML as an input language and MathSpeak™ as an output language, students with visual impairments can independently access an algebra textbook on a computer with ReadHear.

Science

In science classes, students with visual impairments can benefit from the aforementioned assistive technologies for reading, writing, and even mathematics, which is often needed in science. However, in science classes, particularly more advanced and lab-based science classes, students with visual impairments would also benefit from additional assistive technology. Such science assistive technology can include three-dimensional models, tactile graphics, tools to aid in data collection for science experiments, and programs to help analyze data collected during science labs (Mulloy et al., 2014; Smith & Smothers, 2012). Examples of assistive technology to support data collection for science experiments can include a talking scale or a sensor probe that emits sounds with different pitches based on the clarity of a liquid (Rule, Stefanich, Boody, & Peiffer, 2011). Rule and colleagues also discussed teachers and students making models with different textures and braille labels to help deliver understanding of scientific concepts (e.g., modeling the earth's surface using such items as clay, beads, fuzzy balls, and pipe cleaners to represent mountain ranges, earthquake zones, volcanoes, and tectonic pipes, respectively) (Supalo, 2010).

Daily Living

Technologies also exist to support an individual with a visual impairment navigate his/her environment and/or daily life. For example, as part of Universal Design, many intersections now have talking stoplights telling you when to cross. In addition, both handheld GPS devices (e.g., Trekker Breeze by Humanware) as well as GPS apps on smartphones can support independent navigation (Loeding, 2011). Yet one of the most commonly associated technologies to support daily living for students with visual impairments is the white cane. A cane serves multiple purposes, including helping an individual navigate his/her environment independently by detecting obstacles as well as identifying to others that the individual has a visual impairment. Different types of canes exist, including the traditional white cane as well as collapsible canes, laser canes, and sonar canes (Loeding, 2011).

Outside of navigation, everyday objects can also be made accessible to individuals with visual impairments. While not exhaustive, examples include a device that emits sound when placed in a cup to alert an individual that the level is near the top, talking microwaves, talking tape measures, and talking watches. There are also stand-alone devices that will read one's money and tell the denomination of the bills (i.e., Note Teller 2 by BryTech®) as well as ones that will tell an individual the color of an object the device is placed against (i.e., Color Teller by BryTech®).

Of course, many of the functions of stand-alone devices like these can now be replaced by an app on a smartphone or mobile tablet. For example, the app Money Reader by LookTel (for purchase) reads paper currency and voices the denomination; to date, 21 different currencies are recognized (e.g., U.S. dollar, British pound, Indian rupee). Another example is the Color ID (free) by GreenGar Studios, which names colors of objects. The Recognizer (for purchase), also by LookTel, describes everyday objects to the user. An individual builds a library of objects, and the app will then later recognize and tell the individual the specific object (e.g., distinguishing Diet Coke from Diet Pepsi or chicken noodle soup from tomato soup). Digit-Eyes by Digital Miracles (2014; for purchase) is an app similar to the Recognizer (see http://www.digit-eyes.com/). It allows users to scan a product code from a manufacturer, such as grocery items, and will state the product. Within Digit-Eyes, users can scan preprinted washable labels to be sewn into clothing and create their own labels. All of the aforementioned examples use the built-in camera features of a smartphone or mobile tablet.

Low-tech assistive technology options also exist for students and individuals who are blind or low vision in terms of play or leisure and recreation. For example, one can purchase wooden alphabet blocks for children with letters printed in ASL. Similarly, playing cards can be purchased with braille in addition to standard print as well large-print, high-contrast options. Dice and dominoes with raised dots can also be found. Different games, such as chess, checkers, and tic-tac-toe, can be purchased with tactile identification. Games like Monopoly and Scrabble can also be played together by students with and without visual impairments through purchase of ones that include braille and large print. Low-tech options also exist to make participation in sports more accessible, including different balls (i.e., football, soccer, volleyball, tennis, and basketball) with sounds inside, such as bells jingling, when in motion.

Assistive Technology for Hearing

Assistive technology for hearing also includes the spectrum from low tech to high tech to support students who are deaf or hard of hearing. In this chapter, we will focus on technology to support communication and daily living.

Communication Technologies

Common technology to support students with hearing impairments involves technology to assist or substitute for hearing; these technologies are related to communication. The most commonly associated technologies for individuals with hearing impairments include sign language (an unaided augmentative and alternative communication [AAC] device) and hearing aids.

Hearing Aids. Hearing aids are devices that amplify sound. They work by detecting sound, amplifying the sound, and transmitting it to the ear canal (Loeding, 2011). Different types of hearing aids exist: digital programmable, conventional analog, and analog programmable (American Speech-Language-Hearing Association [ASHA], 2014b). Digital programmable hearing aids are newer technology and the most expensive of the options (ASHA, 2014b; Loeding, 2011). Digital hearing aids transmit sound as digital signals and are able to detect noise from speech (Loeding, 2011; Ricketts, 2011). Conventional analog hearing aids are the least expensive option and are used much less nowadays than digital hearing aids. Conventional analog hearing aids do not discern speech and noise, and, thus, both are amplified equally (ASHA, 2014b). Analog programmable hearing aids are based on conventional analog hearing aids but allow programming of the hearing aids to account for an individual's profile (ASHA, 2014b). Hearing aids also come in different styles. These styles include ones that fit in the ear canal, ones that fit into the outer part of the ear, and ones worn behind the ear (ASHA, 2014a) (see ASHA's "Different Styles of Hearing Aids" at http://www.asha.org/public/hearing/Different-Styles-of-Hearing-Aids/ for pictures of the different options; see also Figure 6.3). Hearing aid selection occurs with an **audiologist**.

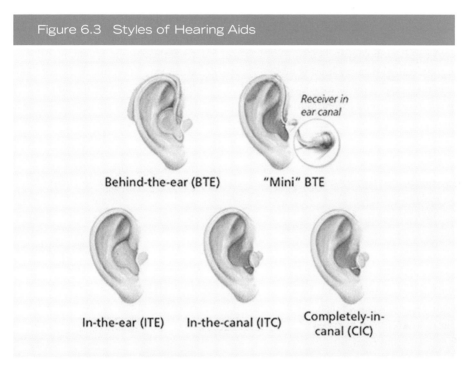

Figure 6.3 Styles of Hearing Aids

Behind-the-ear (BTE)

Receiver in ear canal

"Mini" BTE

In-the-ear (ITE)   In-the-canal (ITC)   Completely-in-canal (CIC)

Source: The National Institute on Deafness and Other Communication Disorders. Retrieved from http://www.nidcd.nih.gov/health/hearing/pages/hearingaid.aspx. Gargiulo (2015).

Implants. Another type of hearing support or substitute technology is implants; the most well-known hearing-based implants are **cochlear implants**. Other types of implants include implantable middle-ear hearing devices, bone-anchored hearing aids, auditory brain stem implants, and auditory mid-brain implants (Loeding, 2011). A cochlear implant is an electronic device consisting of three parts: one part is surgically implanted, another sits behind a person's ear, and the third is a magnetic piece attached externally to an individual's head (Loeding, 2011; National Institute on Deafness and Other Communication Disorders [NIDCD], 2014b; see Figure 6.4). Unlike hearing aids, cochlear implants do not amplify sound. Instead, cochlear implants stimulate the auditory nerve; the signals are then sent to the brain (NIDCD, 2014b).

Audiology is covered as a related service for students with disabilities—such as students with hearing impairments, including deafness—under IDEA (2004; Yell, 2012). Under IDEA Part B, audiology includes identifying students who have a hearing loss; determining the extent of the hearing loss, including referring the child to a medical professional; providing services, such as language, lip reading, or auditory training; providing counseling to students, parents, or children; and determining, selecting, fitting, and evaluating an appropriate aid (e.g., hearing aid or FM system) (Johnson, & Seaton, 2011; Yell, 2012). IDEA Part B also mandates that schools are responsible for assessing the functioning of hearing aids worn by students (Johnson & Seaton, 2011).

Case Study 6.4

Mr. Ferguson is an elementary special education teacher. On his caseload is Marleigh, a second-grade student with a hearing impairment who wears hearing aids. One afternoon, Mr. Ferguson receives a phone call from Marleigh's general education teacher indicating that Marleigh is seeming not to pay attention during reading and is fidgeting or playing with her hearing aid. Mr. Ferguson checks in on Marleigh and realizes that Marleigh's hearing aids need new batteries. Marleigh retrieves her extra batteries that she carries with her from her backpack, and Mr. Ferguson installs the new batteries while also showing Marleigh how to change the batteries herself. Marleigh returns to class, and Mr. Ferguson returns to his classroom and uses an app on his

iStock/CEFutcher

smartphone to create a reminder for himself every day to check the batteries on Marleigh's hearing aids. He also creates an event on his calendar to continue to reinforce to her how to change her own batteries during a more conducive time than reading instruction. Mr. Ferguson is aware of research about the importance of teaching students with hearing impairments how to troubleshoot their own technology challenges (Punch & Hyde, 2011).

Probably true for many assistive technologies (when appropriate)

Figure 6.4   Cochlear Implant

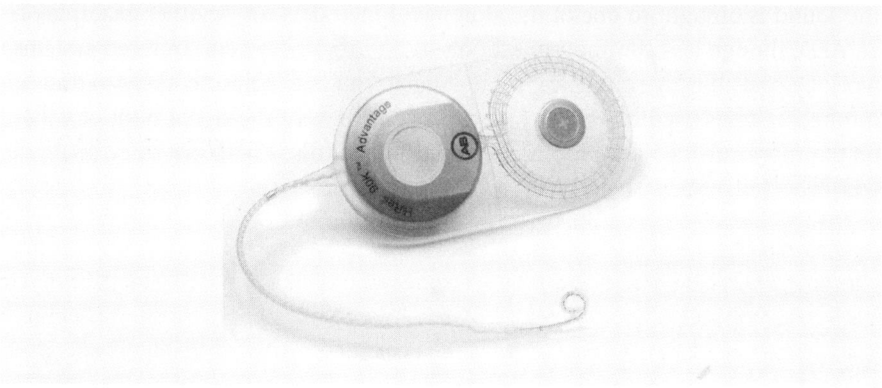

Source: Advanced Bionics. Reproduced with permission.

Controversy surrounds cochlear implants for children and adults who are deaf (Loeding, 2011). One aspect of the controversy is that many in the Deaf culture see cochlear implants as a way to fix deafness; yet they don't view deafness as a disability. Those in the Deaf culture with this perspective worry that a child who is deaf can lose his or her identity with cochlear implants (Rashid, 2010). Note, the Deaf culture "refers to individuals who are deaf who share similar values, attitudes, and practices" (Gargiulo, 2015, p. 431). In the United States, Deaf culture uses American Sign Language (ASL) and values that language as the primary means of communication (National Association of the Deaf, n.d.). In their position statement on cochlear implants, the National Association of the Deaf (2000) argued that such technology does not remove one's deafness and success can depend on whether an individual was born deaf or acquired deafness after exposure to language. To learn more about the different perspectives on cochlear implants, one can watch an older but informative documentary titled *Sound and Fury* (2000). The documentary examines the struggle of an extended family considering cochlear implants for their children and themselves. The director, Josh Aronson, also reconnected with part of the family to revisit their story in his shorter documentary titled *Sound and Fury: Six Years Later* (2006).

Assistive Listening Devices. Assistive listening devices (ALDs) also support communication, as they transport sound closer to an individual (Educational Resource Center on Deafness, n.d.). An example of an ALD is an FM system (i.e., frequency modulation), which allows a speaker's voice to be sent directly to a hearing aid, cochlear implant, or speakers around the room using radio waves (Loeding, 2011). The FM system operates on radio waves. To use the FM system in a classroom, a teacher wears a microphone (transmitter), and the sound is brought to one of the aforementioned devices. Another example of an ALD, though less common in schools, is an infrared system. Infrared systems work by transmitting sound via infrared light. You may be more likely to find infrared systems used in a court of law, as walls prevent the signal from passing on to others outside of the room, or at one's home to use with one's personal television (NIDCD, 2011).

Case Study 6.5

Levon is a student in Mrs. Anderson's fourth-grade classroom. Levon is identified as hard of hearing and wears hearing aids. In addition to the hearing aids, his IEP team determined that the use of an FM system would benefit Levon in the classroom. Mrs. Anderson wears the FM system around her neck, and Levon hears Mrs. Anderson's voice amplified. Mrs. Anderson has also learned that it is important for her to reiterate questions and answers from other students to ensure that Levon also has access to others' conversation. Mrs. Anderson has noted that she feels other students, besides Levon, have benefited from her use of the FM

iStock/GlobalStock

system in class, including Kaden, who is identified as a student with ADHD and struggles with inattention.

Sign Language. As previously mentioned, another common assistive technology for students who are deaf is sign language. Sign language is considered an unaided **AAC** (refer to Chapter 3 for information on AAC) (ASHA, n.d.; Beukelman & Mirenda, 2013; NIDCD, 2014a). The most common sign language in the United States is American Sign Language (ASL). ASL is its own language, and, thus, ASL contains its own rules for grammar as well as word order. Like other languages, ASL has variations or accents based on regions

(NIDCD, 2014a). Aside from sign language, some students who are deaf may use finger spelling, in which words are spelled using the individual sign with each of the 26 English alphabetical letters (see Figure 6.4). Finally, some students may elect to use manually coded English, such as Signing Exact English, that provides a literal interpretation of English.

Although sign language is considered an unaided AAC, or a low-tech form of assistive technology, sign language has also gone digital. In other words, computer-based technology exists surrounding sign language. For example, researchers developed 3D animation technology, including a virtual learning environment in which the mathematics and science are signed to teach this content to students who are deaf (Adamo-Villani & Wilbur, 2010). In other

Figure 6.5   Signs for the 26 Letters of the English Alphabet

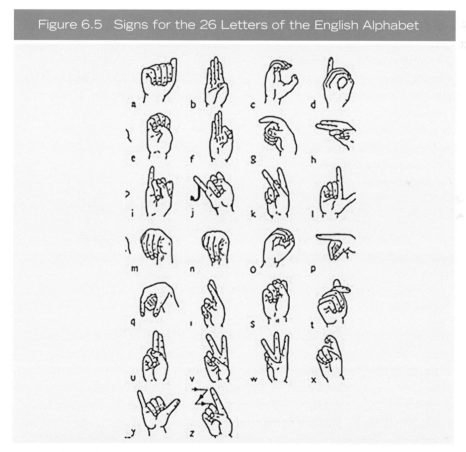

Source: National Institute on Deafness and Other Communication Disorders. Retrieved from http://www.nidcd.nih.gov/health/hearing/pages/asl.aspx

Case Study 6.6

Paige is a second-grade student who is deaf and attends her general education second-grade class as well as receives support from the special education teacher for reading as she is below grade level. Paige communicates via sign language, and a sign language interpreter accompanies her to all her classes. The interpreter, legally provided by the school under the IDEA (2004) as well as Section 504 of the 1973 Rehabilitation Act, translates between English and ASL for Paige and her teachers and peers. The sign language interpreter and Paige's teachers work together to ensure the classroom is as suitable as possible for Paige, including considering how to

iStock/ktaylor

position the teacher, Paige, and the interpreter and removing any obstacles to Paige's visual access to the classroom activities and instruction. In addition, Paige's special education and general education discuss how to use low-tech assistive technology, like visual aids, to better support Paige's comprehension of concepts presented.

words, mathematical and scientific concepts are presented to students who are deaf via their natural language (i.e., sign language) through computer-based technology. It is argued that computer animation offers a low-cost opportunity to provide a signed translation of academic content (Adamo-Villani, Popescu, & Lestina, 2013).

In terms of marketed technologies, the company Vcom3D offers a Sign Smith Studio, which allows educators to take their content (e.g., science) and have an avatar sign the material to a student. In addition, Vcom3D also sells their *Signing Science Dictionary*, which they suggest is an interactive 3D science dictionary. (Please see ASL "The Forest" at https://www.youtube.com/watch?v=80L2XcOK8Jg for an older version of a signing avatar.) If one is interested in learning sign language, Vcom3D also has created a signed English translator (Sign 4 Me) for iOS devices that the company claims teaches one sign language instruction using 3D.

Daily-Living Technologies

Students and individuals who are deaf or hard of hearing also benefit from technologies to support or enhance daily living. Some of these technologies, such as closed captioning, support the premise of **Universal Design** (refer to Chapter 1) in that they benefit a range of individuals, not just those who are deaf or hard of hearing. Closed captioning is when the audio portion of a program appears in text on the screen, similar to subtitles that can exist in movies. Closed captioning can make educational videos accessible to students who are deaf or hard of hearing; by federal law, television programs are now to be closed captioned for any individual who is deaf or hard of hearing (Federal Communications Commission, 2014). Closed captioning is also frequently used in workout facilities and airports. *universal design*

Another mandated technology to make an everyday activity accessible to individuals who are deaf or hard of hearing involves telecommunication (i.e., a phone). Before everyone had access to texting and FaceTime with smartphones or mobile tablets, text telephones (also referred to as TTY or Telecommunication Device for the Deaf [TDD]), allowed individuals who were deaf or hard of hearing to communicate with individuals who were not hard of hearing on a traditional telephone (AboutTTY.com, n.d.). Now, however, Apple advertises their FaceTime app as a means of accessibility for individuals who are deaf or hard of hearing. Apps such as Skype also create telecommunication accessibility for individuals who are deaf or hard of hearing on phones, mobile tablets, and computers.

Daily-living technologies to support students who are deaf or hard of hearing include vibrating alarms (including both alarm clocks as well as watches) and flashing signals, such as doorbells, smoke detectors, and even those that signal the changing of classes in a school. Toys and products for leisure and recreation also exist for children and adults who are deaf. For example, puzzles and games (e.g., bingo) with sign language exist to help teach and support sign language. Likewise, options exist for purchasing dice in which the numbers are printed in sign language.

Assistive Technology to Support Students Who Are Deaf-Blind

Students who are deaf-blind refers to students who have a particular degree of both visual impairment and hearing impairment. Most individuals who are identified as deaf-blind are not profoundly deaf and totally blind; most students identified as deaf-blind have some degree of hearing and/or sight (National

Consortium on Deaf-Blindness, 2007). Students identified as deaf-blind can use many of the assistive technology tools and devices previously discussed to support vision and hearing (e.g., a braille notetaker and TTY) (Bhattacharyya, 2009). In terms of communication, students identified as deaf-blind may use tactile signing. Tactile signing involves physical contact of hands during signing (Chen, Downing, & Rodriguez-Gil, 2001). In terms of daily living, students identified as deaf-blind may rely on tactile alarms, such as a bed shaking, rather than ones that involve sounds (e.g., siren) or sights (e.g., flashes) (Pasupathy, 2010). It should be noted that the Internet can, in many cases, provide independence (e.g., online shopping) and socialization (e.g., communication) for students and individuals identified as deaf-blind (Minnesota Department of Human Services, 2012).

Web 2.0 Resources and Apps

In addition to the different devices and tools mentioned throughout the chapter, Web 2.0 technologies and apps exist to support students in terms of vision and hearing. Apps to support vision previously mentioned in this chapter include the Color ID app, which uses the camera from a phone or tablet and provides the user with the color of the object within the camera's frame. Another app mentioned was the MoneyReader, which tells a user the value of bills from a variety of different currencies. And yet another app that uses a phone or tablet's built-in camera is Magnifying Glass with Light (Falcon in Motion LLC, 2014), which magnifies the object or text within the frame of the camera. The user can increase the magnification level within the app. In terms of academic support and access to books, students can use Bookshare's Read2Go app for iOS devices or Go Read for Android devices (see http://read2go.org/ for a video showing

how Read2Go works on an iOS device). To support students with hearing loss, Sign Smith Studio and Sign4Me, both from Vcom3D, were previously discussed as ways of displaying sign language via 3D.

Students and individuals with sensory disabilities can also take advantage of the built-in accessibility features on iOS mobile devices (e.g., FaceTime, texting, screen readers, dictation, zoom, color inversion, vibrating alerts, and hearing aids made for the iPhone) and Android mobile devices (e.g., captioning, increase text size, audio passwords, text-to-speech, and BrailleBack, which allows a refreshable braille device to be connected). Please refer to Table 6.1 as well as Chapter 5 regarding accessibility features on mobile devices as well as computers that can support students with visual impairments and hearing impairments.

Table 6.1 Select Accessibility Features from Mobile Devices and Computer Operating Systems

Apple OS X (Mac)	Apple iOS (iPhone, iPad)	Windows 7 or 8 (PC)	Android Devices
• Reads computer screen; text-to-speech (reads any highlighted text) • Zoom (magnifies screen) • Dictation (speech recognition to navigate or compose text) • Contrast options (change screen and text color) • Cursor size (change size of cursor) • Screen flash (screen flashes as an alert) • Sticky keys (press keys consecutively instead of simultaneously to perform task) • Word completion (word prediction in certain apps)	• Font adjustments (makes size of font in iOS apps bigger) • Made for iPhone Hearing Aids (manage hearing aids from iPhones) • AssistiveTouch (change gestures required for interacting with device and apps) • Keyboard shortcuts (create customized text shortcuts/abbreviations) • Guided Access (disables Home button so one cannot exit app or can limit time allowed on an app) • Safari reader (provides just the content of articles on Safari)	• Speech recognition (operate computer via speech or dictate documents/e-mails) • Magnifier (magnifies the entire screen or particular parts of a screen) • On-screen keyboards (on-screen keyboard with choice of selection mode) • Narrator (provides audio description of all actions on a computer) • High contrast (increases color contrast of text and screen) • Visual notifications (notifications presented visually and not aurally) • Mouse keys (operate mouse functions with arrow keys)	• TalkBack (screen reader to provide auditory information and feedback as one uses the device) • Captions (turn on closed captioning) • Large text (increase the text size) • BrailleBack (connects to refreshable braille display)

Source: Apple (2015a, 2015b); Google (2015); Microsoft (2015).

Concluding Considerations

Assistive technology can benefit students with visual impairments, including blindness, and hearing impairments, including students who are deaf. In fact, technology is typically an everyday facet of the lives of students with visual or hearing impairments, whether it is using a cane to aid in navigation, wearing a hearing aid, accessing a textbook on a computer or mobile device, or communicating via sign language. IEP teams, often including teacher consultants for the visually impaired or teacher consultants for the hearing impaired, will make decisions about assistive technology to support the access and success of students with visual impairments and hearing impairments. Of course, in making these decisions, IEP teams consider the individual student, inclusive of preferences and attitudes, and his/her environments and tasks. IEP teams should also consider a teacher's content and pedagogical approaches when considering assistive technology, in addition to individual student consideration, when recommending assistive technology. However, it is also important for educators to be aware of the limited research regarding assistive technology and students with both visual impairments and hearing impairments, especially with regard to examining assistive technology as an intervention (Ferrell, Bruce, & Luckner, 2014; Smith & Kelly, 2014). Smith and Kelly (2014) also urge educators to consider that just because a technology may be more efficient, it does not mean that it is more effective. In other words, newer, more sophisticated, or more innovative technology does not always more adequately address a challenge for the student. To refer back to the TPACK framework, as discussed in Chapter 1, educators need to consider the content and the pedagogy as well as context when deciding on technology options to support students (Koehler & Mishra, 2009; Mishra & Koehler, 2009). Of course, student preferences and abilities should also be factored in for individual decision-making (Zabala, 1995, 2005).

KEY TERMS

abacus, p. 135

braille, p. 127

closed-circuit television, p. 129

cochlear implant, p. 139

deaf-blind, p. 125

hearing impairments, p. 125

print disabilities, p. 130

universal design, p. 145

visual impairments, p. 125

EXTENSION ACTIVITIES

- Show the National Center for Technology Innovation's "I Can Soar: Sean" video (http://www.nationaltechcenter.org/index.php/ 2007/03/05/vid-sean/) in class or have students watch individually. Engage in a discussion regarding the assistive technology Sean uses.

- Show the National Center for Technology Innovation's "I Can Soar: Stacey" video (http://www.nationaltechcenter.org/index .php/2007/03/04/vid-stacey/) in class or have students watch individually. Engage in a discussion regarding the assistive technology Stacey uses.

- Show "Assistive Technology in Action— Meet Mason" from the Family Center for Technology and Disability (https://www .youtube.com/watch?v=xMHuWGUEu2M &list=UUOmFlteIOXvxWs7TNJOwJ1g). Engage in a discussion regarding the assistive technology Mason uses.

- Show *Sound and Fury* and/or *Sound and Fury: Six Years Later* in class or have students watch individually. Engage in a discussion regarding cochlear implants and the information presented in the two documentaries.

- Read about Brennan's story with Bookshare on the Bookshare blog (http://bookshareblog .wpengine.com/2014/07/youngster-reads-e-books-in-braille/).

- Show the "Accessible Instructional Materials (AIM): Simply Said" video (http://aem.cast. org/about#.VjDrGWtjI2x) in class or have students watch individually. Engage in a discussion regarding the different types of accessible instructional materials (AIM) and how decisions are made regarding AIM.

APPLICATION ACTIVITIES

- Explore the accessibility features on an iOS or Android mobile device that are focused on supporting vision or hearing. Consider how these accessibility features can support students in school and/or in daily-living activities.

- Explore some of the apps discussed in Chapter 6 that can support vision and hearing, especially those that are free (e.g., Color ID or Magnifying Glass with Light). Consider how these apps can support students in school and/or in daily-living activities.

- Explore and interact with the IRIS Center module on Bookshare (http://iris.peabody .vanderbilt.edu/module/bs/).

DISCUSSION QUESTIONS

1. What different options exist to support a student with a visual impairment gain access to text, and when might you use each option?

2. What is the challenge of using a traditional text-to-speech program to read algebra and other higher mathematics to a student who is blind?

3. In what ways are apps replacing stand-alone devices to support students with visual impairments in activities of daily living?

4. What is the controversy surrounding cochlear implants?

5. When might educators use technology that translates content into sign language for a student who is deaf?

RESOURCES/ADDITIONAL INFORMATION

- The Council for Exceptional Children (CEC)'s Division for Communicative Disabilities and Deafness (http://community.cec.sped.org/DCDD/home)

- The CEC Division on Visual Impairment and Deafblindness (http://community.cec.sped.org/DVI/Home/)

- The American Speech-Language-Hearing Association (http://www.asha.org/)

- The National Association of the Deaf (http://nad.org/)

- American Foundation for the Blind (http://www.afb.org/default.aspx)

- American Printing House for the Blind, Inc. (http://www.aph.org/)

- National Center on Deaf-Blindness (https://nationaldb.org/)

SUGGESTED ENRICHMENT READINGS

- Ferrell, K. A., Bruce, S., & Luckner, J. L. (2014). *Evidence-based practices for students with sensory impairments* (CEEDAR Document No. IC-4). Retrieved from http://ceedar.education.ufl.edu/wp-content/uploads/2014/09/IC-4_FINAL_03-30-15.pdf

- Nelson, L. H., Poole, B., & Munoz, K. (2013). Preschool teachers' perception and use of hearing assistive technology in educational settings. *Language, Speech, and Hearing Services in Schools, 44,* 239–251. doi:10.1044/0161-1461(2013/12-0038)

- Zhou, L., Ajuwon, P. M., Smith, D. W., Griffin-Shirley, N., & Parker, A. T. (2012). Assistive technology competencies for teachers of students with visual impairments: A national survey. *Journal of Visual Impairment & Blindness, 106*(10), 656–665.

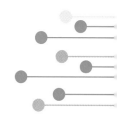

CHAPTER 7

Assistive Technology to Support Behavior and Organization

Chapter 7 focuses on assistive technology to support students with disabilities in terms of behavior and organization, broadly defined. Specifically, Chapter 7 explores a range of low-tech to high-tech assistive technology to support students with skills related to organization, self-management and self-monitoring, and social skills. This chapter also addresses sensory-based assistive technology as well as technology to support teachers with classroom management. The chapter presents stand-alone technology options as well as apps to support behavior or organization.

This chapter will examine technology to support students with behavior, which includes developing social skills, self-control, attention, socioemotional development, and sensory integration as well as such areas as self-monitoring, planning and prioritizing, and organization (Morin, 2014; O'Reilly et al., 2014). Throughout this chapter, we will focus on a variety of students with disabilities—including students with autism spectrum disorder, emotional/behavioral disorders, and ADHD, among others—who may need support for behavior or executive functioning. Assistive technology can and should play a role in supporting students and teachers in addressing behavior and organization, both broadly defined.

Organization

Different technologies can assist in helping students with disabilities get and stay organized, including low-tech assistive technology. Low-tech assistive technology

Chapter Objectives

After reading the chapter, the reader will be able to do the following:

1. Provide concrete examples of low-tech and high-tech assistive technology to support students in terms of organization and self-monitoring

2. Consider the different technology teachers can use to monitor, manage, and support classroom behavior

3. Understand the potential and limitations of sensory-based assistive technology

- Missy is a ninth-grade student identified with ADHD (that is, a student identified under the IDEA category of Otherwise Health Impaired). Missy struggles with inattentiveness and disorganization. Missy's general education and special education teachers know that Missy pays better attention in class when she is receiving more stimulation. Her teachers are also aware that Missy needs supports to keep her organized and on task.

- Ty is a fifth-grade student identified with an emotional/behavioral disorder. Ty attends general education courses and also receives support from his special education teacher and a school social worker. Ty is working on monitoring his own behavior and determining not only when he is on task but also when he is making good choices with his behavior in terms of respecting others' spaces and focusing on positive peer interactions.

- Caleb is a second-grade student identified with autism spectrum disorder. In

iStock/milanrajce

addition to Caleb's struggles with communication and social interaction, Caleb's parents have noted the benefits of sensory integration. In other words, Caleb's parents feel he benefits from engaging in activities that address his need for sensory input.

Based on the brief case studies provided, what assistive technology would you consider evaluating for Missy, Ty, and Caleb? Please keep in mind that the technology should address the student's environments and tasks, and, of course, be something each student is willing to use.

options include planners or planning notebooks (e.g., students write in their assignments, and teachers sign the notebooks), color-coding work and folders, and using highlighters and sticky notes. Educators can also use picture or visual schedules for students who need visual reminders about their days (i.e., typically young children or students with autism spectrum disorder). Visual schedules are considered an evidence-based practice for students with autism spectrum disorder (Knight, Sartini, & Spriggs, 2015).

Mid-tech and high-tech assistive technology can also support the organizing, planning, and prioritizing skills of students with disabilities. For example, one mid-tech assistive technology to help with organization is audio recorders. With audio recorders, students, parents, or teachers repurpose the tool to record and provide prompts, cues, or reminders for later. Another technology that could be repurposed to support the organization and memory of students is a Livescribe smartpen. The Livescribe pen allows students to write notes on special paper while simultaneously recording audio. A student can then retrieve the audio that corresponds to what they recorded within their written notes. In addition to supporting students with taking class notes, students can also record their assignments for each class as well as record reminders for themselves throughout the day.

Rather than these stand-alone devices, students now may be more likely to access apps on smartphones or tablets to support organization in the same or similar manner. Common apps involve the standard reminder or calendar apps on smartphones and tablets included in the operating systems. In addition, teachers and parents can also take advantage of other apps to support students with planning, managing time, or organizing their in-school and out-of-school lives (see Table 7.1).

Table 7.1   Examples of Apps to Support Student Organization

App and OS	Information
iHomework (iOS) (For purchase)	• Keeps track of student's school work, assignments, and grades across iOS and OS X platforms
	• Provides reminders for out-of-school or nonschool activities
	• http://www.element84.com/ihomework/iOS.html
Evernote (Free)	• Allows users to type notes, including adding images as well as audio, and to sync these notes across different devices (e.g., computer, smartphone, tablet)
	• Allows sharing of notes
	• https://evernote.com/
inClass (iOS) (Free)	• Keeps track of classes and assignments
	• Allows students to take notes, including video or audio
	• http://www.inclassapp.com/

(Continued)

Table 7.1   (Continued)

App and OS	Information
Studious (Android) (Free)	• Creates a schedule and reminds students about assignments and tests • Allows notes to be created and stored • Turns phone to silent when in class automatically • https://www.studiousapp.com/
What's Today (iOS) (For purchase)	• Creates and maintains schedules for young children • Provides voice support • http://www.whatstodayapp.com/
Choiceworks (iOS) (For purchase)	• Creates visual schedules • Includes other boards for supporting feelings and waiting • http://www.beevisual.com/
WatchMinder™ (iOS) (For purchase)	• Provides reminders • An app version of the WatchMinder stand-alone device • http://www.watchminderapp.com/

Case Study 7.2 Recap: Missy

Missy's IEP team decided Missy should try a combination of assistive technology, at various levels of sophistication. To address her need for organization, Missy's IEP team decided to have Missy carry either her smartphone throughout the day and, at the end of each class or after an assignment is given, record the daily assignments as well as reminders of upcoming projects, quizzes, major assignments, or tests into the app inClass. (Note that if Missy had an Android device, her IEP team would recommend Studious.) In addition, her IEP team suggested that Missy use the app Voice Recorder, a free app that works on her iPhone, to record audio reminders for herself as well. Finally, Missy has worked with her special education teacher to color-code her class materials. Working with Missy's parents, Missy obtained five different colored notebooks and matching folders and binders, as necessary for the course.

Management and Monitoring

Classroom Management

One aspect of management is **classroom management**. Teachers can use technologies to manage, monitor, and evaluate individual-student or whole-class behaviors. Teachers may use low-tech means to address classroom management, such as using colors of paper to represent what level students are on (e.g., green is making good decisions and red is not making good decisions) or clips and a scale printed on a strip of paper to move students from one level to another. For individual students, teachers can also use paper and pencil means to record student behavior. However, it can be challenging to keep a piece of paper and pencil handy as one is teaching, and research suggests teachers tend to forget the longer it is between noting a behavior and recording (Taber-Doughty & Jasper, 2012).

[handwritten margin note: Stop light chart]

Educators can use more sophisticated technology to monitor and evaluate student behavior, such as smartphones and tablets and their apps. One popular app to record and evaluate student behavior is Class Dojo (see https://www.classdojo.com/). Class Dojo allows teachers to record positive or negative behaviors throughout a school day for each student. Teachers can individually select what behaviors (e.g., responsible use of time or ready to learn) they are going to monitor and what they are going to call them. Class Dojo actually involves more than one app; there is an app for teachers to record behaviors on a mobile device (they can also record from the Internet on a computer) and an app for parents to monitor their student's behavior and check reports. Class Dojo has been used successfully by teachers with students in Grades K–12 and works with both iOS and Android devices. See Table 7.2 for examples of other apps to support classroom management.

Table 7.2 Examples of Apps to Support Classroom Management	
App and OS	**Information**
TooNoisy (iOS & Android) (For purchase)	• Provides different graphics that measure noise in a classroom and provides visual signals (e.g., happy face) • http://toonoisyapp.com/
Classroom Carrots (iOS) (Free)	• Operates similar to Class Dojo but is geared toward younger children • Provides reinforcement and incentives to teachers for using the app • Allows teachers to record positive student behaviors • http://www.classroomcarrots.com/

(Continued)

Table 7.2 (Continued)

App and OS	Information
Stick Picks (iOS & Android) (For purchase)	• Allows teachers to randomly select a student • Enables teachers to store and share information • http://stickpickapp.blogspot.com/
Teacher Kit (iOS) (Free with in-app purchases)	• Allows teachers to record and evaluate students' attendance, behavior, and grades • Enables teachers to communicate with parents • http://www.teacherkit.net/
Kids Countdown (iOS) (Free)	• Provides visual and auditory support for time management for kids • https://itunes.apple.com/us/app/kids-countdown-visual-timer/id786114488?mt=8
Kids Timer (Android) (Free)	• Provides visual and auditory support for time management for kids • https://play.google.com/store/apps/details?id=nl.skywise.kidstimer&hl=en

Self-Management

In contrast to classroom management, in **self-management** students take responsibility for managing their behavior; the responsibility shifts from the teacher to the student (Briesch & Daniels, 2013). Self-management is an evidence-based practice for students with disabilities (Carr, Moore, & Anderson, 2014; Maggin, Briesch, & Chafouleas, 2013). Self-management is typically thought to include such areas as self-monitoring, self-recording, self-evaluation, self-reinforcement, and goal setting (Epstein, Mooney, Reid, Ryan, & Uhing, 2005).

Self-Monitoring. Self-monitoring is probably the most common or well-known aspect of self-management (Briesch & Daniels, 2013). **Self-monitoring** is defined as identifying and regulating one's behavior and represents a common intervention for addressing certain behavior. With self-monitoring, students are taught to identify a behavior and then adjust it through continual identification and recording (Ackerman & Sharipo, 1984; Agran, 1997; Rafferty & Raimondi, 2009). Self-monitoring typically involves two approaches: self-monitoring of performance and self-monitoring of attention (Reid, Trout, & Schartz, 2005). Self-monitoring of performance involves students monitoring their academic

Class Dojo is a relatively new tool, and not a lot of research exists to date regarding its use in inclusive or special education classes. However, Class Dojo does provide a means to help educators collect and analyze data relative to the implantation of positive behavior intervention and supports (PBIS) in schools (O'Brien & Aguinaga, 2014; Sugai et al., 2000). The use of PBIS in schools is a practice supported by policy as well as research (Gable, Tonelson, Sheth, Wilson, & Park, 2012; Technical Assistance Center on Positive and Behavioral Interventions and Supports, n.d.).

Can Class Dojo provide data on schoolwide behavior?

Case Study 7.3

Mr. Keusch is a first-grade teacher. He uses Class Dojo in his classroom to monitor his students' behavior and as part of the data collection system for his school's Multi-Tiered System of Supports (MTSS). Prior to school starting, Mr. Keusch sent home a note to parents explaining Class Dojo— how to sign up their students and how to create their parent accounts. Mr. Keusch also examined his choice of behaviors to monitor, both the positives (e.g., responsible use of time) and the ones that indicated students had work to do (e.g., blurting out). Mr. Keusch told the parents that his goal for each of the students was 80% positive across a day and week, but 90% was a worthy goal for each

iStock/michaeljung

child. In class, Mr. Keusch carries his tablet and notes the behavior of his students. He does not record each positive behavior but uses them intermittently. With Class Dojo, each student can create their own avatar, and he projects the avatars on his class SMART Board at different times throughout the day. Students can see the positive behaviors they have earned

(Continued)

(Continued)

(i.e., the avatars have green positive numbers for ones earned), but they cannot see any indications that they need work. He speaks with students individually about behaviors that need improvement. Mrs. Click's son Troy is in Mr. Keusch's class. She can check daily as well as weekly on Troy's behavior. At home, she reinforces the positive behaviors that were noted (e.g., on task or responsible choices) and discusses any behaviors that were noted by the teacher as needing improvement (e.g., unprepared, off task, or disrespectful). Mrs. Click found that Troy likes to get on the app to check his report every night and engage in conversations about the day based on the report. Troy expresses feelings of pride when he receives responsible choices or responsible use of time. They also discuss any red or "needs work" behaviors (e.g., blurting out) that occur, how everyone is going to get some, and that a few are acceptable.

performance, such as in terms of productivity or accuracy (Reid, 1996). Self-monitoring for attention involves monitoring attention-based behavior (e.g., being on task).

There are two ways in which assistive technology can support self-monitoring. One way is to provide the cue to monitor one's behavior or performance (e.g., an audio tone versus a teacher's hand signal), and the other is to serve as the means of recording one's monitoring (e.g., paper and pencil versus a student response system). In terms of recording, the most common means is the low-tech option of paper and pencil. With paper and pencil, students can record or monitor their behavior, such as being on task for attention monitoring or correctly answering problems for performance monitoring (see Figure 7.1).

Students can also record their performance (i.e., task completion as well as accuracy) with paper-and-pencil self-monitoring. For example, students who are engaged in completing a series of tasks, such as cooking, can use a self-monitoring checklist to indicate they completed each step (see Figure 7.2).

Of course, both types of self-monitoring can also occur via more sophisticated technology. For example, students can self-monitor their behavior or performance via apps on a smartphone or tablet (e.g., Upad, TickTick, Remember the Milk, Do It [Tomorrow], and Wunderlist). Note, many of these apps suggested are not designed for education. However, the apps can be

Figure 7.1   Sample Self-Monitoring for On-Task Behavior with Paper and Pencil

On-Task Behavior	Off-Task Behavior
• Hands used appropriately • Sitting in chair • Materials placed in correct area • Eyes on teacher	• Getting out of seat • Disruptive talking, including shouting out responses, talking to classmates, or talking to self

Please check Y (YES) or N (NO) for each question each time when given the signal by your teacher:

	Am I following class expectations?	Am I completing my assignments?
Time 1		
Time 2		
Time 3		
Time 4		
Time 5		

repurposed from tools to support individuals in everyday life with productivity and staying organized to tools to support students with disabilities with self-monitoring their performance or task completion at school (Bouck, Shurr, Tom, Jasper, Bassette, Miller, & Flanagan, 2012; Mishra & Koehler, 2009).

Educators can also repurpose educational technology for students to self-monitor. Szwed and Bouck (2013) successfully taught three elementary students to self-monitor their on-task behavior using student response systems (i.e., Clickers). The teacher already used the same student response systems in her classroom so the students having them at their desks and using them to self-monitor did not draw attention or create any stigmatization. The teacher signaled the students subtly with her hand, and they used their clickers to respond to the prompts on whether they were meeting class expectations and if they were completing their assignments.

While a hand signal can be a common way for teachers to signal to students to self-monitor, whether with paper and pencil or with technology, students can also receive signals via technology. Signals can also be transmitted visually through low-tech means, such as a sign or symbol. A mid-tech means of providing a prompt to self-monitor is an audio signal (e.g., beep, tone, or voice), which can be transmitted through technology (e.g., recorders) (McDougall, Morrison, & Awana, 2011).

Educators and researchers have also explored using tactile prompts, which allow students to feel the prompts or cues to self-monitor. One such example of a tool to provide tactile prompts is the MotivAider® (see Figure 7.3). The MotivAider® is a small beeper-like device that vibrates. Note, one can also obtain MotivAider as an app for iOS and Android devices. In another example, Bedesem and

Figure 7.3   The MotivAider®

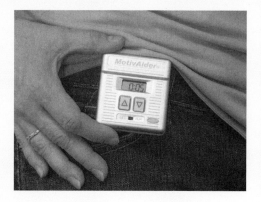 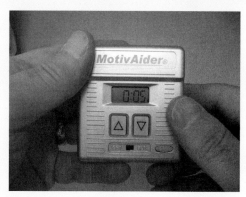

Source: Behavioral Dynamics. Reproduced with permission.

Dieker (2014) recommended a cell phone to both provide cues to students to self-monitor their behavior as well as to record their behavior. Through texting and using the vibrate mode on a cell phone, a student can receive cues to self-monitor his or her behavior as well as respond if he or she is on task.

Another specifically designed product to deliver prompts and reminders is the WatchMinder® (see http://watchminder.com/). WatchMinder is a programmable sports watch that can set 30 alarms (e.g., study for test or take medication) as well as 65 preprogrammed messages (see Figure 7.4). The WatchMinder is also available in app form (see http://www.watchminderapp.com/), which provides messages at random or set times throughout the day. In addition to providing prompts or cues for students (e.g., relax), students can also use the app to self-monitor their behavior, as this app provides the cues as well as serves as a means of self-monitoring.

Self-Operated Prompting Systems. A type of technology that acts as a self-management strategy is **self-operated prompting systems** (Mechling, 2007). Self-operated prompting systems offer students antecedent cues that support them in engaging in particular behaviors or completing a task; self-operated prompting systems can support students in terms of self-instruction (Ayres, Mechling, & Sansosti, 2013; Taber-Doughty, 2005; Savage, 2014). Self-operated prompting systems include picture, audio, and video modeling or prompting. (Note that video modeling involves a student watching the entire video before performing the tasks, whereas video prompting involves a student

Perspective 7.2

Research to Practice
....

Research exists supporting the use of the MotivAider in prompting students to self-monitor their behavior or performance. Moore, Anderson, Glassenbury, Lang, and Didden (2013) found that three middle school–aged students in the general education classroom improved their on-task behavior following self-monitoring of their behavior; they were cued to self-monitor by the MotivAider that vibrated every three minutes.

McDougall et al. (2011) found use of the MotivAider improved student performance with secondary students with ADHD or emotional/behavioral disorder when used to self-monitor if they were completing their classwork. Most recently, Briesch and Daniels (2013) found use of the MotivAider to prompt self-monitoring improved the on-task behavior of three middle school students with behavioral challenges.

Figure 7.4   WatchMinder

Source: Laurence D. Becker, PhD, child psychologist and inventor of the WatchMinder. Reproduced with permission.

watching each step of a task and then subsequently performing that step repeatedly until the entire task is completed [Ayres et al., 2013].)

Technology for picture prompts includes low-tech pictures, such as photographs, icons, or drawings. Picture prompts can help cue students, for example, to identify and correctly locate grocery items or complete a vocational

At his case conference meeting, Ty's IEP team decided to implement self-monitoring. While the IEP team decided to try paper-and-pencil self-monitoring, they also decided to use technology to cue Ty to self-monitor if he is on task and doing what is expected of him in each class. Although the IEP team considered repurposing Ty's iTouch to provide the cues, they worried the technology might be distracting or raise attention since Ty's school does not allow students to use their MP3 players in class. As a result, they decided to have Ty try the WatchMinder to cue him to self-monitor his behavior. Ty's parents also liked that the WatchMinder was a technology that looked like a typical watch and would not attract the attention of peers and potentially create more stigmatization for Ty. Ty keeps his self-monitoring sheets in his class notebooks for ease of recording. In addition to Ty monitoring his own behavior, his parents also asked for increased communication and data on Ty's IEP goals of positive peer interactions and respecting others' space. The IEP team decided to have Ty's general education and special education teachers use Class Dojo in class, as they could record data on their own smartphones or tablets, and Ty's parents could receive daily reports.

task. A range of mid-tech options can deliver audio prompts. The technologies to deliver audio prompts have advanced over the years, moving from tape recorders to CD Walkmans to audio recorders and MP3 players or smartphones. Video modeling or video prompting can be delivered via a desktop, laptop, tablet, or even smartphone; more commonly now, we see video-based self-operated prompting systems delivered via portable or handheld technology (Ayres et al., 2013).

Prompting systems are used to support students with disabilities in a variety of areas, including academics, communication, employment or vocational skills, leisure, transitioning, and social skills (Cihak, Fahrenkrog, Ayres, & Smith, 2010; Kagohara et al., 2013; Kaghoara, Sigafoos, Achmadi, O'Reilly, & Lancioni, 2012; Mechling, 2007; Reed, Hyman, & Hirst, 2011). While not exclusively, much of the attention on self-operated prompting systems occurs for students with intellectual disability or students with autism spectrum disorder.

Perspective 7.3

Do It Yourself . . .

Teachers can create their own self-operated prompting systems, including picture prompting, audio prompting, or video prompting (or video modeling). While Table 7.3 provides an overview for developing a self-operated picture, audio, or video system, more detailed information about how to construct audio and video self-operated prompting system exists in recent articles in *TEACHING Exceptional Children* (see Savage, 2014; Weng, Savage, & Bouck, 2014). These articles provide extensive information about how to create self-operated prompting systems, including discussions about what technology to use and step-by-step instructions.

Table 7.3 Steps for Developing a Self-Operated Picture, Auditory, and Video System

Self-Operated Picture Prompting System	Self-Operated Auditory Prompting System	Self-Operated Video System
1. Identify target task.		
2. Develop a task analysis.		
3. Determine the types of pictures to use (drawings, photos, or icons [e.g., Boardmaker by Mayer-Johnson]).	3. Determine the "script" of auditory prompts.	3. Determine if the student will use video prompting or video modeling
4. Identify words (if any) that will accompany pictures.	4. Determine who will be the "voice" on the audio system (student, teacher, favorite paraeducator, or parent) or whether a "tone" will be used to prompt the student to the next step.	4. Decide video point of view. (Will it be from the student's perspective? Will it depict the student or a different known or unknown individual engaged in the task?)
5. Identify how pictures will be presented (e.g., communication notebook, paper, or an electronic system such as a tablet or smartphone).	5. Determine the system for delivering auditory prompts (e.g., audio recorder, tablet, smartphones, or MP3 player). Also, determine if headphones are needed.	5. Identify the system for delivering videos (e.g., DVD player, computer, tablet, or smartphone).
6. Develop prompting system, and ask two novel individuals to complete the task using the self-operated system. Make edits based on individuals' performances.		
7. Determine if students will use self-management skills when using the self-operated system. Will students self-monitor their progress using a checklist? Will they engage in self-evaluation?		
8. Evaluate student performance as he or she uses the self-operated system.		

Source: Adapted from *Footsteps Toward the Future: Implementing a Real-World Curriculum for Students With Disabilities,* by E. C. Bouck, T. Taber-Doughty, and M. N. Savage, 2015, p. 35. Copyright 2015 by Council for Exceptional Children.

Social Skills and Social Emotional Development

Social Skills

Another component to behavior is **social skills**, which are skills that help individuals make appropriate decisions in various situations. In other words, when one has good social skills, one understands how to interact with others (e.g., verbal and nonverbal communication) and, generally, how to make good decisions that are appropriate. However, some students struggle to learn as well as display consistent, positive social skills, for example, initiating conversations and responding to others, appropriate play skills, social conventions, and regulating emotions (Reed et al., 2011). Educators, including teachers and school social workers, among others, provide interventions to teach and support social skills. One avenue to consider is how assistive technology can support the development of social skills.

Two mechanisms already discussed in this chapter in which technology can support the learning and displaying of positive social skills are self-monitoring and self-management (such as self-operated prompting systems). In fact, Otero, Schatz, Merrill, and Bellini (2015) suggested video modeling was one of the most fruitful interventions for teaching social skills to students with autism spectrum disorders. Teachers and educators can create their own self-operated prompting systems for social skills, such as video models or video prompts; however, a few commercially available options also exist. For example, Model Me Kids® created videos that model social skills for students (see http://www.modelmekids.com/autism-behavior.html).

similar to social stories books

Other technology can also support the teaching or development of social skills. For students with autism spectrum disorder, a common low-tech form of assistive technology is social stories or social narratives (Gray & Garand, 1993). A social story is a story written with images (i.e., icons or pictures) in the first-person point of view that targets a social skill. When using social stories, educators and students read them together. The student might then be asked comprehension questions or asked to role-play the skill discussed (Kassardjian et al., 2014). In addition to paper-and-pencil social narratives and stories, educators can also use more sophisticated technology. For example, Ben-Avie, Newton, and Reichow (2014) indicated teachers were able to use the app StoryMaker™ for Social Studies (available from Handhold Adaptive for purchase) to develop and use social narratives for students with autism spectrum disorders. Other app options, such as I Create . . . Social Skills Stories (available from I Get It for purchase) and Stories About Me (available from Limited Cue for purchase), also exist.

More sophisticated or high-tech assistive technologies also exist to support students with developing social skills. For students with autism spectrum disorder, virtual environments or virtual reality are explored as avenues to teach and promote appropriate interactions (Boucenna et al., 2014; Newbutt, 2014). For example, Cheng and Ye (2010) found students with autism spectrum disorder who interacted in a collaborative virtual learning environment experienced increases in positive social interactions and behavior. Similarly, Cheng, Chiang, Ye, and Cheng (2010) found individuals with autism spectrum disorder increased their capabilities to recognize empathy in others through interaction in a 3D virtual environment.

Robots are another type of technology increasingly examined to support students with autism spectrum disorder (Senland, 2014). Robots have been used to support students with autism spectrum disorder in developing social skills, understanding emotional expressions, and improving social interaction (Feil-Seifer & Matarić, 2011; Scassellati, Admoni, & Matarić, 2012; Tapus et al., 2012). One such example of a robot marketed to work with students with autism spectrum disorder is NAO by Aldebaran (see https://asknao.aldebaran.com/). NAO is considered a humanoid robot and works with apps or games to support students. Research by Tapus et al. (2012) found individual differences among the four young children with autism spectrum disorders in terms of interacting with NAO, ranging from no social interaction impact to increased eye gaze and motor imitation. Other researchers examining NAO, including Bekele et al. (2013), found students with autism spectrum disorder preferred to look at the robot as compared to a human. Diehl et al. (2013) found students with autism spectrum disorders experienced greater improvement in terms of social behaviors with applied behavior analysis when using NAO than without.

Socioemotional Development

Socioemotional or **social emotional development** in children can also be developed and supported through assistive technology. Apps that support the socioemotional development focus on recognizing and understanding emotions in children, particularly those that struggle or have special needs. These include, for example, Touch and Learn – Emotions (available from Innovative Mobile Apps for free) and Social Emotional Exchange (SEE; available from saym basheer for purchase). Another option for technology for socioemotional development, although without a substantial research base, is the use of robotic animals. In place of live animals, students interact with robotic animals, which are tools

Expanding Our Considerations

While the section on social skills and assistive technology tended to focus heavily on students with autism spectrum disorders, they are not the only students who struggle with social skills. Students with and without disabilities alike can struggle with social skills. In Table 7.4, additional technology resources to support positive social skills are presented.

Table 7.4 Examples of Technology to Support Positive Social Skills	
App or Web 2.0 Resource	**Information**
Arthur's Big App (iOS & Android) (For purchase)	• Produced by PBS • Provides games that support positive social skills • http://pbskids.org/apps/filter/app/
What Would You Do at School If . . . Fun Deck (iOS) (For purchase)	• Created by Super Duper Publications • Provides visual and audio flash cards that present a scenario (e.g., you see a classmate cheating) and asks students what they would do
The Social Express (Web 2.0) (For purchase)	• Presents students with animated social problems to solve

designed to look and feel like real animals (Bouck et al., 2012; Stanton, Kahn, Severson, Ruckert, & Gill, 2008).

Sensory

Students with a range of disabilities or challenges can benefit from sensory input, including, but not limited to, students with emotional-behavior disorders, ADHD, and autism spectrum disorders. Sensory input is often used with children with sensory processing disorder, although this is not a category or classification under IDEA. Sensory-based therapies involve providing students with sensory input or sensory stimuli, including, but not limited to, sensory rooms. Often, the forms of sensory stimuli involve low-tech assistive technology, such as sitting on a therapy or exercise ball, holding Silly Putty, and wearing weighted vests or blankets (Lang et al., 2012).

Additional Information

Sensory processing disorder (SPD) is not a disability covered under IDEA. In fact, the American Academy of Pediatrics developed a policy statement against the diagnosis of sensory processing disorder citing a lack of accepted diagnosis framework and the failure of the field to understand if this represented an actual disorder or if the sensory challenges were characteristics of other disorders, such as behavior disorders, autism spectrum disorder, or other developmental disabilities (Zimmer & Desch, 2012). Those that advocate for sensory processing disorder refer to it as a condition in which an individual does not make appropriate responses to sensory signals; in other words, a child has trouble processing sensory stimuli or information (for example, tactile, visual, or auditory) (SPD Foundation, n.d.).

Low-tech sensory-based assistive technology options can include options for seating or positioning. For example, some students use therapy or exercise balls in place of traditional chairs for sitting at one's desk. Other students may use a specific type of seat cushion, including ones that are filled with air, beads, beans, and foam (see Figure 7.5). Of course, in contrast to purchasing or making any supportive seating or positioning assistive technology, teachers can allow students to stand at their desks. Standing can occur at a traditional desk or with adjustable height desks. Please see Chapter 4 for additional discussions regarding seating and positioning for students with disabilities.

Figure 7.5   Cushion for Seating

Source: Toymarketing International, Inc.

Low-tech assistive technologies like seat cushions, Silly Putty, or Koosh balls might benefit students with ADHD, based on the optimal stimulation theory as proposed by Zentall (1975, 2005). With optimal stimulation theory, Zentall proposed that students with ADHD need more stimulation rather than less. Hence, students with ADHD should not be removed from potential distractions but provided greater stimulation through sensory input (e.g., color and music) (Zentall & Zentall, 1983). For practice, this means that the additional stimulation students with ADHD receive from touching Silly Putty or Koosh balls, sitting on a seat cushion, or doodling benefits students; these interactions are not distractions.

Aside from seat cushions or therapy balls to provide stimulation for seating and positioning, other low-tech sensory-based assistive technology includes handheld objects, sometimes referred to as fidget toys. These handheld objects, or fidget toys, include options that are specifically marketed to provide sensory stimulation (e.g., theraputty or textured or hairy tangles) or that are everyday toys repurposed to serve as assistive technology. Such repurposed objects can include Silly Putty, Koosh balls, or kinetic sand. Similarly, doodling can be used to help students pay attention and focus. Research with adults suggested an individual's concentration and memory improved when doodling (Andrade, 2010). There is also a doodle revolution (see http://sunnibrown.com/doodlerevolution/) to change perception that doodling is a distraction rather than helping individuals focus.

Sensory-based assistive technologies also address areas of **sensory integration**. Sensory integration refers to "the neurological process that organizes sensation from one's body and from the environment and makes it possible to use the body effectively within the environment" (Ayres, 1972, p. 11). Sensory integration is connected to sensory processing disorder. A key proponent of sensory integration, or sensory integration intervention (i.e., Ayres Sensory Integration®), was Ayres, an occupational therapist (May-Benson & Schaaf, 2015). Within sensory integration, such low-tech assistive technology as weighted vests or weighted lap blankets may be used. Some students may even use repurposed wraparound weights to provide the stimulation. In addition, squeeze balls, tactile rings, tactile blankets, vibrating pillows, or therapressure brushes may also be used. Sensory integration can also involve wave or bubble panels or swings. Often students with autism spectrum disorder, students with sensory integration disorder, or students with behavioral challenges use sensory-based assistive technology.

Despite the commonality of sensory integration therapy, sensory stimuli, or sensory rooms for students with autism spectrum disorders (Zimmer & Desch, 2012), the research is mixed at best and, more aptly, unsupportive of these approaches. For example, in a review of research on sensory integration therapy for students with autism spectrum disorder, Lang et al. (2012) found sensory integration therapy effective in only three of the 25 studies reviewed. In contrast, 14 reported no benefits were obtained for students, and eight suggested mixed findings. Another study that systematically reviewed the literature on sensory-based therapies for young children (i.e., under age 9) with behavior or developmental disabilities also concluded that there was a lack of research to support the benefits of sensory-based interventions (Barton, Reichow, Schnitz, Smith, & Sherlock, 2015). Lastly, in a meta-analysis of research on sensory integration therapy, Leong, Carter, and Stephenson (2014) concluded the evidence for use of such intervention was weak for individuals with disabilities. We are discussing sensory-based assistive technology in this text because, as suggested by Barton and colleagues, they are likely to continue to be used in schools and requested by parents.

Case Study 7.5 Recap: Caleb

Although Caleb's parents feel he benefits from sensory integration, the educators who work with Caleb are more reserved given the lack of research supporting the practice in terms of benefits. However, in the IEP meeting, it is agreed upon that the occupational therapist working with Caleb will work with Caleb's teachers to implement some sensory-based technologies in his classrooms. For example, they agree to allow Caleb to sit on either a therapy ball or a seat cushion in a traditional chair. They also agree that Caleb can keep a fidget toy with him as long as it does not become something that distracts him from what is occurring in class. His parents suggested Silly Putty or small Koosh balls, which worked well at home and in other out-of-school situations.

Web 2.0 Resources and Apps

The Web 2.0 resources and apps discussed in this chapter have largely focused on apps students can use to self-monitor or organize themselves. However, apps also exist for teachers to monitor student behavior or IEP goals (see Table 7.5 for examples of apps teachers can use to monitor student behavior).

Educators can also use technology to help students collectively manage time in school. While a traditional digital or analog clock might work, teachers can also use apps to support students in understanding how much time they have to work on an activity. For example, the iOS device Kids Countdown (free) provides a visual countdown clock for young children. For a similar app for Android devices, educators can elect to use Kids Timer (free). For those educators without a mobile device, they can explore different types of online stopwatches (http://www.online-stopwatch.com/classroom-timers/). Educators can set up the apps or website on their personal computer or mobile device or broadcast it visually for the whole class via an LCD projector or **SMART Board** (i.e., interactive whiteboard).

Table 7.5 Examples of Apps and Web 2.0 for Teachers to Monitor Student Behavior or IEP Goals	
Technology	**Information**
	Apps
Percentally (iOS) (For purchase)	• Allows educators to track a student's goals and organize data • Also records time per each session • http://expressive-solutions.com/percentally/
Tracknshare (iOS) (Lite version is free) (For purchase)	• Allows educators to track whatever data they might want to monitor for a student • Allows data to be graphed and shared • http://www.trackandshareapps.com/
IEPPal (iOS) (Free app but requires subscription)	• Collects and charts data on students' IEP goals and/or objectives • Turns data into reports and graphs • http://www.ieppal.com/

(Continued)

Table 7.5 (Continued)

Web 2.0 Resources	
Google Docs (Free)	• Allows educators to create forms that collect information and data • Produces databases of data and graphs • Can be shared with other educators or parents • https://docs.google.com/

Concluding Considerations

Assistive technology to support behavior and organization, both broadly defined, ranges from low tech to high tech and includes emerging (e.g., robots) as well as research-supported (e.g., paper-and-pencil self-monitoring) options. Technology can support students with disabilities in terms of organization, social skills, and self-management, inclusive of self-monitoring. All students can occasionally struggle with social skills, paying attention, staying on task, staying organized, and regulating one's emotions or making good choices. Technology can support these students as well as students with disabilities who continually struggle with these areas, inclusive, but not limited to, students with autism spectrum disorders, emotional/behavior disorders, ADHD, and learning disabilities.

KEY TERMS

classroom management, p. 155

self-management, p. 156

self-monitoring, p. 156

self-operated prompting systems, p. 161

sensory integration, p. 169

SMART board, p. 172

social emotional development, p. 166

social skills, p. 165

EXTENSION ACTIVITIES

• Show the Sunni Brown TED Talk (http://www.ted.com/talks/sunni_brown) in class or have students watch individually. What message do you take away from this TED Talk with respect to doodling in K–12 classes? Should doodling be allowed,

encouraged, or discouraged? If it should be allowed or encouraged, when?

• Show examples of video modeling (see https://www.youtube.com/watch?v=makIg B4X3q8 and https://www.youtube.com/

watch?v=3zYVR5PDom8) from Spectrum Keys in class or have students watch individually. Discuss how video modeling might, as in the given examples, support students with disabilities. Also, consider how teachers might develop or use picture or audio prompting in these situations in place of video.

- Show a video from AldebaranRobotics about the NAO robot on the *Engadget Show* (https://www.youtube.com/watch?v=oiURYf_og8M) in class or have students watch individually. Based on your understanding of NAO robots, how do you think the NAO can support and help students with disabilities? If you want to consider examples from the company of how NAO can support students with disabilities, please see the "Ask NAO: Be Part of the Journey" video (see https://www.youtube.com/watch?v=_AxErdP0YI8).

- Show "Assistive Technology in Action—Meet Jean" (http://bit.ly/1HXOU1U) in class or have students watch individually. Engage in a discussion regarding how an iPad serves as an instructional support for Jean.

APPLICATION ACTIVITIES

- Read (a) Savage, M. N. (2014). Self-operated auditory prompting systems: Creating and using them to support students with disabilities. *TEACHING Exceptional Children, 47*(1), 266–275. doi:10.1177/0040059914542763, and/or (b) Weng, P.-L., Savage, M. N., & Bouck, E. C. (2014). iDIY: Video-based instruction using iPads. *TEACHING Exceptional Children, 47*(1), 231–239. doi:10.1177/0040059914542764. Based on the information in the articles, develop your own audio- or video-based self-operated prompting system.

- Discuss the pros and cons to using picture-, audio-, and video-based self-operating prompting systems. Also, consider when and where you might use the different systems and what factors might influence your decision.

- Explore the different apps discussed in Chapter 7 (see Tables 7.1, 7.2, 7.4, and 7.5 as well as Class Dojo). Consider how the apps might help you as a teacher, you as a student, or the future students you will educate and support.

DISCUSSION QUESTIONS

1. How can technology support students with self-monitoring their behavior?

2. What low-tech and high-tech options can help teachers to address classroom management or monitor IEP goals relative to behavior?

3. What sensory-based assistive technology is used with students with disabilities?

4. How can technology support students with disabilities to be more organized?

RESOURCES/ADDITIONAL INFORMATION

- The IRIS Center provides modules on behavior and classroom management. See Classroom Management Part 1 (http://iris .peabody.vanderbilt.edu/module/beh1/) and Classroom Management Part 2 (http:// iris.peabody.vanderbilt.edu/module/ beh2/#content)

- The Council for Children with Behavioral Disorders of the Council for Exceptional Children (http://www.ccbd.net/home)

- The Division on Autism and Developmental Disabilities of the Council for Exceptional Children (http://daddcec.org/)

SUGGESTED ENRICHMENT READINGS

- Myles, B. S., & Rogers, J. (2014). Addressing executive function using assistive technology to increase access to the 21st century skills. In N. R. Silton (Ed.), *Innovative technologies to benefit children on the autism spectrum* (pp. 20–34). Hershey, PA: IGI Global.

- Temple, C. (2013). Executive function skills and assistive technology. *Perspectives on Language and Literacy*, 39(4), 15–17.

Assistive Technology as Instructional Aids

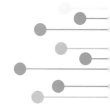

Chapter 8 focuses on assistive technology to serve as instructional aids for students with disabilities. While perhaps skewed towards students with more high-incidence disabilities, Chapter 8 presents assistive technology considerations for students with disabilities across the disability spectrum, with a focus primarily on reading, writing, mathematics, and study skills. The text highlights low-tech, mid-tech, and high-tech options as well as free and for-purchase technology. In addition to providing clear examples of assistive technology to support students with disabilities in the classroom, the chapter also addresses online or hybrid learning for students with disabilities.

When we think about assistive technology for instructional aids, we are considering both assistive technology to support access and achievement as well as to support delivery, such as alternative formats like online or hybrid learning. For many students with disabilities, assistive technology serves as an instructional aid. In other words, assistive technology supports students in reading, writing, mathematics, science, and social studies in terms of access and independence. While assistive technology to support instruction was discussed in previous chapters, such as Chapter 5 relative to access to computers and Chapter 6 relative to vision and hearing, Chapter 8 will focus explicitly on free and for-purchase tools and devices for academics and online education for the range of students with disabilities, including students with high-incidence and low-incidence disabilities.

Chapter Objectives

After reading the chapter, the reader will be able to do the following:

1. Provide clear examples of assistive technology to serve as instructional aids for reading, writing, and mathematics

2. Evaluate the positives and negatives of low-tech, mid-tech, or high-tech reading, writing, and mathematics assistive technology as instructional aids

3. Consider apps and Web 2.0 technologies to support instruction for students with disabilities

4. Provide clear examples of technology to support cognitive study skills for students with disabilities

- Alex is an upper elementary student with a learning disability in reading. After going through the response-to-intervention (RTI) process at his school, Alex was referred for additional testing by the school psychologist. The testing indicated Alex had an IQ of 109 with a 23-point discrepancy for word recognition and a 26-point discrepancy for reading comprehension. It takes Alex significantly longer to read than his classmates, and even when he finishes reading, he still struggles to fully comprehend what he read.

- Jacob is a middle school student with ADHD who does well with expressing himself with language but struggles with written expression. Specifically, Jacob struggles with organizing his ideas and thoughts as well as editing his written products and spelling. In addition, his teachers, and even Jacob, find it difficult to read his written work.

- Justine is a secondary student with a mathematics learning disability. Specifically, Justine struggles with mastery of her basic number facts, a struggle that has persisted into high school. However, once beyond her challenge with basic facts, Justine is able to understand the advanced mathematical concepts presented in her mathematics (i.e., Algebra II) class.

Based on the brief case studies provided, what assistive technology would you consider evaluating for Alex, Jacob, and Justine? Keep in mind that the technology should match with the content (e.g., mathematics) as well as with a teacher's pedagogical approach and work within the context of the particular school. Also, please keep in mind that the technology should address the student's environments and tasks and, of course, be something each student is willing to use.

Reading

Reading is typically considered the most critical, albeit complex, academic skill (Strangman & Dalton, 2005). The current conception of reading instruction focuses on five areas: phonemic awareness, phonics instruction, fluency, vocabulary, and reading comprehension (National Reading Panel, 2000). Despite its use in all other academic areas, national assessment data from the National

Assessment of Educational Progress (NAEP) continue to suggest reading remains a struggle for students with and without disabilities. The most recent data of fourth and eighth graders indicate 33% and 24%, respectively, scored below a basic level. A basic level on the NAEP "denotes partial mastery of prerequisite knowledge and skills that are fundamental for proficient work at each grade" (National Center for Education Statistics, 2011b, p. 6). The rates more than doubled when just examining data for students with disabilities: 68% of fourth-grade students with disabilities and 70% of eighth-grade students with disabilities scored below the basic level.

The challenges students with disabilities face in reading are real and can be daunting. Technology, however, can help address some of the issues, such as those related to access and independence, as well as to compensate for challenges with decoding. The portion of the chapter on assistive technology to support reading will focus on low-tech, mid-tech, and high-tech options to support reading and will also focus on both free as well as for-purchase tools and devices (see Table 8.1 for examples of assistive technology to support reading across all levels of technology).

Low-Tech Assistive Technology for Reading

As you will recall from Chapter 1, low-tech assistive technology is generally technology that does not require a power source, is lower in cost, and requires less training. Low-tech assistive technology to support students with disabilities

Table 8.1   Examples of Assistive Technology for Reading

	Low Tech	Mid Tech	High Tech
Free	• Reading window, guide, or ruler • Changing font size • Picture symbols	• Books on tape or CD (from public library) • Free e-books	• Bookshare • Rewordify • Text-to-speech from built-in accessibility on computer operating systems
For purchase	• Highlighter strips or highlighter tape • Post-it notes or flags • Page holders	• Reading pen • Talking dictionaries • LeapReader™	• Text-to-speech from Kurzweil 3000-firefly • Text-to-speech from Read&Write GOLD

in reading can include the use of highlighters, highlighter strips, or highlighter tape. While students can use traditional highlighters, if concerns exist about the permanence of color in a book, Crayola markets erasable highlighters. Additional nonpermanent options include removable highlighter tape or Post-it notes (Cumley, 2009). Another option is highlighter strips, which are laminated, thinly cut pieces of neon-colored transparency that students can place over words or sentences when reading. Related to the use of highlighter strips are color overlays, such as Irlen color overlays (see http://irlen.com/). Although research is mixed and lacking in rigor regarding their effectiveness (Gregg, 2009), color overlays are allowed as an accommodation on some standardized tests for individuals with learning disabilities, such as the GED (Gregg, 2012), and thus are still being used (Gregg, 2009, 2012). Finally, educators can consider making a reading window or reading guide, which typically involves taking a piece of cardboard, posterboard, or notecard and cutting out a space large enough for a word or sentence that the student can move along their text to isolate words as they read (Shvimer, Kerbel, & Friedmann, 2009).

[handwritten margin note: leaves books "reusable" by future students]

Other low-tech assistive technology to support reading for students with different disabilities includes changing the font size of the text (i.e., providing students with enlarged text) or adding images or pictures to support the written word (Shurr & Taber-Doughty, 2012). To create visual supports for text, teachers can print out and attach their own pictures to existing books or reformat books. The use of visual supports to assist students with comprehension, such as students with autism spectrum disorder and students with intellectual disability, is supported in the literature (Knight & Sartini, 2014; Shurr & Taber-Doughty, 2012). Outside of teachers creating their own, for-purchase products exist in which visual supports are added to text to support students' comprehension. For example, News-2-You (see https://www.n2y.com/products/news2you/) is a newspaper that supports four different reading levels (with varying visual support). Teachers can print out the content-based newspapers, have students read online with text-to-speech, or access them via an iPad app.

Mid-Tech and High-Tech Assistive Technology for Reading

Multiple mid-tech (i.e., typically requiring a battery source, increased training, and increased cost) and high-tech (i.e., generally computer-based, more sophisticated technology requiring increased training and increased cost) assistive technology exist to support students with disabilities in reading. While

The research on text-to-speech in terms of student impact is mixed for both the use of text-to-speech in daily class activities to access materials as well as its use as an accommodation on standardized assessments. Researchers within the last decade found that text-to-speech used for a minimum of 30 min a week in daily class activities resulted in no gains in vocabulary or reading comprehension by students with reading disabilities or at-risk for reading disabilities (Stodden, Roberts, Takahishi, Park, & Stodden, 2012). However, increasing the time of using text-to-speech, along with the provision of vocabulary supports, resulted in positive comprehension gains (Stodden et al., 2012). In contrast, Meyer and Bouck (2014) found no gains in comprehension when students with learning disabilities accessed grade-level expository text via text-to-speech. In terms of text-to-speech as an assessment accommodation, Flowers, Kim, Lewis, and Davis (2011) found that although text-to-speech allowed the students to be more be independent and work at their own pace, which decreased student frustration, students with disabilities actually scored higher when a human read the test aloud as opposed to using text-to-speech to read the test.

not exclusive, many of the mid-tech and high-tech tools to support reading involve reading printed text for students with disabilities; in other words, they are text-to-speech devices. **Text-to-speech** is printed or digital text produced aurally, such that a voice output occurs. Text-to-speech can replace having a student read the material to his or herself or having another individual (e.g., teacher or paraprofessional) read the text for a read-aloud accommodation. Despite its common use and advocacy for its use, the research on text-to-speech is mixed regarding impact (Strangman & Dalton, 2005).

Perhaps the most commonly associated text-to-speech technology is via a computer. Both free and for-purchase text-to-speech programs exist (see Table 8.2 for examples of popular text-to-speech programs). For example, one product that has existed for about 40 years is Kurzweil. In 1976, the Kurzweil Reading Machine debuted. It was a device that could read printed text (Kurzweil Technologies, 2015). The current product is the Kurzweil 3000-firefly, which is marketed as an educational software for supporting students in literacy across multiple computer platforms (i.e., Windows and OS X) as well as on tablets and the Internet. Kurzweil 3000-firefly provides text-to-speech with multiple languages and provides access to webpages, PDFs, and documents. Students can also take notes and highlight, among other features, with the Kurzweil 3000-firefly (Kurzweil Education, n.d.).

Table 8.2	Examples of Text-to-Speech Computer Programs
Free	**Natural Reader (NaturalSoft Limited, 2013)** • See http://www.naturalreaders.com • Can be used on the website or downloaded • Free version, although paid options exist that provide natural-sounding voices • Highlights text as it is read on Word documents, websites, PDFs, and e-mails • Compatible with PC and Mac computers as well as an iPad app
For Purchase	**Read&Write GOLD (Texthelp, 2013)** • See http://www.texthelp.com/North-America • Reads text while simultaneously highlighting text on a computer • PC and Mac versions as well as apps for Google Chrome and iPads • Includes reading support (i.e., text-to-speech) as well as dictionary, spell checker, word prediction, speech-to-text, and a translator, among other features

In addition to programs, both OS X and Windows operating systems provide built-in accessibility features, including text-to-speech options (refer to Chapter 5 for additional information on built-in or standard accessibility for different computer and mobile-device operating systems). For example, OS X comes standard with a voice-over feature to read the computer screen, often referred to as a screen reader, as well as text-to-speech that reads highlighted text. The popular suite of productivity software, Microsoft Office for PC or Mac computers, also comes with built-in or standard accessibility features, including text-to-speech as well as a read mode that removes tools and buttons so an individual can read text with minimized distractions (Microsoft Corporation, 2014). Browser-specific text-to-speech options also exist. For example, SpeakIt! (sketchboy.com, 2014) is an extension for Google Chrome that translates into speech any text from the browser. Likewise, Text to Voice (ViJo, 2012) is an add-on for Firefox that translates text from the Firefox browser to speech.

Beyond computer-based text-to-speech, stand-alone devices also exist. For example, the Quicktionary 2 is a handheld **optical character recognition system** that scans and then reads printed text (Higgins & Raskind, 2005; WizcomTech, 2012) (see Figure 8.1). Limited research exists on using handheld reading pens, such as the Quicktionary 2. Two studies with high school students contradict each other on whether the use of a reading pen increases the comprehension of students with reading disabilities (Higgins & Raskind, 2005; Schmitt, McCallum, Rubinic, & Hawkins, 2011). A third study focused on college students with reading disabilities failed to show comprehension benefits for two out of the three students in the study (Schmitt, McCallum, Hennessey, Lovelace, & Hawkins, 2012).

Some reading pens, like the Quicktionary 2, will read any printed text as long as its size fits within the scanner. However, other reading pens are designed to work only with specific books or under specific conditions. For example, LeapFrog™ developed a reading pen that can read specifically designed LeapFrog books that are loaded onto the pen. The reading pen, which is now called LeapReader™ Reading and Writing System (formerly called the LeapFrog Tag Reading System), will read the specially designed books at the level of page, sentence, or word and will question the student for comprehension. The LeapReader is targeted to students aged 4 to 8; LeapFrog also markets a LeapReader Junior for children ages 1 to 3 with books designed at their level. A similar product, AnyBook Personal, does not require one to purchase specifically designed books as it allows an individual to record a story from any book, using his or her own voice http://www.anybookreader.com/. The person doing the recording places stickers in the book, which operate like bar codes. These connect the recording to the book page. A student can then use a handheld device to listen to the book by selecting the sticker for a particular page to be played. The reading pens represent concrete examples of repurposing assistive technology (refer to Chapter 1) as neither the LeapReader nor the AnyBook Personal are marketed as assistive technology, yet they can easily support students with disabilities. However, another device, Bookworm, allows a teacher or other individuals to take books and make them switch-accessible; it was specifically designed to support students with disabilities (see Figure 8.2). With Bookworm, educators can record any book for students with disabilities to access via a switch (see Bookworm Audio in

Figure 8.2   Bookworm by AbleNet

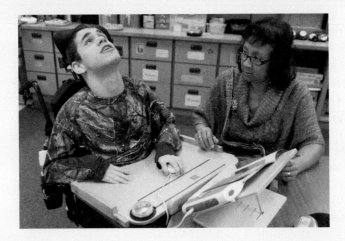

Source: AbleNet. Reproduced with permission.

YouTube [https://www.youtube.com/watch?v=2YLAP2wWb40&t=119] for a video of how Bookworm works).

Related to text-to-speech is **eText** or **supported eText**. eText is electronic text; it may also be referred as digital text or e-books. Supported eText is eText with additional features to benefit students with disabilities, such as dictionaries or text-to-speech (Anderson-Inman & Horney, 2007). eText or digital text in and of itself may not produce access, but with supported eText, students with disabilities take advantage of the additional features.

eText can be accessed from a variety of places. For example, digital books can be purchased from Amazon, iTunes, or Barnes and Noble and accessed on each company's own eText reader (i.e., Kindle, iBooks, and Nook, respectively). Project Gutenberg (see https://www.gutenberg.org/) offers over 46,000 free e-books (Ahrens, 2011) and Loyal Books (see http://www.loyalbooks.com/) also offers free audiobooks and downloadable e-books. For students with documented print disabilities, Bookshare® (see https://www.bookshare.org/cms) provides over 300,000 free accessible e-books to students in the United States. For students who are eligible for Bookshare, they can select from different options as to how to read their accessible text: (a) a computer using Bookshare's own web readers (e.g., Bookshare Web Reader or Read: Outloud—Bookshare Edition 6) or separate free or for-purchase text-to-speech readers (e.g., Kurzweil,

Recall that the National Instructional Materials Accessibility Standard (NIMAS) was discussed in Chapter 1. NIMAS was included in the 2004 reauthorization of IDEA. NIMAS is related to eText or digital text in that NIMAS mandates that students with **print disabilities** be provided accessible instructional materials through such options as large print, braille, audio, and digital text (National Center on Accessible Instructional Materials, 2011). Under NIMAS, students with print disabilities—inclusive of students with reading-based learning disabilities, visual impairments, and physical disabilities that impact access to printed text—are to receive textbooks and other school materials in an accessible format (Loeding, 2011).

Read&Write GOLD, ReadHear; (b) Bookshare's Go Read Android app or Read2Go iOS app; (c) other text-to-speech apps; or (d) DAISY audioplayers (e.g., ReadHear by gh, LLC) or braille notetakers (Bookshare, n.d.).

Three other text or book-based tools can support students with disabilities in reading. One is Wiggleworks, marketed by Scholastic (see http://teacher .scholastic.com/products/wiggleworks/index.htm). Wiggleworks is a program that provides technology-based reading instruction in the five areas of reading identified by the National Reading Panel (2000) (i.e., phonemic awareness, phonics instruction, fluency, vocabulary, and reading comprehension) for students in Grades preK–3. The leveled books include reading supports and scaffolds, including reading the whole text, reading words to the students, as well as teachers being able to record their own supports (e.g., teachers making a connection between a word in the title of a book, such as peanut, to the ongoing class discussion regarding compound words). Wiggleworks also allows students to write responses to prompts or engage in the story by writing via the technology. Similar, albeit free, technology is provided by the Center for Applied Special Technologies (CAST) UDL Book Builder (see http://bookbuilder.cast .org/; refer to Chapter 1 regarding a discussion of UDL and CAST products). UDL Book Builder allows individuals, such as teachers, to create a digital book that includes supports and scaffolds for students with disabilities. Such supports can include the student recording his or her voice as well as scaffolds and prompts to aid in comprehension. Another alternative to CAST's UDL Book Builder is the Tarheel Reader (http://tarheelreader.org), which provides free accessible books that can be used with a variety of technology, including switches and alternative keyboards. The Tarheel Reader also allows individuals to author books to share.

Finally, a stand-alone device that supports students' reading is a talking dictionary. Talking dictionaries can support students in the area of vocabulary when reading. Talking dictionaries include the Elementary Children's Speller and Dictionary by Franklin (see Figure 8.3) and the Middle Schooler Merriam-Webster Intermediate Dictionary by Franklin. These handheld talking dictionaries are portable, making them easy for student use.

Case Study 8.1 Recap: Alex

Alex's individualized education program (IEP) team, including Alex, determined that Alex might benefit from using a product that read text to Alex. After an unsuccessful and frustrating trial with the Reading Pen, the IEP team decided that a computer-based text-to-speech program might be appropriate. However, Alex did not want to stand out by using something different from his classmates, so he was not happy about the possibility of having to go to a desktop computer at the back of his general education classroom to access either Natural Reader or Kurzweil 3000-firefly. His special education teacher suggested Alex try

©Digital Vision/Photodisc/Thinkstock

Read&Write for the Cloud, which would provide him with text-to-speech as well as highlighting and dictionary features, but it could be used on the Google Chromebooks that his teacher used regularly in her classroom. With small, discrete headphones, Alex could get access to the text-to-speech he needed.

Writing

Writing is also a critical, complex, and multifaceted skill that cuts across almost all content areas (National Commission on Writing for America's Families, Schools, and Colleges, 2005). Writing involves not just the motor aspects of writing (i.e., handwriting) and other technical elements (e.g., spelling) but also composition, which consists of planning, organizing, generating and drafting text, editing, and revising (Flower & Hayes, 1981). Students with and without disabilities can and do struggle with these different components (Mason, Harris, & Graham, 2011; National Center for Education Statistics, 2012c). Data from the 2011 NAEP writing assessment indicated only 27% of eighth and 12th graders were above a basic level with respect to writing. Stated differently, over three-fourths of eighth and 12th graders were at or below a basic level on the NAEP writing assessment. The 2011 NAEP writing data were not disaggregated for students with disabilities.

Students with disabilities face real and daunting challenges with writing. As noted previously, these challenges can occur in terms of handwriting, spelling, and then composing a written product. Assistive technology can support students with disabilities in writing, including both the technical elements as well as the creation of a written product. The discussion of assistive technology to support writing in this chapter will focus on low-tech, mid-tech, and high-tech options across the different facets of writing (e.g., handwriting, planning, and editing). In addition, free and for-purchase options will be discussed (see Table 8.3 for examples of assistive technology to support writing).

Figure 8.3   Children's Speller and Dictionary

Source: © iStock/ayaka_photo

Table 8.3   Examples of Assistive Technology for Writing

	Free	For Purchase
Handwriting	• Colored pencils • Make a window with an index card	• Typing on computer or tablet • Pencil grips • Raised-line paper • Ergonomic pencils or pens
Spelling	• Microsoft Word spell-checker	• Handheld spell-checker
Prewriting	• Paper-based concept maps • Computer-based concept maps (Cmap or the Visual Understanding Environment [VUE])	• Computer-based concept maps (Kidspiration, Inspiration, or Webspiration)

(Continued)

Table 8.3 (Continued)

	Free	For Purchase
Writing	• Speech-to-text (Dictation for Mac computers or Windows Speech Recognition for PC computers) • Dragon Dictation app for iOS devices	• Speech-to-text (Dragon Naturally Speaking) • Word prediction (Co:Writer 7, Co:Writer app, or Co:Writer Universal)
Postwriting	• Text-to-speech (Natural Reader) • Grammar-checker (Ginger) • Built-in text-to-speech with Microsoft Office and/or operating systems	• Text-to-speech (Read&Write GOLD) • wordQ + speakQ

Low-Tech Assistive Technology for Writing

Low-tech assistive technology exists to support students with disabilities in writing, from handwriting to the writing process. Handwriting can be challenging for students with disabilities, and a variety of low-tech, usually low-cost, options exist. For example, a classic low-tech assistive technology to support students with disabilities in handwriting is the pencil grip (see Figure 8.4). A variety of different types of pencil grips actually exist, so teachers and/or related service providers (for example, occupational therapists) may need to experiment with different types to see what works best for a student. Everyday items can also be repurposed to serve as pencil grips, such as squishy balls and pink-foam hair rollers. As an alternative to a pencil grip, some students with handwriting challenges might benefit from the Handiwriter® (see http://www.handithings.com/handiwriter.htm), which is a knit band that goes around a student's wrist with a portion sticking up through in which to put a pencil. The tool also has a charm that the student holds in his or her palm. Students may also benefit from different-size writing utensils, such as larger/thicker or thinner pencils, pens, or even crayons (for example, see Crayola). Alternative pens also exist, such as the ergonomic evo.millennium pen (see http://www.evopen.com/evopenproducts.html).

As paper and pencil are key ingredients to traditional writing and handwriting, an alternative to using an adapted pencil is using adaptive paper. Students with disabilities can benefit from some paper adaptions, such as

Figure 8.4   Pencil Grips: A Low-Tech Assistive Technology for Writing

Source: The Pencil Grip, Inc. Reproduced with permission.

raised-line paper (a student can feel the lines of the paper), darker line paper, and enlarged-line paper. Educators could make raised-line paper using such items as Elmer's glue or a for-purchase product like Wikki Stix (see http://www.wikkistix.com/). Additional options include students using alternatives to paper, such as gel boards, whiteboards, or even shaving cream in lower grades to practice letters, writing, and spelling. Finally, some students might benefit from elevating the surface on which they are writing, such as using a slant board.

Low-tech assistive technology can also support students with disabilities with the writing process: prewriting (i.e., planning and organizing), writing

Ms. Koontz is an elementary special education teacher who supports her third-grade students with disabilities in their general education settings as well as back in her special education classroom. In the general education settings, Ms. Koontz has worked with the general education third-grade teachers to implement some low-tech assistive technology through the idea of Universal Design for Learning (UDL). Specifically, in a basket in the middle of each group of four desks in the classrooms sit enough pencil grips, color highlighter strips, and sticky notes for each student. Individually, students can select different pencil grips and use them on their own pencils or pens when writing, changing as needed or desired. Students can also choose to use the color highlighter strips when reading their textbooks or their own self-selected books for fun during silent reading time, choosing among neon yellow, green, yellow,

iStock/5second

pink, and orange. By making these low-tech assistive technology devices available to all students, Ms. Koontz's students do not face stigmatization from using the tools, and students who are not identified for special education but who may need additional support for a variety of reasons benefit.

(i.e. composing text), and postwriting (i.e., editing and revising) (Flower & Hayes, 1981). Use of advanced organizers, also referred to as procedural facilitators or think sheets, is common in order to support students with disabilities in the writing process (Englert, Zhao, Dunsmore, Collings, & Wolbers, 2007). Particularly advanced organizers, such as concept maps or graphic organizers, can support the planning and organizing portion of the writing process. While many options exist, two examples include POWER (planning, organizing, writing, editing, and revising) and the hamburger paragraph (see Reading Rockets' "Paragraph Hamburger" at http://www.readingrockets.org/strategies/paragraph_hamburger for two downloadable templates) (Mariage & Bouck, 2004; Mariage, Englert, & Garmon, 2000). Outside of these preexisting think sheets, students, when instructed on such an organizational approach, can simply make a concept map on a piece of paper to organize their thoughts for writing.

Mid-Tech and High-Tech Assistive Technology for Writing

A number of mid-tech and high-tech assistive technologies exist to support students with disabilities across the writing process as well as in the technical elements of writing. In terms of the technical element of handwriting, a computer or portable word processor can serve as an alternative to handwriting. Rather than students writing their own answers or written products or relying on a **scribe**, some students with disabilities might benefit from **typing**, via a computer, word processing machine, or computer-like device, such as mobile tablet with a keyboard. Portable word processors, such as the Forte or the Fusion by the Writer Learning Systems (see http://www.writerlearning.com/), allow students access to a word processor, like Microsoft Word, but at a fraction of the cost of a computer. In addition to typing on portable word processors, these tools often come standard with a variety of accessibility features that have already been or will be discussed in this chapter, including word prediction and text-to-speech.

Computer-supported written documents allow for easy spelling checks with their **built-in spell-checkers**, such as the one in Microsoft Word. When not on a computer, students can check spelling with a **portable spell-checker** or combination portable spell-checker and dictionary. Franklin® produces both stand-alone spelling assistants (e.g., the Assistant—Webster's Spelling Corrector Plus) as well as handheld portable devices for both checking spelling and serving as a dictionary (e.g., the Elementary Children's Speller & Dictionary) (see http://www.franklin.com/for-children).

Computer-based concept maps support students in the planning and organizing phases of the writing process. Educators can use free computer-based concept-mapping programs, such as CmapTools (Institute for Human & Machine Cognition, n.d.) and the Visual Understanding Environment (Tufts University, 2008). However, for-purchase programs, such as Inspiration, Kidspiration, and Webspiration (Inspiration Software, 2012), generally include more options and are easier to use. Some computer-based concept-mapping programs have built-in additional supports, such as text-to-speech, speech-to-text, and pictures to represent ideas.

Students can take advantage of a variety of assistive technology devices as they move into the writing phase of the writing process. In terms of actually getting words onto paper, students can type with a keyboard, use alternative keyboards, or use speech-to-text, among other options. Students with difficulties with handwriting or composing can try speech-to-text, in which a computer program translates spoken text into text that appears in a document on a computer (MacArthur, 2009). Students can use speech-to-text to create an essay in a Word document as well as e-mails and other digital documents. Both for-purchase and free speech-to-text options exist. One of the most common speech-to-text programs is the for-purchase Dragon Naturally Speaking (Nuance, 2013) that works on both PC and Mac computers. Note that there is also a free Dragon Dictation app for iOS devices. Both Windows and OS X computers offer free, built-in speech-to-text programs. Windows operating systems come standard with Windows Speech Recognition (Microsoft Windows, 2012) and Mac computers with the Mountain Lion or newer operating system provide Dictation (Apple, 2013) as a standard feature. Both are relatively easier to use than the for-purchase Dragon Naturally Speaking and typically require less training. The reader is invited to refer to Chapter 5 for a complete discussion of assistive technology for computer access, including alternative keyboards, switches, and mouse options.

another example of AT now commonly integrated into "regular" tech.

Word prediction is another computer-based program that can support writing. Nowadays most people are probably more familiar with word prediction than in the past, given its use in texting (e.g., QuickType for iOS devices). Word prediction is when a program predicts the word an individual is typing prior to him or her finishing the word. Based on the letters typed, the program offers suggestions. For example, one types H-O, and a word prediction program might suggest *home*, *house*, or *hole* (MacArthur, 2009). While a few free computer-based word prediction programs exist (e.g., eType [eType, 2012]) and Turbo Type [Soft Grup Construct SRL, 2012]), these are usually only compatible with a Windows-based operating system. It should be noted that they can include advertisements or need rebooting after a period of time. For-purchase word prediction programs include Co:Writer 7 (Don Johnston, 2015), which is compatible with both PC and Mac computers; SoothSayer (Applied Human Factors, 2013), which works on any Windows-based operating system; wordQ+speakQ (GoQ, 2011); and Read&Write GOLD, which runs on both PC and Mac computers (texthelp, 2015). SoothSayer and Co:Writer 7 both also

Limited current research exists regarding technology to support the writing process for students with disabilities (Batorowicz, Missiuna, & Pollock, 2012). In other words, more research exists from the 1990s and early 2000s than from 2010 and beyond. Older research suggests benefits from using spell-checkers to revise written work if students are trained, with the caveat that not all errors will be detected (Batorowicz et al., 2012). The existing research base regarding speech recognition for producing and revising text shows some mixed results; some research suggested high-quality writing with the use of speech recognition technology as compared to handwriting (Batorowicz et al., 2012). Positive prior results are found with regard to concept mapping to plan or organize a paper on such outcomes as length and quality (Batorowicz et al., 2012).

---

offer text-to-speech and spell-check. Read&Write GOLD and wordQ+speakQ are more comprehensive, offering word prediction, text-to-speech, and speech-to-text. In a relatively recent study, Evmenova, Graff, Jerome, and Behrmann (2010) examined six students with disabilities using three different word prediction programs. The researchers found all three programs resulted in increased spelling accuracy; results for writing performance and composition rate varied across students and programs.

In the postwriting phase, students focus on editing and revising their work. Spell-check, grammar-check, and text-to-speech can support student success in this phase. Students can check their spelling using built-in spell-checkers within programs, such as Microsoft Word. Often, however, these programs check just for spelling and not words in grammatical context. A free grammar-check program is Ginger (Ginger Software, n.d.). Ginger checks spelling and grammar in documents, e-mails, and text to be placed on websites; additional features can be purchased with Ginger. Ginger understands context. It can correctly suggest deer instead of dear when one types, "I saw a dear." Also, with revising and editing, students and educators can take advantage of the free Review or Track Changes features within Microsoft Office, which allow either oneself, a peer, or an adult editor to suggest changes to a typed document, and the author can then accept or reject those changes. Google Docs online also has a similar feature in which an individual can make suggested edits.

gramonarly ↓ newer than book?

Finally, text-to-speech supports editing and revising. Hearing text can assist students with identifying errors and lack of clarity to be fixed in their own written product (Kelly, Kratcoski, & McClain, 2006; Madraso, 1993). While this can be accomplished by having students read their own text out loud, text-to-speech offers additional support when the written product is typed. As previously noted, a variety of text-to-speech options exist, including built-in accessibility options for computers and mobile devices, free downloadable programs, free online or web-based programs, and comprehensive for-purchase options.

Case Study 8.1 Recap: Jacob

Jacob's IEP team determined that computer-based supports might work best for Jacob given his struggle with handwriting. Specifically, they thought that with a laptop computer and different software options, Jacob's struggles with handwriting, organizing, spelling, and editing could be addressed. Jacob felt being able to use a computer in class was pretty cool, and he already possessed decent typing skills. Once a laptop was procured, the IEP team had Jacob try out a few different pieces of software, including concept-mapping applications and spell-check and grammar-check applications. Jacob enjoyed the free trial of Inspiration and felt he could handle the program with greater ease than the free Cmap and VUE concept-mapping tools he tried. Also, he was able to read his concept maps and outlines, which was an advantage for him over paper-and-pencil options. He also felt that Ginger was a better alternative for checking his spelling and grammar than the options already built into Microsoft Word. Finally, Jacob did like the free version of Natural Reader to read his written product back to him so he could make edits.

Mathematics

Mathematics poses challenges for students with disabilities, from fluency with basic facts to problem solving and from fractions to algebra (Calhoon, Emerson, Flores, & Houchins, 2007). The 2011 NAEP mathematics assessment data indicated only 55% of fourth graders with disabilities were at or above a basic level, as compared to 85% of fourth graders without disabilities. In eighth grade, the rate for at or above the basic level decreased for both students with and without disabilities—35% of students with disabilities and 77% of students without disabilities (National Center for Education Statistics, 2011a).

Technology is actually a critical component to mathematics education for all students. In fact, in the most recent version of the National Council for Teachers of Mathematics (NCTM, 2000) Standards, technology was listed as one of the six principles of a quality mathematics program. NCTM stated, "Technology is essential in teaching and learning mathematics; it influences the mathematics that is taught and enhances students' learning" (p. 24). Low-tech and mid- to high-tech options exist to support students with disabilities, although often the assistive technology in mathematics is technology to support all learners (see Table 8.4 for examples of assistive technology to support mathematics).

Table 8.4 Examples of Assistive Technology for Mathematics

Low Tech	Mid Tech	High Tech
• Concrete manipulatives • Number lines • Graph paper	• Calculators (e.g., four-function, graphing, or talking) • Coin-U-Lator	• Virtual manipulatives • Anchored instruction • Apps (e.g., ISolveIt)

Low-Tech Assistive Technology for Mathematics

Low-tech assistive technology is generally common in mathematics classrooms. While often considered an instructional tool for mathematics teaching and learning, concrete manipulatives, graph paper, and number lines can also serve as assistive technology for students with disabilities. Concrete manipulatives are generally considered an evidence-based practice for teaching mathematics to students with disabilities. In practice and research, concrete manipulatives have been successfully used to support students with disabilities in understanding algebra, area and perimeter, integers, and fractions (Cass, Cates, Smith, & Jackson, 2003; Jordan, Miller, & Mercer, 1998; Maccini & Hughes, 2000; Maccini & Ruhl, 2000). Number lines, graph paper, and hundreds charts can also serve as low-tech assistive technology to support students with disabilities in accessing mathematics. For example, number lines are used to support the teaching and learning of addition and subtraction with younger students as well as price comparison by secondary students with intellectual disability and students with autism spectrum disorder (Weng & Bouck, 2014).

Case Study 8.3

Matt is a 10th-grade student identified with autism spectrum disorder and moderate intellectual disability (full scale IQ of 47). Matt is able to identify numbers up through 20 and identify prices in a store but has an IEP goal of comparing the prices of two items to determine the lower price. Matt's teacher implemented a number line system and taught Matt to use the low-tech assistive technology to compare each digit, as needed, between the prices of two items to determine the lower price. Specifically, the teacher laminated a number line containing the numbers 0–9 and provided Matt with a dry-erase marker and eraser. Matt circled each number in the price starting with the ones and going through the tenths and hundredths, as needed, to determine the lower price.

Concrete manipulatives, number lines, and graph paper can act as instructional aids for all students or as assistive technology for students with disabilities. These same tools can also be implemented in a manner consistent with Universal Design for Learning (refer to Chapter 1 for additional information on UDL). By applying a UDL framework to the use of these tools, educators can make the tools freely available to all and allow students to decide how and when to interact with them, offering all students multiple means of engagement as well as expression and flexibility in their learning (Council for Exceptional Children [CEC], 2005).

Mid-Tech and High-Tech Assistive Technology for Mathematics

Calculators, virtual manipulatives, anchored instruction, and computer-assisted instruction represent mid-tech or high-tech assistive technology to support students with disabilities in mathematics (Bouck & Flanagan, 2009). Calculators are one of the most common accommodations in IEPs for students with disabilities (Maccini & Gagnon, 2000; 2006). Whether four-function, scientific, graphing, fraction, talking, online, or app-based, calculators support students with disabilities with basic facts. Calculators allow students with disabilities to access mathematics (e.g., problem solving) without be constrained by their struggles with basic facts or working-memory challenges (Bouck, Hunley, & Bouck, in press).

Depending on a student's needs, mathematics content, preferences, and age, educators can consider the range of different calculator options. Often, classrooms may allow students access to the basic four-function calculator, a scientific calculator, or a graphing calculator, depending on students' ages and mathematical content being taught (e.g., graphing calculators for algebra and above). Of course, some students may need a talking calculator, which allows for the numbers a student is typing in as well as the output to be voiced. For students who primarily use their computers for accessing information and content, online calculator options exist and can be compatible with switches, a mouse, or other alternative means of accessing a computer. Finally, app-based calculator options are increasingly popular, including ones that solve the problem a student writes on the mobile device with his or her finger, such as MyScript Calculator, or ones that talk, such as Talking Calculator (Croser, 2013). For students with more moderate or severe disabilities who are focusing on money skills, a specifically designed money calculator (i.e., the Coin-U-Lator) can assist in adding or subtracting money, including dollars, quarters, dimes, nickels and pennies.

Virtual Manipulatives

A digital or virtual counterpart to concrete manipulatives can also support students with disabilities (Bouck & Flanagan, 2009). Virtual manipulatives were traditionally Internet-based; however, now there are app options for mobile devices. For Internet-based virtual manipulatives, a popular website is the National Library of Virtual Manipulatives (NLVM; http://nlvm.usu.edu/) (Cannon, Dorward, Duffin, & Heal, 2004); see Figure 8.5 for a screen shot of the NLVM. Educators are also able to access the NLVM offline and customize it via the NLVM app, which allows users to install the NLVM on individual computers or servers (see https://www.mattimath.com/). With the computer app, students can save work as well as print, and teachers, as previously noted, can customize or design an activity with virtual manipulatives. Other websites include Illuminations by the National Council for Teachers of Mathematics (n.d.) (see http://illuminations.nctm.org/ActivitySearch.aspx) and Interactivate by the Shodor Education Foundation (n.d.) (see http://www.shodor.org/interactivate/) (Bouck & Flanagan, 2010).

To date, limited research exists that explicitly examines students with disabilities being supported by virtual manipulatives. One of these studies found elementary-aged students with autism spectrum disorder were supported in solving

Perspective 8.4

Research to Practice

As common as calculators are—almost every cell phone now includes one—use of calculators is not without controversy, especially their use as an accommodation for students with disabilities. Previous research found that students with high-incidence disabilities benefit from use of a calculator on mathematics assessments (Bouck, 2009; Bouck & Bouck, 2008; Lee, Wells, & Sireci, 2010) and answer more problems correctly with a calculator (Bouck et al., in press). However, students with disabilities often do not elect to use calculators (Bouck, Joshi, & Johnson, 2013). Teachers should ensure that students with disabilities not only have access to calculators but also know how to use each type of calculator proficiently prior to providing them as an accommodation (Bouck, 2010).

subtraction problems using both virtual and concrete manipulatives, although the students were more successful with the virtual manipulatives (Bouck, Satsangi, Taber-Doughty, & Courtney, 2014). The other study found that high school students with learning disabilities increased their performance in solving area or perimeter problems using virtual manipulatives (Satsangi & Bouck, 2015).

Figure 8.5   Base-10 Blocks from the National Library of Virtual Manipulatives

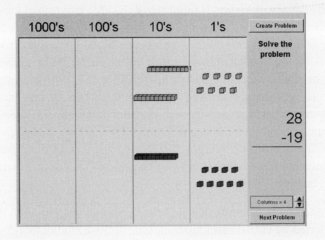

Source: Utah State University (2015). Reproduced with permission.

Two final technologies for mathematics, which are usually considered **instructional technology** but can be repurposed to be assistive technology for students with disabilities, are anchored instruction and computer-assisted instruction (CAI). Anchored instruction is the alternative presentation of a mathematics problem or lesson situated in a real-world context; a common medium in the past, albeit now an outdated technology, was CD-ROM (Bottge, 1999). Bottge and colleagues (cf. Bottge, Heinrichs, Mehta, & Hung, 2002; Bottge, Rueda, Serlin, Hung, & Kwon, 2007; Bottge, Rueda, & Sivington, 2006) found anchored instruction and enhanced anchored instruction helped students with disabilities in problem solving. While anchored instruction was focused on problem solving and developing conceptual understanding, the majority of CAI for students with disabilities is focused on rote memorization or basic skills. However, the research on CAI, like that of anchored instruction, is positive as to its impact on student outcomes (Bouck & Flanagan, 2009).

Case Study 8.1 Recap: Justine

Justine advocated in her IEP meeting for use of a calculator in her mathematics classes and classes that involved mathematics, such as chemistry. While Justine's IEP team was open to a handheld calculator, Justine and her parents pushed back and suggested that she use the MyScript Calculator app for the iPad she already owned and carried with her at school. The app was free, and Justine already used the device at home and felt very comfortable with it.

Science and Social Studies

Assistive technology can also support content area learning in science and social studies; however, few specifically designed technologies exist for these domains. Often educators use literacy-based assistive technologies (e.g., reading pen or speech-to-text) to support students in science and social studies given the often heavy use of textbooks or other reading and writing activities in these content areas (Scruggs, Mastropieri, & Okolo, 2008). However, one specific assistive technology to support students with disabilities in science is the CAST UDL Science Writer (see http://sciencewriter.cast.org/), a free online tool. The UDL Science Writer supports secondary students with disabilities in constructing science reports. The technology scaffolds the writing of the science report as well as uses built-in assistive technologies, such as text-to-speech, to edit and revise their written reports.

Study Skills

In addition to supporting students with disabilities in content area instruction, technology can support students with disabilities in **study skills**. Study skills refer to skills or strategies students use for "acquiring, recording, organizing, synthesizing, remembering, and using information presented" (Hoover & Patton, 1995; Paulsen & Sayeski, 2013, p. 40). Study skills have been broken down into those for management (e.g., self-management) and those for cognition (e.g., note-taking). For the purposes of this chapter, we will discuss cognitive study skills; please see Chapter 7 for self-management skills.

One component of study skills is note-taking, and one technology to aid students in note-taking is a Livescribe™ smartpen (see Figure 8.6). Currently, two different models of a Livescribe pen exist: the Pulse and the Echo (Shrieber & Seifert, 2009). The Livescribe smartpen looks similar to a regular pen, but a student writes on special paper. In addition to writing notes, the pen also records a lecture or class discussion. After class, the student can retrieve the audio by going back to his or her notes and tapping on their notes on the special paper. With the Livescribe pen, the student has written and auditory notes. An alternative computer-based option to the Livescribe pen might be Evernote (see https://evernote.com/). Evernote allows users to type in notes, including adding images as well as audio, and sync those notes across different devices, such as a computer, smartphone, or other mobile device. Notes can even be shared. Likewise, another collaborative online note-taking device is Google Drive (https://www.google.com/drive/), in that students can type notes into a Google Doc and share with others. Those with whom the document is shared can just review, edit, or add notes, depending on the manner in which it is shared.

Quizlet

Other options to support study skills include digital flash cards or study aid apps, such as Brainscape or Study Blue. Brainscape (see https://www.brainscape.com/) provides flash cards on a computer or mobile device. Teachers or students can make their own flash cards or use sets from those that are freely available with the program. Similarly, two other study apps are Study Blue (see https://www.studyblue.com/), which can include flash cards, review sheets, study guides, and quizzes; and Quizlet (see http://quizlet.com/), which can similarly support flash cards and study games.

Source: Livescribe. Reproduced with permission. Retrieved from http://www.livescribe.com/blog/noteworthy2/press-resources/

Of course, low-tech options exist to support study skills. Aside from another individual taking notes for a student with a disability, such as a scribe, students can be given guided notes. An older low technology to support students with disabilities who struggled with note-taking was having a student with strong note-taking skills take notes on carbon copy paper, and a copy would be shared with the student with a disability. Nowadays, when more sophisticated technology is not used, a more common method may be to photocopy or scan a student's notes to share. Likewise, flash cards for studying can still be made on notecards. Another low-tech option, discussed to a greater extent in Chapter 7, is a checklist (i.e., self-monitoring) to support a student's study skills.

Online and Hybrid Education

Aside from instructional assistive technology to support students in academics, assistive technology for instruction should also consider the mode of delivery, such as online learning. Online-learning experiences are increasingly becoming a reality for students with disabilities. Over 50% of states offer fully virtual or online schools as an option for students (Watson, Pape, Murin, Gemin, & Vashaw, 2014). Additionally, some states use virtual schools to offer courses to supplement student learning.

For students with disabilities, online learning can offer advantages as well as challenges. For example, with online learning, instructors can implement practices aligned to Universal Design for Learning (refer to Chapter 1 for in-depth information regarding UDL). For example, instructors can post videos as well as text transcriptions (Hashey & Stahl, 2014). Online courses can also contain built-in opportunities for engagement with the learning through different online means as well as allow students to rewatch, read, or engage

What Is Online Learning?

What is online learning? **Online learning** is virtual learning. In other words, learning via a course that occurs, nowadays, on the Internet. Online-learning experiences can be fully online, wherein the entire course occurs online and there are no face-to-face meetings, or use **blended** or **hybrid** approaches, in which some learning or course meetings occur face-to-face and some occur virtually. Within online courses, there are different means of interaction: **synchronous** and **asynchronous**. Synchronous courses involve real-life interactions, like a live face-to-face class or texting or chatting. Asynchronous courses involve interactions separated by time, such as discussion forums or e-mail (Hashey & Stahl, 2014).

with something multiple times (Serianni & Coy, 2014). Some online-learning experiences are designed to allow students to move at their own pace. Yet online learning may not be differentiated to all students' needs, and not all students handle a more self-initiating environment (i.e., going at one's own pace) (Greer, Rowland, & Smith, 2014; Serianni & Coy, 2014). It should also be noted that despite federal laws (i.e., the Americans with Disabilities Act and Section 504 of the Rehabilitation Act), not all online learning is accessible to students with disabilities (Center on Online Learning and Students with Disabilities [COLSD], 2012).

Multiple technologies support online, hybrid, or flipped classes for students with and without disabilities. For one, there are for-purchase as well as free **learning management systems** (LMS) that educators can use to teach online or flipped classes or use for online discussions. Two free LMS choices are Edmodo (see https://www.edmodo.com/) and Schoology (see https://www.schoology.com/). Each allows teachers to create classes and students to enroll for free. In Edmodo and Schoology, students can engage in online discussions, receive and post homework, and complete quizzes, among other features. Both Edmodo and Schoology are available online as well as for mobile iOS and Android devices.

Beyond LMS options, other types of technology can support instruction. For example, for students who might need or want additional instruction or support outside of school, some options exist, such as Khan Academy (see https://www.khanacademy.org/). Khan Academy is a free website that provides personalized learning to students. In other words, students can go at their own

Perspective 8.6

What Is Flipping the Classroom?

....

Flipping the classroom refers to inverting traditional teaching (Fulton, 2014). Rather than teaching the lesson within the classroom, teachers record lectures or content presentations in advance, often with technology (e.g., interactive whiteboards, SMART Boards, or video recordings), and post these for students to access. Students access the teacher instruction prior to the class, such as at home the night before, and then classtime is spent doing exercises, extending the learning, or engaging in projects (Fulton, 2014).

pace, using practice exercises and instructional videos on a variety of subjects (e.g., mathematics procedures, computer programming, and science). Khan Academy offers options for students as young as kindergarten and can be used to support learning outside of school. Another option for teachers creating online or flipped experiences is using TED Ed (see http://ed.ted.com/). TED Ed allows educators to create a lesson featuring a TED talk (see http://www.ted .com/) or other videos available on YouTube. The lesson features opportunities for students to watch the video, think about the video by answering questions, dig deeper by exploring additional resources, and engage with other students in discussion. Of course, teachers can go to YouTube to find videos to support or enhance their instruction without these additional features as well as create their own videos. Teachers can use the for-purchase product Camtasia to create their own videos to support student learning outside of the classroom (http:// www.techsmith.com/camtasia.html). Camtasia allows video to be recorded not just of the individual but also creates a record of what is occurring on one's computer screen. For example, an educator can present and narrate using a PowerPoint with Camtasia, and the PowerPoint will be on the video, along with the person recording (i.e., his or her image as well as his or her voice). These videos can then be uploaded to an LMS site or YouTube for dissemination.

A final technology consideration to help students with disabilities with instruction is interactive whiteboard apps, such as ShowMe and Educreations. These apps allow educators to record lessons or support videos while diagramming or explaining on a whiteboard app. These recordings can support a flipped classroom or support students in or out of class who may need additional assistance. ShowMe and Educreations are both free apps, although one can purchase additional features and options with Educreations.

Educators, students, and parents can check the accessibility of products for online learning as well as websites. For example, COLSD provides information regarding the Voluntary Product Accessibility Template (VPAT) for different products. COLSD applied Section 508 requirements to products, such as learning and/or content management systems, e-readers, social-networking sites, document creation tools, and progress-monitoring sites, among others (see http://centerononlinelearning.org/resources/vpat/) (Hashey & Stahl, 2014; Smith & Basham, 2014). This evaluation by COLSD can be important with research suggesting that the majority of K–12 online and virtual education is provided by for-profit vendors and, thus, needs to be evaluated as to its match with the desired goals and support (Patrick, Kennedy, & Powell, 2013; Queen, Lewis, & Coopersmith, 2011). WebAIM offers a free website accessibility check (see http://wave.webaim.org/). By plugging in a website, WAVE (Web Accessibility Versatile Evaluator) provides information about the website's accessibility, including errors and alerts (i.e., areas of potential concern). Errors can include, for example, images in which alternative text is not presented (Hashey & Stahl, 2014). While the errors and potential errors can be overwhelming, Hashey and Stahl (2014) recommended focusing on three features: (1) if text can be read by a screen reader, (2) if a site's navigation, which would allow items to be read by screen order, is in the correct order, and (3) if alternative text exists for images or videos.

Web 2.0 Resources and Apps

Throughout the text, multiple Web 2.0 resources and apps were mentioned to serve as assistive technology for instruction. These same ones as well as others are reinforced in Tables 8.5 and 8.6, which focus on free and for-purchase supports for literacy and mathematics. Yet the table is not an exhaustive list. Teachers may also want to consider other Web 2.0 resources or apps. For example, Remind is a Web 2.0 resource or app technology that allows a teacher to communicate with students or parents via texting, without either group needing to provide the other with their actual phone numbers (see https://www.remind.com/). Another teacher tool is TeachersPayTeachers (see https://www.teacherspayteachers.com/), which allows teachers to sell or provide for free their lessons and activities to other teachers (or parents). A variety of lessons exist on this site, many which support all students as well as specific lessons for supporting students with disabilities. Teachers, parents, or other educators can opt to access free material or purchase resources and materials.

Other Web 2.0 resources and apps educators may want to consider, which can be repurposed as assistive technology for students with disabilities, include BrainPOP (see https://www.brainpop.com/) and BrainPOP Jr. (see https://jr.brainpop.com/); BrainPOP Jr. is designed for students in Grades K–3. Both can be accessed online or via an app. BrainPOP and BrainPOP Jr. work with students to support learning in traditional classrooms, serve as instructional resources in flipped classrooms, or act as additional support or reinforcement for students who might be struggling with content. Both versions offer free and for-purchase options. An additional app to consider is Gizmos by ExploreLearning (2014) (Greer et al., 2014). The Gizmos app provides teachers and students in Grades 3 through 12 with free science and mathematics simulations focused on developing understanding of concepts. Gizmos can also be used on the Internet (see http://www.explorelearning.com/), but there is a license cost.

Table 8.5 Examples of Free Literacy and Mathematics Web 2.0 Resources and Apps as Assistive Technology to Support Instruction		
	Web 2.0 Resources	**Apps**
Reading	• Rewordify (see https://rewordify.com/) – Free online website that simplifies language pasted from document or URL; includes learning sessions to teach students words	• Natural Reader (see https://itunes.apple.com/us/app/naturalreader-text-to-speech/id598798210?mt=8) – Free app that reads documents (e.g., Word, PDFs, and websites) on a mobile device as well as words typed into the app's browser
Writing	• Ginger (see http://www.gingersoftware.com/) – Free Google Chrome or Safari extension that can check for spelling or grammar errors	• Ginger (see https://itunes.apple.com/app/ginger-page-writing-compass/id822797943?ls=1&mt=8) – Free app that checks spelling and grammar as well as suggests rephrases before texting, e-mailing, or uploading to social media from a mobile device; includes text-to-speech
		• Dragon Dictation (see https://itunes.apple.com/us/app/dragon-dictation/id341446764?mt=8) – Free app that provides speech-to-text capabilities for iOS devices

(Continued)

Table 8.5 (Continued)

	Web 2.0 Resources	Apps
Mathematics	• NLVM (see http://nlvm.usu .edu/) – Free website that provides virtual manipulatives in such areas as numbers and operations, algebra, geometry, measurement, and data and probability for Grades preK–12	• ISolveIt (see http://isolveit.cast.org/home) – Two free math puzzle apps (MathSquared and MathScaled) from CAST built following UDL • MyScript Calculator (see https://itunes.apple .com/us/app/myscript-calculator-handwriting/ id578979413?mt=8) – Free app that performs calculations based on writing problem on mobile devices

Table 8.6 Examples of For-Purchase Literacy and Mathematics Web 2.0 Resources and Apps as Assistive Technology to Support Instruction

	Web 2.0 Resources	Apps
Reading	• ClickHear™ (see https://www.gh-accessibility.com/ software/clickhear) – For-purchase downloadable tool that reads webpages as well as alt text and buttons; also comes as a mobile (nondownloadable) option	• Prizmo (see https://itunes.apple.com/ us/app/prizmo-scanning-ocr-speech/ id366791896?mt=8) – For-purchase app that allows users to take a picture of a printed document and the app will read the document
Writing	• Webspiration (see http://www .mywebspiration.com/) – For-purchase online productivity tool to support writing, including planning and organizing	• Inspiration Maps VPP (see https:// itunes.apple.com/us/app/inspiration-maps-vpp/id510173686?mt=8) – For purchase app that allows students to engage in the previously downloadable computer program Inspiration on iOS devices
Mathematics	• Gizmos (see http://www.explorelearning .com/) – For-purchase math and science interactive online simulations connected to the Common Core State Standards; note that it is also available as an app (see https://itunes.apple.com/us/app/ gizmos/id692838319)	• Math Manipulatives (see https://itunes .apple.com/us/app-bundle/math-manipulatives/id973557973?mt=8) – For-purchase virtual manipulative; seven-app bundle, including algebra tiles, base-10 blocks, connecting cubes, color tiles, number lines, pattern blocks, and number rods

KEY TERMS

asynchronous, p. 200

blended course, p. 200

eText, p. 182

flipped classroom, p. 201

hybrid course, p. 200

instructional
   technology, p. 197

learning management
   systems, p. 200

online learning, p. 200

optical character recognition
   system, p. 180

study skills, p. 198

supported eText, p. 182

synchronous, p. 200

Text-to-speech, p. 179

EXTENSION ACTIVITIES

- Show the video "K–12 Using Assistive Technology for Math and Science" (http://bit .ly/1Isvbgr) in class or have students watch individually. Engage in a discussion regarding the assistive technology tools and devices discussed to support mathematics and science.

- Show "Assistive Technology in Action—Meet Brody" (http://bit.ly/1GLNgPb) in class or have students watch individually. Engage in a discussion regarding the assistive technology tools used to support Brody and what supports these tools provide.

- Show "Assistive Technology in Action—Meet Joe" (http://bit.ly/1InjYMd) in class or have students watch individually. Engage in a discussion regarding the assistive technology tools used to support Joe and what support these tools provide.

- Show "Assistive Technology in Action—Meet Jean" (http://bit.ly/1HXOU1U) in class or have students watch individually. Engage in a discussion regarding how an iPad serves as an instructional support for Jean.

APPLICATION ACTIVITIES

- Explore the free Web 2.0 discussed in Chapter 8 to support instruction in reading, writing, mathematics, and science for students with disabilities. Specifically, students can explore the CAST products (e.g., UDL Book Builder, CAST Science Writer; see http://www.cast.org/ learningtools/), the NLVM, Rewordify, and Ginger (i.e., refer to Table 8.5).

- Explore the free apps discussed in Chapter 8 to support instruction in literacy,

mathematics, and science for students with disabilities. Students can explore the apps discussed in Table 8.5 (e.g., Ginger or ISolveIt) as well as throughout the chapter.

- Explore the free teacher tools discussed in Chapter 8, including, for example, Edmodo, Schoology, Teachers Pay Teachers, Remind, ShowMe, and Brainscape.

- Download and explore trial versions of for-purchase products that support reading and writing, such as Inspiration (http://www .inspiration.com/Inspiration) or Kidspiration (http://www.inspiration.com/Kidspiration), wordQ (http://www.goqsoftware.com/), and Read&Write GOLD (http://www .texthelp.com/north-america/our-products/ readwrite/features-pc). Consider how these for-purchase options do or do not provide additional supports or features to benefit students with disabilities as compared to their free alternatives (e.g., CmapTools or Natural Reader).

DISCUSSION QUESTIONS

1. How can assistive technology for reading help students with disabilities who struggle with decoding? Comprehending?

2. When would low-tech versus mid- or high-tech assistive technology be appropriate to support students with disabilities in writing? When would free versus for-purchase products be appropriate?

3. How can different technologies that support mathematics teaching and learning for students with disabilities be implemented in a manner consistent with Universal Design for Learning?

4. Describe some of the positives and negatives of using mid- to high-tech assistive technology to support cognitive study skills for students with disabilities.

RESOURCES/ADDITIONAL INFORMATION

- The Center for Applied Special Technology (see http://www.cast.org/)

- Technology and Media Division of the Council for Exceptional Children (http:// www.tamcec.org/)

- *The Journal of Special Education Technology*

SUGGESTED ENRICHMENT READINGS

- Knight, V., McKissick, B. R., & Saunders, A. (2013). A review of technology-based interventions to teach academic skills to students with autism spectrum disorders. *Journal of Autism & Developmental Disabilities*, 43(11), 2628–2648.

- Berkeley, S., & Lindstrom, J. H. (2011). Technology for the struggling reader: Free and easily accessible resources. *TEACHING Exceptional Children*, 43(4), 48–55.

- Bouck, E. C., Meyer, N. K., Hunley, M., Satsangi, R., & Savage, M. (2015). Free computer-based assistive technology to support students with high-incidence disabilities in the writing process. *Preventing School Failure*, 59, 90–97.

CHAPTER 9

Assistive Technology to Enhance Independence and Transition

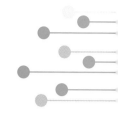

Chapter 9 focuses on assistive technology to support individuals with disabilities as they transition from K–12 school into postschool life. Specifically, Chapter 9 discusses assistive technology to support individuals with disabilities in postsecondary education, employment, and independent living. This chapter presents examples of assistive technology to help individuals with disabilities be independent in higher education, employment, and in daily living, including dressing, food preparation, and safety.

The goal of secondary education is to prepare *all* students for a successful life after exiting school (Gargiulo, 2015; Wehman et al., 2014). Students with disabilities receive special services under the Individuals with Disabilities Education Act (IDEA, 2004) to support their move from school to postschool life, called **transition services**. Transition services include instruction, related services (e.g., assistive technology), daily-living skills, employment-focused support, and other community experiences (Gargiulo, 2015; IDEA, 2004; Test, Aspel, & Everson, 2006). The goal of transition services is to provide students with disabilities a set of coordinated, individualized activities focused on their post-school success (i.e., postsecondary education, employment, and independent living). Legally, under the federal IDEA (2004), transition-planning services must begin when a student is 16 years of age (Yell, 2012). States can require statements of transition services to appear in an individualized education program (IEP) for students younger than age 16 (Yell, 2012).

Chapter Objectives

After reading the chapter, the reader will be able to do the following:

1. Understand assistive technology can support individuals with disabilities across the lifespan

2. Provide examples of assistive technology to support individuals with disabilities in postsecondary education

3. Provide examples of assistive technology to support individuals with disabilities in employment

4. Provide examples of assistive technology to support individuals with disabilities in independent or daily-living activities

Despite receiving transition services (i.e., transition services were included in IDEA since 1990) (Yell, 2012), students with disabilities continue to struggle in the major life domains after exiting school. Data from the National Longitudinal Transition Study-2 (NLTS2) suggest that while the majority of students with disabilities report attending postsecondary education within eight years of exiting school (60%), their postsecondary education option is more likely to be a two-year or community college (Newman et al., 2011). The rates of postsecondary education varied greatly via disability category (e.g., 75% of students with hearing impairments attended postsecondary education while only 29% of students with intellectual disability attended). Within eight years of exiting high school, 63% of students with disabilities reported living independently (i.e., on own or with roommate or spouse) or semi-independently (i.e., college dormitory or military) (Newman et al., 2011). Within six years of exiting high school, 71.1% of students with disabilities reported having a paid job, yet the rate of employment also varied greatly by disability category (e.g., 29.8% of students identified with deaf-blindness versus 78.6% of students with learning disabilities) (Sanford et al., 2011).

Assistive Technology for Transition and Postschool Experiences

Assistive technology can support students with disabilities across transition and postschool experiences. Students with disabilities can use assistive technology in postsecondary education, employment, and aspects of independent living. Often assistive technologies used in transition and postschool are the same or similar to that used in students' K–12 schools. In other words, many assistive technology devices are tools that can support individuals with disabilities across the life span. As such, the reader should consider that the augmentative and alternative communication devices discussed in Chapter 3, the instructional technologies referenced in Chapter 8, the technologies for computer access from Chapter 5, the technologies for vision and hearing from Chapter 6, the technologies for organization and self-management from Chapter 7, and the technologies for mobility and positioning from Chapter 4 can continue to support individuals with disabilities in their postschool experiences.

Students with disabilities benefit from assistive technology provided during K–12 education. Likewise, individuals with disabilities benefit from the provision of assistive technology during postschool activities, such as postsecondary education, employment, and aspects of independent living. Yet researchers suggest a decline occurs between the provision of assistive technology in

K–12 education and that for individuals with disabilities postschool (Bouck & Flanagan, in press; Bouck, Maeda, & Flanagan, 2011). Researchers have also found that despite studies showing benefits of using assistive technology in terms of greater access, skill acquisition, learning, and increased independence while in school, students who receive assistive technology in school do not experience better postschool outcomes (Bouck & Flanagan, in press; Bouck et al., 2011). However, older research suggests a relationship between receiving assistive technology in postschool experiences (e.g., in postsecondary education or employment) and positive outcomes, including increased GPA, lower attrition rates, and successful employment (Langton & Ramseur, 2001; Raskind & Higgins, 1998).

Legal Issues Involving
Transition and Assistive Technology

As students transition from preK–12 education to education in postschool settings, they also shift from being served under the protections of IDEA and Section 504 of the 1973 Rehabilitation Act (i.e., Section 504) to being protected under Section 504 and the Americans with Disabilities Act (ADA; refer to Chapter 1 for additional information regarding laws). Section 504 essentially prohibits discrimination against individuals with disabilities from entities that receive federal funding, including public K–12 schools and institutions of higher education (Yell, 2012). Individuals with disabilities, who are broadly defined under Section 504, are granted physical access to programs and activities as well as the right to receive reasonable accommodations at no cost. Reasonable accommodations in postsecondary education and employment can include assistive technology (Dell, 2010). The ADA is a federal law passed in 1990, and its focus is to prevent discrimination against individuals with disabilities. Unlike Section 504, ADA covers both private as well as public organizations (Kinsell, 2014). ADA regulates the provision of assistive technology as a means of an accommodation or auxiliary aids and services (Dell, 2010).

With Section 504 and ADA, students attending postsecondary education must request accommodations and auxiliary aids and services. Unlike preK–12 schools, postsecondary institutions are not required to seek out students with disabilities (Dell, 2010). Students with disabilities enrolled at institutions of higher education must identify themselves as having a disability and work with an institution's office of disability rights. The self-identification includes requesting assistive technology the students needs to access and participate in the learning. Under Section 504 and ADA, institutions of higher education are not required to provide the specific technology a student wants. As long

Section 504 defines an individual with a disability as "any person who (i) has a physical or mental impairment which substantially limits one or more of such person's major life activities, (ii) has a record of such an impairment, or (iii) is regarded as having such an impairment" (Rehabilitation Act of 1973, Section 504, 29 U.S.C. § 706[7][B]). Under Section 504, individuals can be covered if they have a condition impacting a bodily system, such as the digestive or neurological, as well as mental illness, learning disabilities, or intellectual disability (Rehabilitation Act of 1973, 34 C.F.R. § 104.3[j][2][i]).

as institutions can demonstrate their technology and/or accommodation are as effective, institutions do not have to give a student exactly what he or she requests (Dell, 2010).

In the adult services arena, assistive technology, outside of postsecondary education institutions, is likely provided by through vocational rehabilitation. Vocational rehabilitation counselors can support individuals in terms of determining what, if any, assistive technology is needed to support them in obtaining and maintaining employment (Homa & DeLambo, 2015; Lindstrom, Kahn, & Lindsey, 2013; McDonough & Revell, 2010). As noted, the provision of assistive technology, if needed, during employment is covered under ADA.

Postsecondary Education

The assistive technologies that supported students with disabilities in preK–12 education can also support students with disabilities in accessing and achieving in postsecondary education, including two-year or community colleges, four-year colleges or universities, and vocational or trade schools. However, students with disabilities do report a decline in receipt of assistive technology from K–12 to postsecondary education (Bouck et al., 2011; Cawthon & Cole, 2010). This decline may be a result of students deciding to not self-identify, as researchers suggest that less than one third of students with disabilities inform postsecondary education institutions of their disability. Of this one third, only 19% received accommodations or supports, such as assistive technology, from the postsecondary institutions they attended (Newman et al., 2011). Recent research suggests students with disabilities in postsecondary education may own their assistive technology for personal use (e.g., computer or mobile phone) and, thus, contribute to the low number seeking support from the postsecondary institution (Seale, Georgeson, Mamas, & Swain, 2015). It also suggests that students with disabilities may not be using assistive technology because of perceived stigmatization or the attitudes or policies of instructors (Lang et al., 2014). Little research exists regarding the impact or effectiveness of assistive technology use at the postsecondary education level for students with disabilities (Lang et al., 2014).

Older research, while dated, suggests the following are the most commonly reported assistive technologies provided in postsecondary education settings: adaptive furniture, document conversion, and then hardware or software (Stodden, Roberts, Picklesimer, Jackson & Chang, 2006). For students with learning disabilities, commonly reported assistive technologies used in postsecondary education are those that assist in reading (e.g., text-to-speech) and writing (e.g., word processors and speech-to-text) (Abreu-Ellis & Ellis, 2006; Sharpe, Johnson, Izzo, & Murray, 2005). Other researchers reported the following assistive technology used in institutions of higher education: voice recognition systems, reading machines (e.g., Kurzweil), frequency-modulated (FM) listening systems, recording tools, and tools to support planning (Lang et al., 2014; Seale et al., 2015). Nowadays, handheld reading pens, text-to-speech, or a digital textbook on a laptop or tablet are common reading machines. However, all assistive technology used in postsecondary education may be underreported because it may be underutilized (Lang et al., 2014).

Although previously noted in other chapters, the following are examples of assistive technology that can support students with disabilities in postsecondary education, especially when one considers the amount of reading, notetaking, and writing that occurs in higher education. One such assistive technology, which is fast becoming a mainstream technology, is e-books or digital text (Stachowiak, 2014). Students without disabilities are electing to use digital textbooks for ease (i.e., carrying a tablet as opposed to textbooks) and cost (Reynolds, 2011; Sloan, 2012). For students with disabilities, digital textbooks can provide text-to-speech as well as other supportive features (e.g., highlighting and text color contrast). One such program to provide additional supports to students with disabilities beyond just digital text (e.g., text-to-speech and highlighting capability) is the Kurzweil 3000-firefly. Kurzweil 3000-firefly is a technology that supports students with disabilities across different computers, tablets, and the Internet. With Kurzweil 3000-firefly, postsecondary students can create voice-based notes, create flashcards, and take notes, among other features (Steinberg & Murphy, 2012).

Floyd and Judge (2012) conducted a study on the use of a reading pen (i.e., Classmate Reader) by postsecondary students with learning disabilities to access printed text. Floyd and Judge (2012) found all six of the students with learning disabilities answered more comprehension questions correctly when using the technology than without. However, in another study examining the impact of reading pens (i.e., Readingpen® Advanced Edition) and the comprehension of college students, Schmitt, McCallum, Hennessey, Lovelace, and Hawkins (2012) found that not all students benefit. In their study, two of the undergraduate participants did not improve in terms of comprehension when using the reading pen. Together, these studies suggest the importance of individualizing assistive technology for *all* students, including students at the postsecondary level, and allowing students to experiment with different assistive technologies to determine what fits their needs, strengths, and preferences and positively impacts their learning.

Technology to support note-taking can include a Livescribe™ smartpen. With a Livescribe smartpen, a student can record audio while simultaneously writing notes. However, with such a tool, a user needs to purchase the pen as well as special paper. In contrast to a stand-alone tool, students with disabilities in postsecondary settings may elect to use an app. For example, a popular notetaking app is Notability (available from Ginger Labs for purchase). Notability allows a student to handwrite notes as well as record audio, and, as with the Livescribe smartpen, the audio notes are linked to what a student wrote. Notes on Notability can also be shared with others. Another app with similar features is Evernote (available for free), which allows users to take notes on mobile devices and computers and sync all the devices.

Case Study 9.1

Lawson is a 12th-grade student with a learning disability and ADHD who is getting ready to graduate and attend college. During high school, Lawson took general education courses with a special education study period that supported him by providing him with extra time to get work done; addressing his struggle with organization and study skills; and offering tutoring, preteaching and reteaching to complete general education courses. One of Lawson's major struggles relates to note-taking. Even as he approaches graduation, Lawson still struggles with listening intently in class, deciphering the most important elements, and transferring the verbal information onto his paper in a legible fashion that can later be read. Given that Lawson did not want to stand out in his general education high school classes, his high school IEP team focused on technology that could be repurposed to be assistive technology. The IEP team eventually tried the LiveScribe pen for Lawson, and he was able to successfully use the pen to record the audio in his classes, focus on the major points to write on his paper to attach to the recorded audio, and then repeatedly listen to the notes as needed. As Lawson is preparing to graduate, he and his IEP team are preparing for his transition and discussing with him accommodations and assistive technology he will need to advocate for himself in college. Of course, they discussed the success of the

iStock/Photodjo

LiveScribe pen and the benefits Lawson experienced while in high school. Although Lawson enjoyed the LiveScribe, he has done some research on his own. At this IEP team meeting, he told his teachers and parents that he plans to use the app Notability on his iPad to support his note-taking at college this fall. He liked that Notability has similar features as the LiveScribe pen, but the iPad is more multifunctional, including allowing him to read his digital textbooks on the device. In addition, he hoped that he could connect with other students who use or are willing to use Notability, and they can share notes.

Technology to support students with disabilities in postsecondary education extends beyond literacy to also support students in science, technology, engineering, and mathematics (STEM) courses and pursuing STEM careers. Similar to K–12 settings, higher education institutions need to provide students, including students with physical challenges or visual impairments, among others, with accessible science labs (Burgstahler, 2012). Examples of accessible technology include adjustable tables, handles on beakers, lab equipment with braille, use of plastic equipment in contrast to glass, and technology to enlarge microscopic images (e.g., video camera) (Burgstahler, 2012).

Postsecondary education institutions also must provide students with disabilities with means of accessing computers, including different input options. As discussed in different chapters (see Chapters 5 and 6), alternative input options to a keyboard, mouse, or trackpad include, for example, switches, joysticks, trackballs, speech-to-text or voice recognition, and braille input devices (e.g., BrailleNote Apex).

Inaccessibility in Postsecondary Education. Aside from assistive technology, most instructors in postsecondary education settings use some sort of technology in their teaching (Schmid et al., 2014). And this technology (e.g., student response systems, podcasts, Prezi, and interactive whiteboards) may not be universally accessible to all students with disabilities (Fichten, Asuncion, & Scapin, 2014). Yet some options exist to address this gap. One such option to support students with visual impairments in accessing documents is RoboBraille (see http://www.robobraille.org/convert-file). RoboBraille allows users (i.e., students or teachers) to convert inaccessible documents into more accessible formats (e.g., braille, audio, or e-books) (Goldrick, Stevns, & Christensen, 2014). The challenges of universal accessibility continue with postsecondary education. Online-learning experiences, an increasingly popular medium in higher education, is one of the latest formats to add to this challenge.

Online Learning. One aspect of postsecondary education to further explore is *online learning* and the technologies that can support access to full participation and success for students with disabilities. We invite the reader to refer to Chapter 8 for a discussion of online learning for students with disabilities, with attention to K–12 education. With online learning in postsecondary education, it is essential to keep in mind the accessibility of the course and the materials for students with disabilities, especially textbooks (Ingeno, 2013). In fact, in 2010 the Office of Civil Rights of the Department of Justice and the Department of Education notified colleges and universities that

need to check features of new tech. options!

requiring use of an emerging technology in a classroom environment when the technology is inaccessible to an entire population of individuals with disabilities—individuals with visual disabilities—is discrimination prohibited by the Americans with Disabilities Act of 1990 (ADA) and

Section 508 of the Reauthorized Rehabilitation Act of 1998 stipulated that hardware or software purchased by the federal government must be accessible for individuals with disabilities. In addition, under the Technology-Related Assistance for Individuals with Disabilities Act of 1988 (i.e., the Tech Act), states that receive funding from said act must follow Section 508 requirements (Hashey & Stahl, 2014). Please review the WebAIM Section 508 checklist (see http://webaim.org/standards/508/checklist) for additional information about Section 508 standards. WebAIM also provides information for educators on how to provide accessible Word documents (see http://webaim.org/techniques/word/#create) as well as accessible PowerPoint presentations (see http://webaim.org/techniques/powerpoint/#create). The National Center on Disability and Access to Education (NCDAE) also provides information on making accessible content, including YouTube videos and Adobe products (see http://www.ncdae.org/resources/cheatsheets/).

> Section 504 of the Rehabilitation Act of 1973 (Section 504) unless those individuals are provided accommodations or modifications that permit them to receive all the educational benefits provided by the technology in an equally effective and equally integrated manner. (Office of Civil Rights, U.S. Department of Education, 2010, n.p.)

In institutions of higher education, most of the online courses taken by students, including students with disabilities, are asynchronous (Heiman & Shemesh, 2012). **Asynchronous** refers to when the students are engaged in the learning at different times than when an instructor is presenting (Smith & Basham, 2014). In other words, an instructor records a video or posts information on a website or course management system, and a student interacts with the material at a later time. Asynchronous is in opposition to **synchronous** learning, which is when students and instructors are interacting in real time, such as with video conferencing technology (Smith & Basham, 2014). *Zoom, Teams, etc.*

Online learning creates greater opportunities for access to students with disabilities, as students can work from their own environment and take advantage of their tools and resources (Bastedo & Vargas, 2014). Online learning also creates opportunities for accessibility through instructors utilizing multiple means of representing the learning, including, but not limited to, use of videos, text transcription of videos, text, presentations, and live chats (Barrett, 2014). Online-course instructors need to check the accessibility of the material they produce and use in an online course as well as make sure their **learning management system** is accessible to students with a wide range of disabilities (Bastedo & Vargas, 2014). Instructors of online education for students with disabilities may want to consider common technology that supports accessibility. For example, Google Hangouts, a free video-conferencing tool, allows users to transcribe the contents (i.e., audio) of the Hangout (see https://hangout-captions.appspot.com/ for information about captioning a Hangout and http://www.google.com/+/learnmore/hangouts/ for information on Google Hangout in general). Likewise, captions can be added to videos posted to YouTube (see https://support.google.com/youtube/answer/2734796?hl=en for information on how to add closed captions to a video on YouTube).

Employment

The assistive technologies that support students with disabilities in preK–12 education and individuals with disabilities in postsecondary education can also support individuals in terms of employment. These include assistive technology to support reading, writing, mathematics, access to a computer, mobility and positioning, and augmentative and alternative communication (Bryant, Seok, Ok, & Bryant, 2012). Assistive technology is an accommodation or support that can help individuals with disabilities access and succeed in employment (Lindstrom et al., 2013; Pack & Szirony, 2009).

One type of assistive technology to support students in employment is a mobile device for delivering prompting, such as self-operated prompting systems (see Chapter 7 for a discussion of self-operated prompting systems). Self-operated prompting systems offer students antecedent cues that support them in engaging in particular behaviors or completing a specific task, such as those associated with vocational skills or employment (Ayres, Mechling, & Sansosti, 2013; Taber-Doughty, 2005; Savage, 2014). Self-operated prompting systems include picture, audio, and video modeling or prompting. Video prompting involves students completing each task after viewing it in sequential steps, and video modeling involves students viewing an entire task and then completing it (Taber-Doughty et al., 2011). Picture prompts typically involve photographs, icons, or drawings presented to students on paper or in a book. However, one could also use a photo app on a smartphone to deliver picture prompts (Bouck, Jasper, Bassette, & Shurr, 2015 Walser, Ayres, & Foote, 2012). Audio prompts can be delivered via CD player, MP3 player, smartphone, or audio recorder. Video models or prompts can be provided via computer, tablet, or smartphone.

Educators and students can evaluate the accessibility of products for online or digital learning. The Center for Online Learning and Students with Disabilities (COLSD) provides information regarding the Voluntary Product Accessibility Template (VPAT) for different products by evaluating them in light of Section 508 requirements, including such products as learning and/or content management systems, e-readers, social-networking sites, document creation tools, and progress-monitoring sites, among others (see http://centerononlinelearning.org/resources/vpat/) (Hashey & Stahl, 2014; Smith & Basham, 2014). Educators and students can also evaluate the accessibility of any website using the Web Accessibility Versatile Evaluator (WAVE) from WebAIM (see http://wave.webaim.org/). The WAVE provides information about a website's accessibility errors or potential concerns, including such areas as having alternative text for images or if text can be read by a screen reader.

For students with autism spectrum disorder and intellectual disability, the use of prompting systems (e.g., picture, audio, and video) has a rich history of supporting vocational skills, independent-living skills, and academics (Ayres et al., 2013; Odom et al., 2014). With regard to employment skills, Sauer, Parks, and Heyn (2010) reported the use of different prompting systems encouraged task accuracy, independence, and generalization among individuals with intellectual disability. Although video modeling is considered an evidence-based practice for students with autism spectrum disorder (Franzone & Collet-Klingenberg, 2008; Wong et al., 2014), individuals might react differently to the different prompting systems (see Allen, Burke, Howard, Wallace, & Bowen, 2012). Decisions regarding what self-operated prompting system to use and the technology to deliver the system should be determined based on the individual as well as considerations of the setting or context (i.e., going into a community system might suggest a more portable technology), tasks, and desired teaching or support approach.

In addition to self-operating prompting systems, handheld portable technologies, such as smartphones or tablets, can also support individuals with disabilities by other means, such as apps that provide reminders (e.g., built-in Reminders app with iOS devices) (Gentry, Kriner, Sima, McDonough, & Wehman, 2015). Similarly, individuals with disabilities, like all individuals, can use apps that provide to-do lists. While one can use apps that come standard with an operating system for these features, such as Reminders or Notes for iOS devices, apps also exist that combine both features (e.g., Fantastica 2 by Flexibits [for purchase] and Any.Do by Any.Do [free, with in-app purchases]).

Independent and Daily Living

Assistive technology allows individuals with disabilities to be more independent, including in their everyday lives. Assistive technology can support individuals with disabilities in a wide array of independent and daily-living activities, including, but not limited to, hygiene and dressing, food preparation, and safety (Wehmeyer, Tassé, Davies, & Stock, 2012).

Hygiene and Dressing

Assistive technology for hygiene and dressing include low-tech to high-tech options. Low-tech options to support dressing can include reachers or grabbers (i.e., long handle with pinchers or jaws for grasping objects controlled by a handle) for obtaining objects as well as extended or long-handled shoe horns and devices that assist an individual with independently putting on his or her own socks and shoes (Koehler, 2011). Individuals can also use zipper pulls (i.e., help with zipping pants or coats) and button grippers or hooks (i.e., helps to get a button through a button hole) to help dress more independently (Koehler, 2011). In terms of more mid- and high-tech options, especially for students with visual impairments, the Color Teller device by BryTech®, the Colorino Talking Color Identifier from the American Printing House for the Blind, and Color ID app (available from GreenGar Studios [for free]) help to identify the color of objects, including clothing. Another device that assists with identifying the color of clothing is the PenFriend Audio Labeler. With special labels, one can record information he or she wants about an item, such as a shirt, and, using the PenFriend device, later return and have an audio output of the information one elected to store (e.g., green short-sleeve shirt that says Michigan State University).

In terms of hygiene, different everyday hygiene or daily-grooming tools can be modified or adapted. For example, toothbrushes can be adapted to include enlarged, elongated, weighted, or angled handles, as can hairbrushes or combs. Low-tech options also exist for razors (e.g., straps or extensions) for men and women as well as for devices to aid in clipping fingernails and toenails. Low-tech options also exist to support individuals with the bathing and toileting aspects of hygiene. For example, specifically designed products exist to assist with wiping after toileting (e.g., Buckingham Easywipe or Clean Easy) as well as chairs, stools, bars, and rails for getting in and out of tubs or showers and supporting one when in those spaces. These different products can aid individuals in being more independent (Koehler, 2011). For more devices and images of devices, please see, for example, Patterson Medical (http://www.pattersonmedical.com/).

Food Preparation and Eating

Assistive technology can support individuals with disabilities across the ages with food preparation and eating (Bryant et al., 2012). A variety of adapted dishes and utensils exist. For example, different eating dishes are produced to support individuals with disabilities, including scooper bowls and plates, dishes with partitions, dishes with food guards, and dishes with vacuum or suction bottoms for sticking to surfaces (i.e., table). Adapted cups can include ones with a cut-out for the nose, easier grasps or handles, designs that offer more stability, or options for straws to aid with drinking, such as elongated and/or flexible straws. Utensils can also be adapted in a variety of ways, including curved or angled options, weighted utensils, ones with enlarged handles, flexible utensils, or textured utensils. For images and additional examples of adaptive dishes, cups, and utensils, please see the eSpecial Needs page on dining (http://www.especialneeds .com/dining.html).

Food preparation can also be supported with assistive technology, ranging from low-tech to high-tech options. In terms of actual devices for food preparation, examples include adapted knives (e.g., roller knives, rocker knives, or ergonomic knives), holders that secure mixing bowls to the table or counter, and holders that secure pots on a burner. Adaptive cooking utensil options also include ones with easy grasps for grating, ones for opening jars or cans, and spatulas. Options exist for measuring cups and spoons, such as different angles for easier reading of the measurement, color coding, or printed with braille. Other braille-based kitchen tools exist, such as braille microwaves. Likewise, some kitchen appliances can be purchased with voice capabilities, such as a coffee pot, microwave, or meat thermometer. See, for example, these products and others at such sites as WrightStuff.biz kitchen aids (see http://www.wrightstuff.biz/kitchenaids.html) and My Special World dining needs (see http://www.myspecialworld.net/dining-needs/).

Aside from tools, individuals can use picture-based cookbooks to provide visual supports for each step of cooking (e.g., *Visual Recipes: A Cookbook for Non-Readers* [Orth, 2006]). While not at the same simplified level, an app also exists that provides visual photos of step-by-step directions for different recipes in *The Photo Cookbook: Quick & Easy* (available from ditter.projektagentur GmbH [for purchase]). One can also purchase other photo cookbooks from the same developer for baking, vegetarian options, simple and delicious food, and barbecue grilling (see http://www.thephotocookbook.com/) (see Figure 9.1).

In addition to the picture-based prompting systems for cookbooks, individuals can also use video prompting or video modeling. Video modeling and video prompting have been used to successfully instruct students with disabilities

Showcasing Technology

Please consider watching a short YouTube video from the Assistive Technology Advocacy Center of Disability Rights New Jersey, the state's federally funded assistive technology project. The video shows five low-cost assistive technology options for the kitchen to promote greater independence for individuals with disabilities. See https://www.youtube.com/watch?v=Wj_rsXbRS44 or search "Assistive Technology in the Kitchen" by Jamie Arasz.

Figure 9.1   The Photo Cookbook—Barbecue Grilling: An Example of Picture Prompts for Food Preparation from ditter.projektagentur GmbH

Source: ditter.projektagentur GmbH. Reproduced with permission.

(e.g., mild intellectual disability or autism spectrum disorder) to prepare food (cf. Mechling, Ayres, Foster, & Bryant, 2013; Taber-Doughty et al., 2011). While video models or video prompts are most often created by an instructor (or researcher), some for-purchase options exist (e.g., Look and Cook by Attainment Company) (Mechling et al., 2013). Video modeling and video prompting can be delivered, for example, on a computer (e.g., via DVD or PowerPoint), DVD player, smartphone, or tablet. Using a smartphone or tablet creates more portability for using video prompting in natural (or in vivo) settings.

Purchasing and Money

Purchasing skills for individuals with disabilities can be supported with assistive technology. Common assistive technology to support individuals with disabilities in purchasing skills include prompting systems, such as picture prompts, audio prompts, and video prompts (or models). For example, individuals with disabilities can use

Do It Yourself

If you are interested in learning more about how to create your own video model or video prompt, a recent article by Weng, Savage, and Bouck (2014) in *TEACHING Exceptional Children* provides step-by-step instruction for how educators, parents, or others can create their own video-based instructional tool. Readers should note that video modeling is considered an evidence-based practice, especially for students with autism spectrum disorders (Franzone & Collet-Klingenberg, 2008; Wong et al., 2014). If you are interested in learning more about how to create audio prompting systems, a recent article by Savage (2014) in *TEACHING Exceptional Children* provides step-by-step directions for creating one's own self-operated audio prompting systems. Please note the application activities section at the end of the chapter provides the complete references for the two *TEACHING Exceptional Children* articles.

picture prompts, such as photographs, symbols, or icons, to locate grocery items within a store. To further support individuals, the prompts can be accompanied by aisle numbers (or photographs of aisle numbers) and arranged sequentially as one travels from one end of the store to another. Similarly, individuals can rely on audio prompts, recorded by themselves or others, to provide an item as well as its location; video modeling or video prompting can also be used to provide an item to purchase as well as its location. Of course, with a smartphone or tablet, apps can also support grocery list identification (e.g., Grocery List Free [available from Skript], Shopping List Free [available from hensoft], aisle411 [available from aisle411]). Picture, audio, and video prompting systems can also assist individuals in other components of purchasing, including comparing costs and then buying the object (i.e., paying with cash or debit or credit card) (see Figure 9.2 for an image of video prompting on an iPad for cost comparison).

→ good for anyone to think systematically

Number lines are another assistive technology to support individuals with purchasing and money. One facet of money and purchasing is cost comparison, or understanding which item is cheaper. Low-tech objects like number lines can allow individuals with disabilities to compare prices, often by comparing digits in each place value (i.e., dollars to dollars, tenths to tenths) (Weng & Bouck, 2014). Calculators, including standard as well as adapted (e.g., big displays or talking), can also support students with money and purchasing. A special calculator also exists for adding money (e.g., the Coin-U-Lator). For individuals who struggle with identifying different bills, stand-alone devices, such as the Note Teller 2 by BryTech® and the Franklin Bill Reader by Franklin, read bill

Figure 9.2 Example of Video Prompting for Teaching Price
Comparison

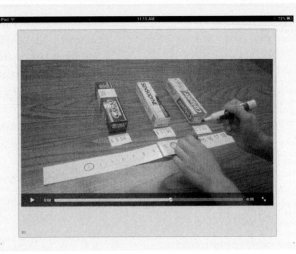

Source: Reprinted from *Footsteps Toward the Future: Implementing a Real-World Curriculum for Students With Disabilities,* by E. C. Bouck, T. Taber-Doughty, and M. N. Savage, 2015, p. 35. Copyright 2015 by Council for Exceptional Children.

denominations and provide audio output. Or individuals can use the Money Reader iOS app by LookTel (for purchase), which also reads the denominations of different bills and provides audio output.

Case Study 9.2

Whitney teaches special education in a secondary life skills classroom. In her classroom, she has a SMART Board and two iPads to use at her discretion. She also has students who have assistive technology specifically designated for them, such as augmentative and alternative communication devices (AAC; refer to Chapter 3 for additional information on AAC). While she has these more sophisticated technologies, one technology she finds herself increasingly incorporating into her life skills instruction is an audio recorder to provide audio prompts to students as they independently engage in life skills in the community, such as grocery shopping. She previously provided picture prompts for students to use in independent grocery shopping during the class's community-based instruction but was concerned about the age appropriateness of picture prompts as well as the dependency her students developed for her to provide them with the picture prompts. While she considered using video prompting on the iPad to support students' grocery shopping, she was concerned about the amount of time it would take her each week to create the video prompts. Hence, she decided to experiment with an inexpensive audio recorder. She felt the audio recorder was more age appropriate and promoted greater independence as compared to the picture prompts, and it was not as time consuming as creating video

iStock/realitybytes

prompts. In fact, although originally Whitney recorded the grocery list for her students, she now has many of her students record the lists themselves. She feels that the audio recorders increased her students' independence.

Safety

When safety is considered for individuals with disabilities, like all individuals, it extends to the home as well as the community. For safety purposes, homes, schools, and businesses are supposed to have working smoke detectors and carbon monoxide detectors. For individuals with hearing impairments, the detectors should flash lights in addition to making a noise. When cooking, as previously discussed in this chapter, using technology to stabilize pots on a stove or appliances equipped with braille can help ensure the safety of the individuals engaged in such activities.

Outside of the home, the community should be designed with safety in mind. As discussed in Chapter 1, the concept of Universal Design provides accessibility in our environments and architecture as well as safety. Curb cuts, for example, benefit a range of individuals (e.g., individuals pushing strollers, pulling suitcases, or riding bikes) as well as provide a safety feature for individuals with visual impairments and individuals who use wheelchairs for mobility. Likewise,

Figure 9.3 Trekker Breeze
by Humanware:
Handheld
Talking GPS

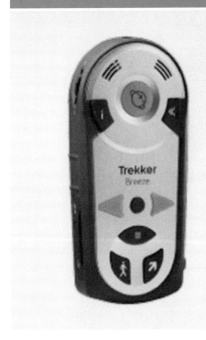

Source: Humanware. Reproduced with permission.

talking and visual pedestrian crosswalks also provide safety for different individuals with disabilities as well as create universal accessibility.

Everyday devices can also assist individuals with safety, such as cell phones. Cell phones allow all users to call or otherwise alert others that they may need assistance. For individuals with disabilities, this can include being lost in the community. Individuals with disabilities can use cell phones to call, text, or even send pictures to someone to indicate they are lost and seeking assistance or to receive assistance. Individuals can also use apps with their smartphones to help them to navigate, such as the Google Maps app.

In contrast to the all-in-one smartphone with its apps, separate devices also exist to aid individuals with disabilities in navigation. While GPS devices are commonly known to help people navigate in a car, handheld GPS devices also exist for walking (e.g., Garmin). For individuals with visual impairments, a specifically designed handheld talking GPS can support navigation within the community. Trekker Breeze by Humanware (see Figure 9.3) is an example of one such device.

Aspects of Home

One way in which assistive technology supports independent living within one's home is through **environmental control units** (ECUs); ECUs can also be known as electronic aids to daily living (EADLs) (Gierach & Stindt, 2009). ECUs enable individuals with disabilities, such as physical disabilities, to independently operate their electronic devices (DO-IT, 2014). In other words, ECUs can help an individual control their lights and television, for example (see "AbleNet ECU Products" on YouTube for an example of how an ECU works [https://www.you tube.com/watch?v=1MSi0L27vcg]).

Would Alexa count?
"Alexa turn on the lights"

Multiple types of ECUs exist, including ones that are operated via, infrared, radio control, and ultrasound (DO-IT, 2014). ECUs also differ in their input options, including, for example, switches, scanning remote controls, computers, and voice activation (Quartet Technology, n.d.). One example of an infrared-based ECU is Primo from AbleNet (see Figure 9.4). While accessories are needed

Figure 9.4   Primo ECU from AbleNet

Source: AbleNet. Reproduced with permission.

Figure 9.5   PowerLink® 4 Control Unit from AbleNet

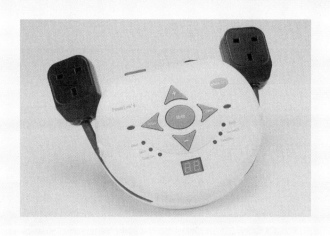

Source: AbleNet. Reproduced with permission.

for some features, the ECUS can control, for example, telephones, AAC devices, lights, and computers. Another example of an ECU is the PowerLink® 4 Control Unit by AbleNet, which allows users to control up to two electrical appliances via switches (see Figure 9.5).

Leisure and Recreation

Leisure and recreation can take many forms, including reading for pleasure, playing games, doing crafts, sports, and engaging with activities in the community (Koehler, 2011; Westling, & Fox, 2009). Individuals with disabilities can access a range of assistive technology to support their individual interests for leisure and recreation. Adapted games exist, such as games in braille (e.g., playing cards or Scrabble) or with large pieces or components (e.g., dice, dominoes, or playing pieces). Individuals can also use card holders to hold playing cards for them when playing a card game (e.g., Rummy or Go Fish) or use a switch-activated spinner (e.g., All-Turn-It® Spinner) in place of dice or a traditional spinner (see Figure 9.6).

Leisure can also involve reading. As noted in other chapters (e.g., Chapters 6 and 8), assistive technology can support individuals with disabilities in terms of reading. In addition to free (e.g., Natural Reader) and for-purchase (e.g., Kurzweil-3000-firefly and Read&Write GOLD) text-to-speech programs, e-books and audiobooks can be used. Individuals can access free e-books, purchase e-books, check out audiobooks from their local public library, or purchase audiobooks. More specifically, e-books can be purchased from, for example, Amazon, iTunes, or Barnes and Noble and accessed on each company's own eText reader (i.e., Kindle, iPad, and Nook, respectively). In

Figure 9.6   All-Turn-It® Spinner

Source: AbleNet. Reproduced with permission.

terms of free e-books, Project Gutenberg (see https://www.gutenberg.org/) offers over 46,000 e-books (Ahrens, 2011). Individuals with documented print disabilities (i.e., visual impairments and those with physical disabilities and learning disabilities if it impacts use of printed materials) can access Bookshare® (see https://www.bookshare.org/cms), which provides over 300,000 accessible e-books. For individuals not in school, there is an annual cost plus a setup free for Bookshare.

In terms of crafts or arts, individuals with disabilities can use specialized scissors, such as Easi-Grip Scissors, dual-control training scissors, or a pair of tabletop spring scissors (see, for example, especialneeds.com). Individuals can also use specifically designed (e.g., Crayola So Big Brush, an enlarged paint brush, or other adaptive grip bushes) or modified products for others aspects of art, such as a universal cuff, mouthwand, or Arthwriter Hand Aid to hold and stabilize a paintbrush. In another example, the Infila Needle Threader supports individuals as it automatically threads a needle by simply pushing a button.

The participation of individuals with disabilities in recreational activities can also be supported by technology. For example, individuals who use wheelchairs for mobility purposes can use specifically designed wheelchairs to engage in different sports, including generic sport wheelchairs or wheelchairs for specific sports (e.g., tennis, racing, and extreme sports). Other mobility-based assistive technologies, as discussed in Chapter 4, can also be used to assist individuals with disabilities to engage in sports. For example, a gait trainer can be used to provide support for mobility for an individual to engage in basketball (see Figure 9.7). In another example, individuals who are blind can use balls that beep or jingle to support their involvement in different sports (i.e., football, soccer, volleyball, tennis, and basketball). Individuals of all ages with disabilities may also be eligible to engage in sports, such as baseball and the Miracle League (see www.miracleleague.com/), if such a league exists in one's area. The technology used in Miracle League baseball involves a field, which typically includes rubberized surfaces that are barrier-free, for individuals who use wheelchairs or have visual impairments.

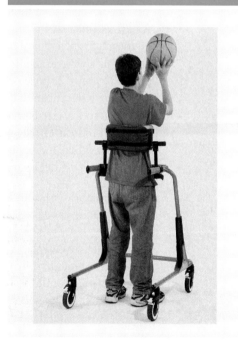

Figure 9.7   Gait Trainer to Support for Sports

Source: Rifton. Reproduced with permission.

Although sports provide socialization opportunities and fun for all individuals, including individuals with disabilities, participation in sporting activities for students with disabilities also presents barriers. For students with motor challenges, such as those who use a wheelchair for mobility, such barriers can include a lack of specialized equipment as well as the cost to not just acquire the equipment but also to participate, including transportation to the events (Bedell et al., 2013). A quick Google search can find prices in the high thousands and beyond for just one type of sports wheelchair, keeping in mind this in addition to the cost of an everyday wheelchair. Wheelchairs can be paid for by a variety of sources, including Medicaid (mostly for children) and Medicare, with a doctor's prescription. Individuals and families can also use private health insurance (WheelchairNet 2006). However, the funding from these sources covers everyday wheelchairs. Wheelchairs for specific purposes, such as sports, or with more options or specifications may need to be purchased privately, which can be cost-prohibitive for many individuals and families.

Three additional elements of recreation that can be supported by technology include bowling, bike riding, and engaging in sports activities via the Nintendo Wii™ (Koehler, 2011). For bowling, individuals can use a bowling ramp, bumpers in the gutters of a typical bowling lane, or adapted balls (e.g., coated foam balls). Individuals with disabilities of all ages can also enjoy adaptive bikes, such as a Rifton Adaptive Tricycle or the different bike options from Freedom Concepts, Inc. (e.g., prone recumbent bikes or semirecumbent bikes) (see http://www.rifton.com/products/special-needs-tricycles/adaptive-tricycles and http://www.freedomconcepts .com/fc_products/f3-bike-series/). Finally, some suggest that engagement in sports video games, like the popular, interactive Nintendo Wii (e.g., Wii Sports or Wii Sports Resort), provides recreational options for individuals with disabilities.

Individuals with disabilities can also take advantage of technology to support and indirectly encourage exercise, in a similar manner as all individuals. For example, researchers found that wearable activity monitors, such as products by Fitbit, increased the physical activity (i.e., number of steps) in adolescents with intellectual disability, autism spectrum disorder, and other developmental disabilities (LaLonde, MacNeill, Eversole, Ragotzy, & Poling, 2014; Ptomey et al., 2015). The devices are not only socially acceptable and popular but allow individuals to independently track their activity, both on the device as well as on the Internet or mobile-device app.

A final aspect of leisure and recreation for discussion is socialization. Although socialization can occur face to face, such as at community events, in places of employment, or in postsecondary education, it also occurs via technology. Just as individuals without disabilities socialize and interact with others through technology, so can individuals with disabilities. This can occur via e-mail, texting, interactive online games, and social media (e.g., Facebook, Twitter, Google Plus, and Instagram) (Bryant et al., 2012).

Communicating plays a large role in socializing. While the previously mentioned technology (e.g., Facebook and texting) provides a virtual means of communicating, technology can also support face-to-face communication, such as through the use of augmentative and alternative communication (AAC). As discussed in Chapter 3, AAC includes both aided (external to the person) and unaided (only one's person, such as sign language or facial expressions) means of communication. Aided communication involves low-tech (e.g., picture symbols), mid-tech, and high-tech (e.g., Proloquo2Go app for mobile devices) options. With app-based AAC, individuals with disabilities can use the device for multiple purposes, including communication as well as a mechanism for other means of socialization (e.g., social media, video chatting, texting, and shared gaming).

Self-Determination

A final area related to independence to consider with regard to technology and individuals with disabilities is self-determination. According to Wehmeyer (1996), self-determination is "acting as the primary causal agent in one's life and making choices and decisions regarding one's quality of life free from undue external influence or interference" (p. 24). In other words, self-determination involves an individual having control over his or her life and making his or her own decisions.

Communication technology, such as AAC, greatly supports self-determination in individuals with disabilities. With AAC, whether low tech, high tech, or unaided, an individual with a disability can communicate and express his or her preferences and choices. Likewise, technology that provides students access to printed materials, such as text-to-speech or a tool that reads digital books, also can promote self-determination. These types of technology provide individuals with disabilities with the independence to access what material they want, using the medium they want, and then to make their own decisions based on what they read (Lee et al., 2011).

Individuals with disabilities can also use technology to advocate for themselves. With advocacy, individuals can use social media, such as Facebook and Twitter. They can also engage in self-advocacy relative to transition-planning meetings and meetings with adult service providers. Van Laarhoven-Myers, Van Laarhoven, Smith, Johnson, and Olson (2014) found positive results from students engaging in self-advocacy in their own transition planning by creating PowerPoints or multimedia presentations that presented their preferences, interests, and wishes for their future in transition to individualized education program meetings.

Concluding Considerations

Assistive technology supports individuals with disabilities throughout their lives, including as individuals age and transition from formal preK–12 schooling to postschool life, whether postsecondary education, employment, or independent living. Assistive technology helps individuals to be more independent, whether that technology is allowing the individual to access a college textbook, use their computer at work (e.g., switch or joystick), or independently dress or prepare one's food. As with assistive technology used in preK–12 education, individuals with disabilities in post-school settings should have opportunities to experience and try out a technology prior to a decision that it should be used. Assistive technology considerations for individuals with disabilities, regardless of their age, should factor in individual preferences, especially an individual's willingness to use the device or tool. Finally, individuals with disabilities should also receive training on how to use the technology independently.

KEY TERMS

environmental control units, p. 224   transition services, p. 207

EXTENSION ACTIVITIES

- Show "Keeping Web Accessibility in Mind" (see https://www.youtube.com/ watch?v=yx7hdQqf8lE) and "Experiences of Students with Disabilities" (see https://

www.youtube.com/watch?v=BEFgnYktC7U) in class or have students watch individually. Engage in a discussion regarding the importance of website accessibility.

- Show "Perfectly Abled: Life on Campus with a Disability" (see https://www.youtube.com/watch?v=kr5hHmZbQHw) in class or have students watch individually. Engage in a discussion regarding the accessibility of postsecondary institutions for students with disabilities. Also, consider what assistive technology Ashley currently uses as well as what other tools might benefit Ashley in college.

- Show "Paul Schulte's Real Life" (see https://www.youtube.com/watch?v=fa1vjER8mJM). Engage in a discussion regarding Paul's participation in the Paralympics.

- Show "Assistive Technology and the Workplace" (see https://www.youtube.com/watch?v=RBWZWYzzIoY) in class or have students watch individually. Engage in a discussion regarding the low-tech, mid-tech, and high-tech options that can support some individuals with disabilities in employment.

APPLICATION ACTIVITIES

- Have students visit the COLSD site at http://centerononlinelearning.org/resources/vpat/. Encourage them to read COLSD's evaluation of how different technologies used in education comply with Section 508.

- Encourage students to submit three different websites into WebAIM's web accessibility evaluation tool, WAVE (http://wave.webaim.org/). Encourage students to select websites (a) they are likely to use as teachers, (b) they know current K–12 teachers are using, and/or (c) they are currently asked to use as college students.

- Using WebAIM (see http://webaim.org/techniques/word/#create or http://webaim.org/techniques/powerpoint/#create) or the National Center on Disability and Access to Education (NCDAE) (see http://

www.ncdae.org/resources/cheatsheets/), create an accessible Word document, PowerPoint presentation, YouTube video, or Adobe document.

- Read (a) Savage, M. N. (2014). Self-operated auditory prompting systems: Creating and using them to support students with disabilities. *TEACHING Exceptional Children*, 47(1), 266–275. doi:10.1177/0040059914542763 and/or (b) Weng, P.-L., Savage, M. N., & Bouck, E. C. (2014). iDIY: Video-based instruction using iPads. *TEACHING Exceptional Children*, 47(1), 231–239. doi:10.1177/0040059914542764. Based on the information in the articles, develop your own audio- or video-based self-operated prompting system to support independent or daily-living activities.

DISCUSSION QUESTIONS

1. Describe how assistive technology supports individuals with disabilities across the life span.

2. In what ways does technology allow individuals with disabilities to be more independent in aspects of daily living? Provide examples of technology devices or tools that support that independence.

3. What technology do you use in your postsecondary education, employment, or independent or daily-living activities? Can this technology also support individuals with disabilities in its current form or via modification or adaptation?

RESOURCES/ADDITIONAL INFORMATION

- Division on Career Development and Transition of the Council for Exceptional Children (http://community.cec.sped.org/dcdt/home/)

- State vocational rehabilitation agency contacts (http://wdcrobcolp01.ed.gov/Programs/EROD/org_list.cfm?category_cd=SVR)

- Americans with Disabilities Act (http://www.ada.gov/)

- Section 504 of the Rehabilitation Act (http://www2.ed.gov/about/offices/list/ocr/504faq.html)

SUGGESTED ENRICHMENT READINGS

- Ayres, K. M., Mechling, L., & Sansosti, F. J. (2013). The use of mobile technologies to assist with life skills/independence of students with moderate/severe intellectual disability and/or autism spectrum disorders: Considerations for the future of school psychology. *Psychology in the Schools*, 50(3), 259–271. doi:10.1002/pits.21673

- Bouck, E. C., Maeda, Y., & Flanagan, S. M. (2012). Assistive technology and students with high-incidence disabilities: Understanding the relationship through the NLTS2. *Remedial and Special Education*, 33(5), 298–308. doi:10.1177/0741932511401037

CHAPTER 10

Assistive Technology for Young Children

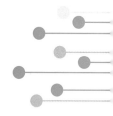

Chapter 10 presents assistive technology considerations for young children with disabilities. This chapter will familiarize the reader with the legal issues surrounding early intervention and early childhood special education as well as concerns about the exposure of young children to technology. Chapter 10 discusses the heavily emphasized areas of assistive technology for young children: communication, mobility and positioning, and interactions with different environments.

Special education services for young children typically refers to early intervention or early childhood special education (Gargiulo, 2015). Early intervention is the coordinated services delivered to young children from birth through two years of age, while early childhood special education is services designed to meet the needs of young children with disabilities ages 3 through 5 (Gargiulo, 2015). Young children who qualify for early-intervention services (i.e., services for children from birth through age 2) are served under Part C of the Individuals with Disabilities Education Act (IDEA, 2004), while young children who qualify for early childhood special education (i.e., ages 3 and up) are served under Part B of the IDEA (Yell, 2012).

From the *35th Annual Report to Congress on the Implementation of the Individuals with Disabilities Education Act* in 2011, 336,895 infants and toddlers between the ages of 0 and 2 were provided services under Part C of IDEA (U.S. Department of Education, 2013). The majority (62.3% in 2011) of infants and toddlers who receive services under Part C later qualified to receive services under Part B when they turned 3 years of age.

Chapter Objectives

After reading the chapter, the reader will be able to do the following:

1. Explain how young children are covered for services under IDEA

2. Understand the main types of technology to support young children

3. Provide clear examples of assistive technology to support young children with disabilities in communication, mobility and positioning, and interactions with different environments

4. Consider the perspectives on the exposure of young children to screen-based technology

Case Study 10.1

Mrs. Cuttell is an early childhood special education teacher. Her classroom consists primarily of children ages 3 to 5 who have been identified with autism spectrum disorder, moderate or severe intellectual disability, and early childhood developmental delay. Throughout her classroom, Mrs. Cuttell tries to integrate low-tech assistive technology. While she is not opposed to mid-tech or high-tech assistive technology and individual students throughout her class have their own devices (e.g., speech-generated AAC device), she knows that low-tech assistive technology can support her students, often requires less training, and is more portable. One way in which Mrs. Cuttell uses low-tech assistive technology is through visual schedules. She has visual schedules for the whole class as well as for individual students. She also incorporates icons for students to make decisions and choices, such as the song for the day during large-group circle time. She

also incorporates an array of options to draw and practice emergent writing. For example, she has secured Crayola jumbo crayons as well as Crayola egg-shaped crayons. In addition, she makes her own by melting down broken crayons into muffin tins, which can be easier to grasp. Mrs. Cuttell also has a variety of different positioning options for students, including specifically purchased seat cushions and corner seats and foam wedges she herself made. Finally, as an example, Mrs. Cuttell has secured as many wooden-knob puzzles as she could. For those without, she has added knobs or extenders to create easier access for her students.

Consistent with the philosophy of early intervention, over three-fourths of the infants and toddlers receiving early-intervention services do so in their homes (86.6%). The 35th annual report also showed that 745,954 young children aged 3 to 5 were served under Part B of IDEA. Speech and language impairments, followed by developmental delay, and then autism spectrum disorder were the most prevalent disability categories of young children (U.S. Department of Education, 2013).

Young children under the age of 3 served under IDEA Part C are provided services (i.e., early intervention) because (a) they are experiencing a developmental delay relative to cognitive development, physical development, social or emotional development, or adaptive development, or (b) they were diagnosed with a "physical or mental condition which has a high probability of resulting in developmental delay" (IDEA 2004, § 632[5][A]). Young children at risk of experiencing a developmental delay are provided services at the discretion of the state in which they reside (IDEA, 2004; Shackelford, 2006) (see the Early Childhood Technical Assistance Center [ECTA, 2014b] for states' Part C regulations and policies). Young children between the ages of 3 and 5 served under IDEA Part B (i.e., early childhood special education) are provided services if they qualify for one of the 13 federal disability categories covered under IDEA (i.e., autism; deaf-blindness; deafness; emotional disturbance; hearing impairment; intellectual disability; multiple disabilities; orthopedic impairment; other health impairment; specific learning disability; speech or language impairment; traumatic brain injury; or visual impairment, including blindness) or under the category of developmental delay (Bitterman, Daley, Misra, Carlson, & Markowitz, 2008; National Dissemination Center for Children with Disabilities, 2012). Children with disabilities can receive services under IDEA Part B between the ages of 3 and 9 under the category of developmental delay; states also define developmental delay for children aged 3 to 9 (Bitterman et al., 2008). Readers can refer to the ECTA to determine how their state defines developmental delay (see http://nectac.org/~pdfs/topics/earlyid/partc_elig_table.pdf).

Part B of IDEA, the section of IDEA that dictates the education of students age 3 through 21, is required of all states. States must provide a free, appropriate public education in the least restrictive environment to, at minimum, students between the ages of 3 and 21 (IDEA, 2004; Yell, 2012). Part C of IDEA, the part responsible for services for young children from birth through age 2, is not required of states. However, currently all states participate in Part C (Center for Parent Information and Resources, 2014a). The provision of early intervention for infants and toddlers with disabilities was established in the reauthorization of the Education for All Handicapped Children Act (later to be known as IDEA) in 1986, referred to as Part H at the time (Center for Parent Information and Resources, 2014a). Under Part C, states receive funding for early-intervention services in exchange for the provision of such services to all eligible children and families.

Early childhood special education services provided under Part B of IDEA offer all the services available to all other students with identified disabilities served under Part B. In other words, young students with disabilities, aged 3 to 5, receiving early childhood special education services are provided a free, appropriate public education in the least restrictive environment with guaranteed procedural safeguards. Students receiving early childhood special education are eligible to receive direct services from a special education teacher as well as other related services (e.g., speech and language therapy, social work, and assistive technology). Early-intervention services, provided as IDEA Part C, also include direct services by providers, such as speech and language therapy, physical therapy, and assistive technology devices and services. However, early-intervention services are mainly focused on families and are most likely to occur in children's natural settings (e.g., homes) (Yell, 2012).

Young students receiving early-intervention services receive an individualized family service plan (IFSP) (IDEA, 2004; Yell, 2012). Students receiving early childhood special education services historically received an individualized education program (IEP); however, federal laws allow students receiving services up through the age of 5 to use an IFSP (Gargiulo, 2015; Lipkin & Schertz, 2008). Like the IEP, a multidisciplinary team develops the IFSP, however, it is reviewed more frequently (i.e., every six months). The IFSP is focused on the family (e.g., resources, priorities, and concerns), the young child's developmental levels, and the provision of services in as natural environments as possible (Gargiulo, 2015). Please refer to the ECTA Center (2014a) and the Center for Parent Information and Resources (2014b) for additional information on IFSPs.

Technology for Young Children

As previously mentioned in the opening chapters of this book, technology benefits students with disabilities, including young children with disabilities. Technology can increase access, participation, and independence. However, there is a caveat for young children with disabilities. Technology for young children in general is not universally supported. In 2010, the American Academy of Pediatrics released a policy statement urging no screen time (e.g., television or computers) for children less than 2 years of age. The American Academy of Pediatrics also recommended limiting the screen time of children over the age of 2 to no more than two hours per day. Concerns about screen time use for young children include associations with decreased academic achievement, lower cognitive or language development, fewer and/or lower quality interactions with adults, and increased potential for obesity (Barr, Lauricella, Zack, & Calvert, 2010; Duch, Fisher, Ensari, & Harrington, 2013; Mendelsohn et al., 2008; Schmidt et al., 2012; Tomopoulos et al., 2010).

However, some researchers, such as Plowman and colleagues, disagree that technology and young children do not mix (Plowman & McPake, 2013). Within their research, Plowman and colleagues did not have parents reporting negative cognitive, behavioral, or health effects of technology exposure on young children (cf. Stephen, McPake, Plowman, & Berch-Heyman, 2008). Parents reported not being overly concerned regarding the negative correlation between technology and young children, yet many recognized a need for moderation (Plowman, McPake, & Stephen, 2010). Earlier research suggested academic gains occurred in young children with exposure to computers and computer applications in such areas as literacy (e.g., letter recognition) and mathematics (e.g., number recognition) (Clements & Sarama, 2007; Penuel et al., 2009; Primavera, Wiederlight, & DiGiacomo, 2001).

Others in the conversation regarding technology and young children suggest it is the content not the medium (i.e., screens) that matter. In other words, some television shows were designed to be educationally relevant and valuable (e.g., Sesame Street). The same is true with some software, websites, apps, and smart toys; the interactiveness versus passiveness of software, websites, and apps should be considered (National Association for the Education of Young Children and the Fred Rogers Center for Early Learning and Children's Media, 2012). The National Association for the Education of Young Children (NAEYC) and the Fred Rogers Center support the *appropriate and intentional* use of technology for young children and provide principles to guide such use by early childhood educators.

To draw from the NAEYC and the Fred Rogers Center's focus on appropriateness and intention, it is important for educators and parents to be aware that a technology (e.g., website, television show, app, or learning or smart toy) labeled as educational is not always educational; there is not a federal agency that supervises the labeling of technology for children as educational. In 2003, Glassy, Romano, and the Committee on Early Childhood, Adoption, and Dependent Care noted the lack of scientific evidence associating educational toys with learning. Others discussed the lack of data to support IQ gains through use of educational toys (Carroll, 2004). In other words, evidence does not support the contention that toys labeled as smart toys or educational toys make kids smarter or more prepared for education (Bouck, Okolo, & Courtad, 2007).

Assistive Technology for Young Children

While the aforementioned debate regarding technology for young children applies to all children, often those engaged in the discussion are excluding or not specifically considering assistive technology for young children. In fact, the NAEYC and Fred Rogers Center (2012) supported technology use for young children with disabilities, suggesting technology empowers and increases their independence in everyday life as well as participation in inclusive environments.

Assistive technology for young children truly embraces the federal definition—"any item, piece of equipment, or product system, whether acquired commercially, modified, or customized, that is used to increase, maintain, or improve functional capabilities of individuals with disabilities" (29 U.S.C. § 2202[2]). Assistive technology for young children can involve commercially produced products, including those used for their intended purpose and also ones repurposed to serve as assistive technology. Young children's use of assistive technology may also include tools educators or parents construct or modify from an existing item to better serve the child (Mistrett, Lane, & Ruffino, 2005). While assistive technology for young children could address almost any of the types or purposes of assistive technology identified in Chapter 1, Lane and Mistrett (2002) suggested three primary areas for considering assistive technology for this population: movement, communication, and interactions with environments (e.g., toys). However, we will also discuss a few other areas in this chapter, such as literacy and assistive technology to support play.

Movement

Young children with orthopedic impairments (e.g., cerebral palsy) or those who struggle with gross-motor movement might benefit from specifically designed assistive technology for movement. While Chapter 5 presents an in-depth discussion of assistive technology for mobility and positioning, this chapter discusses some specific devices or considerations for young children.

One of the most common assistive technology devices for movement is the wheelchair. For young children, there is debate regarding if and when to introduce a power (i.e., electric or motorized) wheelchair as opposed to a manual wheelchair. Researchers suggest the benefit of moving under one's power and suggest young children—sometimes as young as age two—can successfully use power wheelchairs (Guerette, Furumasu, & Tefft, 2013; Jones, McEwen, & Neas, 2012). However, given the expense and some concern with young children using power wheelchairs, there are other creative ways to provide independent mobility

Universal Design for Learning (UDL) is appropriate for young children as well and can help early childhood educators implement technology to support young children with disabilities (Parette & Blum, 2015). Parette and Blum (2013, 2015) proposed a technology integration framework model for early childhood programs based on UDL: EXPECT IT—PLAN IT—TEACH IT—SOLVE IT. In this framework, early childhood educators begin with a learning standard for an activity (EXPECT IT). Then, during PLAN IT, they make decisions regarding instructional strategies, assessments, *and* technology. TEACH IT involves teaching the activity with the decisions made. SOLVE IT is then for young children with disabilities who may need additional supports to participate and succeed in the activity (Peterson-Karlan, Parette, & Blum, 2013).

through modifying existing products. For example, two faculty at the University of Delaware modified off-the-shelf battery-operated vehicles designed for young kids to provide mobility for young children with motoric issues (see Dr. Galloway's website http://www.udel.edu/gobabygo/). Matching the child's needs and his or her motor abilities allows customized mobility options for young children, and by modifying existing products, these cars are available at a fraction of the cost of specifically designed mobility devices for young children (Cheney, 2014; Cheney & Templin, 2014; Huang & Galloway, 2012). Galloway and his partners provide a free manual on their website for parents to engineer these modified cars.

In addition to wheelchairs and customized movable vehicles, other options exist to support the mobility of young children. For example, gait trainers exist in a variety of sizes to support walking for infants through adults (see Table 10.1 for examples of and resources for assistive technology to support movement in young children; see Figure 10.1 for an image of a gait trainer).

Modifications can also be made to assistive technology movement devices for young children, including attaching Velcro to different products with wheels to slow them down for young children and applying tennis balls to walkers to provide a smoother experience for young children (Mistrett et al., 2005). In addition, parents and educators can construct their own mobility-based assistive technology for young children. Help with this can be found at the Office of Special Education Programs' funded research institute Tots 'n Tech (see http://tnt.asu.edu/home/), which provides suggestions for modifying or making

Table 10.1	Assistive Technology to Support Movement in Young Children
Device	**Description**
Rifton Pacer Gait Trainer (see Figure 10.1)	• Supports 9-month-olds through individuals weighing 275 pounds in walking or gait training • http://www.rifton.com/products/gait-trainers/pacer-gait-trainers
Skippi Children's Power Wheelchair	• Adjustable power wheelchair for young children • http://www.ottobock.com/cps/rde/xchg/ob_com_en/hs.xsl/5577.html
Kidz	• Adjustable manual wheelchair designed for toddlers • http://www.sunrisemedical.com/Products/zippie/Manual/ZippieKidz.aspx
Pediatric Walker	• Foldable toddler or child walker • http://www.rehabmart.com/product/guardian-pediatric-folding-walker-10545.html
VTech Sit-to-Stand Learning Walker	• Toy designed to support babies as they transition to walking • http://www.vtechkids.com/product/detail/479/Sit_to_Stand_Learning_Walker

Figure 10.1   Rifton Pacer Gait Trainer

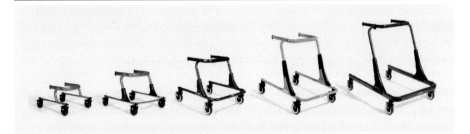

Source: Copyright 2014 by Rifton Equipment. Used with permission.

assistive technology for young children. For example, they share directions to create a Scoot-a-bout, which is a scooter with straps (see http://tnt.asu.edu/ideas/support/scoot%E2%80%90a%E2%80%90bout) (Robinault, 1973).

In addition to mobility, positioning and seating assistive technology may also be considered to support young children with disabilities. Positioning and seating assistive technology is a consideration within mobility-based assistive technologies, such as wheelchairs, but also is important for other aspects. For young children with disabilities, considerations of assistive technology to support positioning might involve devices that support sitting on the floor, in chairs or seats, or in cars or other modes of transportation. Examples of positioning and seating assistive technology include Boppys™, wedges, specifically designed booster seats, and specifically designed bath seats (Mistrett et al., 2005). For-purchase positioning options exist even for babies with special needs served through early-intervention systems, including options for sitting or laying (e.g., Leckey's Squiggles Early Activity System [see http://www.leckey.com/products/] and the Tumble Forms 2 Tadpole Pediatric Positioner [see http://www.tumbleforms.com]).

These positioning assistive technologies can help support play in young children with disabilities, and play is essential to the development and learning of young children (Baker, 2014; Rogers, 2011). For young children with disabilities in school settings, specifically designed seat cushions (e.g., gel, foam, beads, or air) can also help with positioning in a classroom chair. Merritt (2014) found the off-task behavior for preschool-aged children decreased when they used a seat cushion.

As with mobility devices, assistive technology for positioning and seating can be purchased off the shelf, modified, or made new. The Tot 'n Tech (2011) program also provides examples of modified or constructed supports for positioning and seating for young children on their website.

Communication

Communication is a right of all individuals, including young children with disabilities. As discussed in Chapter 3, "Assistive Technology for Communication," augmentative and alternative communication (AAC) can range from low tech to high tech and involves both aided and unaided communication (please refer Chapter 3 for a detailed discussion on AAC). Most existing research on AAC for young children with complex communication needs involves preschool-aged children (i.e., ages 3–5), and the results are positive as to the impact of AAC (Drager, Light, & McNaughton, 2010). However, additional research is needed regarding AAC and young children served through early-intervention services.

Historically, the most common AAC systems used in practice with young children with disabilities included unaided AAC (i.e., gestures), nonelectronic

A meta-analysis of the impact of assistive technology on the communication and literacy skills of preschool-aged children concluded the two types of assistive technology examined (speech-generating devices and computer software or hardware) were effective in improving the communication and literacy abilities of young children (Dunst, Trivette, & Hamby, 2012). Despite the effectiveness of the assistive technology, Dunst and colleagues found these types of technology were not used enough for the preschool-aged population as well as younger children (e.g., toddlers).

aided-communication boards or books, and simple electronic-aided AAC devices with digitized speech (Binger & Light, 2006; Hustad et al., 2005) (see Table 10.2 for sample simple electronic aided AAC devices; see Figure 10.2). AAC decision-making for young children, like assistive technology decision-making for all students with disabilities, follows the premise to start with low-tech or nonobtrusive technology first and then increasingly consider more sophisticated technology.

Table 10.2 Simple Aided AAC Devices for Young Children

Device	Description
Attainment Talkers (see Figure 10.2)	• Six- or 24-message battery-operated AAC devices • Each message (image) includes 10 s of recording time • Not switch compatible • http://www.attainmentcompany.com/attainment-talkers
Talkable 4	• Four-message battery-operated AAC devices • Four different colored buttons with an icon above • Device has a total recording time of 20 s • Not switch compatible • https://www.enablemart.com/speech-and-communication/augmentative-and-alternative-communication/basic-communicators/talkable-4
QuickTalker™	• One-, four-, 12-, or 23-message battery-operated AAC devices • Recording time ranges from 30 s to 20 min based on number of messages

Device	Description
	• Not switch compatible
	• http://www.ablenetinc.com/Assistive-Technology/ Communication/QuickTalker
Seen & Heard App (see Figure 10.3)	• AAC app for iOS devices https://www.ablenetinc.com/ quicktalker-23
	• Visual scene display (VSD) with scenes with recorded voices
	• Also includes Widgit symbols
	• http://www.therapy-box.co.uk/scene_and_heard.aspx

Figure 10.2   Attainment Talker 6

Source: Attainment Company. Used with permission.

Figure 10.3   Scene & Heard App

Source: Therapy Box, Inc. Reproduced with permission.

iStock/Macsnap

Jackson is a 4-year-old young child identified with autism spectrum disorder. He attends his local school district's preschool program, which follows a braided approach (i.e., students who attend are supported by parent-paid tuition, reimbursement from the county or state for children at at-risk, and funding from early childhood special education) (Wallen & Hubbard, 2013). A paraprofessional works with Jackson in the classroom on appropriate social interaction as well as participating in classroom activities. Jackson also receives related services, including speech and language therapy and occupational therapy. Jackson displays echolalia and uses picture symbols to communicate at times.

Jackson's paraprofessional wears a few picture symbols on a keyring attached to her belt loop for him to communicate that he needs a break, a drink, and to use the bathroom (see Figure 10.4). Jackson's paraprofessional also uses a visual schedule with icons to communicate to Jackson his schedule for the day, and they remove the icons, attached via Velcro, after each activity is completed.

Figure 10.4 Visual Symbols from Visual Aids for Learning

Source: Visual Aids for Learning. Reproduced with permission. Retrieved from http://www.visualaidsforlearning.com/

Do It Yourself

Visual schedules, or visual activity schedules, are schedules represented with symbols, such as pictures, line drawings, or photographs (Knight, Sartini, & Spriggs, 2015). They are often used to support students, such as students with autism spectrum disorder, in transitions or completing an activity with multiple tasks or steps. Teachers can create their own visual schedules, for example, by using laminated symbols (e.g., pictures), a laminated strip of paper, and Velcro. The steps or activities can then be laid out sequentially for a student, often vertically. When a student completes an activity, the symbol is removed from the schedule. Knight and colleagues recommended that visual schedules be considered an evidence-based practice.

Teachers can obtain the symbols by taking photographs and printing them out. Often, educators may use a program, such as Boardmaker by Mayer-Johnson to create icons or symbols. Some websites do exist that provide free symbols, such as Visual Aids for Learning (http://www.visualaidsforlearning.com/) and Do2Learn (http://www.do2learn.com/picturecards/VisualSchedules/index.htm) (Simpson & Oh, 2013).

One research-supported AAC practice, especially for young children with ASD, is Picture Exchange Communication Systems (PECS); PECS is a low-tech, aided AAC system that involves students exchanging a picture with a communication partner (Bondy & Frost, 1994, 2001; Sulzer-Azaroff, Hoffman, Horton, Bondy, & Frost, 2009). Other options based on photographs or icons for young children include communication books, where a child might carry about a book with the pictures and select one or ones to communicate (Sadao & Robinson, 2010). Icons or photographs are typically used more in the increasingly sophisticated speech-generating devices as well.

Currently, there is increasing attention to mobile technologies (e.g., iPad) and apps for all individuals who use AAC devices, including young children (Light & McNaughton, 2012a, 2012b). A popular AAC app in practice and research is Proloquo2Go from AssistiveWare (Kagohara et al., 2013; Xin & Leonard, 2014). However, many AAC app options exist, including the PECS Phase II app, which presents the research-supported PECS digitally via a mobile device (Ganz, Hong, & Goodwyn, 2013). An obvious concern for young children is for the child to understand and be able to independently use more complex apps.

Light and McNaughton (2012a) also suggested that AAC devices that present language concepts in context, such as through a photograph, rather than a typical grid display of symbols to select may be more beneficial to younger children. The presentation of language via photographs is referred to visual scene display (Light & McNaughton, 2012a). Please note that VSDs can appear on stand-alone or dedicated devices as well as through apps, such as the one depicted in Figure 10.4.

One consideration with respect to electronic aided AAC devices is the compatibility or accessibility via a switch. A switch allows an individual to use it for either direct selection or scanning of an AAC device. Switches include ones that are pushed (activated) via, for example, a head, foot, hand, or elbow. There are also switches that are activated by puffing, sipping, rolling, or squeezing. (Switches are discussed more in depth in Chapter 5.)

As with assistive technology for movement, AAC for young children can involve devices that parents or educators make or modify themselves. The Tech 'n Tots group provides a variety of resources and suggestions for making or modifying one's own AAC (see http://tnt.asu.edu/helpdesk-communication-social). For example, Tech 'n Tots offers the suggestion from Reed (2003) for creating a floating communication board out of garden kneelers, contact paper or laminate, plastic baggies, Velcro strips, and picture symbols.

Interactions with Environments

Infants, toddlers, and preschoolers with disabilities interact with their environments, including materials in their environments, in a variety of ways. When we consider interaction with environments for this population, we are focused on play and materials that promote play as well as interactions with other materials of daily living.

In terms of toys, educators and family members can look for specifically designed toys for young children with disabilities, can use toys off the shelf as is or modified, and/or can use switches to interact with battery-operated toys. A Google search of "selecting toys for young children with disabilities" will net a variety of websites, including popular toy company chains that advertise catalogs of toys appropriate for young children with disabilities as well as organizations that provide lists of appropriate toys. Many of the toys suggested are ones appropriate for and desired by all young children (e.g., the toy plays music). For example, when it comes to crayons, Crayola developed a range of options, from the original crayons to jumbo crayons, easy-grip crayons, triangular crayons, and egg-shaped crayons. However, educators can also modify crayons themselves for young children with fine-motor issues by doing such things as putting small squishy balls around them (i.e.. inserting the crayon through) or placing small pink-foam hair rollers around the crayon.

A common approach to modifying a battery-operated toy for young children with disabilities involves a switch (Baker, 2014). A common switch for young children with disabilities is a push or touch switch, such as the Big Red Switch® or Buddy Button™. A switch can be attached to a battery-operated toy, and when a young child activates the switch (e.g., presses the jelly bean switch), the toy is activated (e.g., plays music or moves; see Figure 10.5). To convert a battery-operated toy to a switch toy, an educator or a parent would need to use

Figure 10.5 Jelly Bean Switch Attached to Battery-Operated Toy

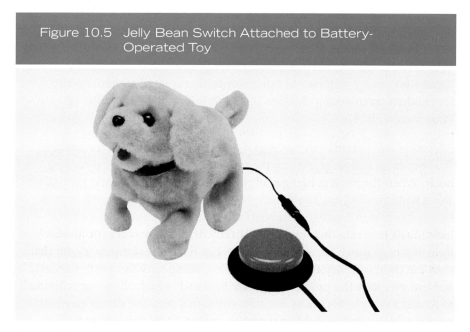

Source: AbleNet. Reproduced with permission.

a battery adapter; battery adapters are inserted between two batteries (e.g., AA batteries) or at the end of a battery (e.g., C or D batteries) and then connected to a switch (Let's Play Project, n.d.). For example, battery device adapters are available through such companies as AbleNet (see http://www.ablenetinc.com/). A variety of different types of switches exist and will be discussed more in depth in Chapter 5.

Mistrett et al. (2005) discussed using assistive technology in the environment of a young child for stabilizing (i.e., holding objects in place or within grasp or vision), attaching (i.e., bringing an object closer or keeping within reach), extending (i.e., enhance objects for easier use), highlighting (i.e., drawing attention to an object), and confining (i.e., preventing an object from moving away). Many of the tools to aid for these purposes can be everyday objects repurposed as low-tech assistive technology; however, specifically designed tools or products are also sold (see Table 10.3).

Literacy

Learning to read or exposure to literacy can and should begin at birth for all children. Educators, pediatricians, and other professionals stress reading to young children and having access or exposure to print (e.g., books) in the home (Leseman & de Jong, 1998; Sénéchal, Pagan, Lever, & Ouellette, 2008). While low-tech books are ideal, technology can also support literacy for young children. In other words, literacy and technology mix for children, even young children (Liang & Johnson, 1999; Miller & Warschauer, 2014).

Educators and parents can use audiobooks to expose students to literacy. This can be as simple as playing the tape or CD of an individual reading the book. When the book is being read, the teacher, parent, or child can follow along with the physical book. Such audiobooks can be purchased or even checked out from a public library. Another option for audiobooks is for individuals to create their own. Specifically designed books exist in which an individual can purchase it and record him or herself reading the story, and then the child can play the audio and follow along with the print. Similarly, one can purchase the product AnyBook Personal, which allows an individual to record a story using his or her own voice on a pen-like device (see http://www.franklin.com/for-children/anybook-reader-30-hour-headphone-edition#sthash.osqtJcmY.dpbs). A young child can then listen to the audio of

Table 10.3 Assistive Technology for Young Children's Environmental Interactions

Purpose	Example of Repurposed Tool	Example of Purchased Tool
Stabilizing	Grip shelf liner	• Suction based dishes (http://www.especialneeds.com/dining-plates-bowls-suction.html)
Attaching	• Velcro	• Boomerings® by Discovery Toys (http://www.discoverytoys.com)
Extending	• Popsicle sticks • Empty pill bottles	• Wooden-knob puzzles (http://www.melissaanddoug.com/wooden-knob-puzzles)
Highlighting	• Colored yarn or thread	• Wikki Stix (http://www.wikkistix.com/)
Confining	• Cookie sheet • Hula hoop	• Inflatable pools

Source: Baker (2014); Mistrett et al. (2005); Sadao and Robinson (2010).

the book by selecting the accompanying stickers on each page. The stickers, operating like a bar code, alert the device to play the audio recorded to correspond to each sticker (i.e., page).

For less labor-intensive audiobooks, other for-purchase products were developed. For example, LeapFrog™ developed a reading pen that reads specifically designed LeapFrog books. The reading pen, which is now called LeapReader™ Reading and Writing System (formerly called the LeapFrog Tag Reading System), reads the specially designed books at the level of page, sentence, or word as well as provides questions to check for comprehension (see Figure 10.6). The LeapReader is targeted to young children ages 4 to 8. LeapFrog also markets a LeapReader™ Junior, which is a separate device for children ages 1 to 3, with books targeting their developmental level (see Figure 10.7). The LeapFrog products are not specifically designed as assistive technology for students with disabilities, rather, they are marketed as products for use at home, implemented at the class level for young

Figure 10.6   LeapFrog LeapReader™ Reading and
Writing System

Source: LeapFrog. Reproduced with permission.

Figure 10.7   LeapFrog LeapReader™ Junior

Source: LeapFrog. Reproduced with permission.

children. However, the LeapFrog products, such as the LeapReader™ Reading and Writing System, can be repurposed to serve as assistive technology for children who struggle with literacy (Bouck, Flanagan, Miller, & Bassette, 2012).

Nowadays, technology and literacy also means e-book or digital books to be accessed on a mobile device, such as a tablet, smartphone, e-reader, or apps that support literacy development for such devices (Miller & Warschauer, 2014). Parents or educators can purchase or select free e-books for their devices for their young children. Outside of just e-books, apps can also support the literacy development of young children with disabilities. A good site for apps for young children and literacy is PBS KIDS (see http://pbskids.org/apps/filter/app/). In researching their own apps, PBS found young children who engaged with the apps Martha Speaks: Dog Party and Super Why experienced gains in reading skills (PBS KIDS, 2010).

Educators or parents who are considering implementing audiobooks, e-books, or literacy apps for young children with disabilities need to carefully select the book or app, as they would a traditional printed book (Miller & Warschauer, 2014). The selection of the e-book or app should involve considerations of the features as well as the quality (Barnyak & McNelly, 2015). For example, educators and parents may want to consider the involvement or interactivity the child has with the technology as well as the encouragement of interactiveness between the adult and the child with the technology. With e-books, the adult may also want to differentiate between a basic e-book, in which a traditional print book is just made digital, and an enhanced e-book, which includes additional features (e.g., music or illuminated text) (Barnyak & McNelly, 2015). In addition, e-books, like all printed books, should be developmentally appropriate and free from violence or bias (Barnyak & McNelly, 2015).

Early childhood educators may elect to implement e-books, in whatever form, during center time. Young children can work individually or with a partner to engage with the e-book. In addition, e-books may be shared as a whole-group activity, such as during circle time in early childhood programs (Barnyak & McNelly, 2015). Of course, e-books can also serve as an accommodation for student with disabilities as a means to gain access to printed text. Parents can use e-books similar to traditional books and share in reading time (Judge, Floyd, & Jeffs, 2015). In addition, parents may elect to use literacy technology, such as the LeapFrog Reader, as an individual playtime activity for young children to gain additional exposure to literacy.

Research exists suggesting young children's acquisition of specific literacy skills (e.g., vocabulary or phonological awareness) does not differ whether exposed to an audiobook or an adult reading the book (De Jong & Bus, 2004; Korat & Shamir, 2007). Other researchers examining technology and literacy for young children found that young children expressed greater interest and engaged more with e-books than traditional print books (Noel, 2013).

Case Study 10.3

Ms. Rubly is an inclusive-preschool teacher, meaning her classroom consists of students who receive early childhood special education services under Part C of IDEA as well as students without documented disabilities. Ms. Rubly is working with her students on emergent reading. To do so, she created multiple reading-based stations and activities that she can integrate into her classroom activities, including during large-group time, small-group time, and free-choice time. For example, Ms. Rubly has secured large books with picture icons to support the words that she makes available on a table during free-choice time. She also does this with both the LeapReader and LeapReader Junior she has in her classroom,

iStock/Christopher Futcher

allowing the books to be an activity the student chooses to do during his or her free-choice time at the start of preschool. Ms. Rubly also has some audiobooks that she and her assistant teachers can use during large or small groups. For some of the audiobooks, she has a small set of paper books so students can turn the pages of the story while it is being read.

Apps for Young Children with Disabilities

Apps are becoming increasingly popular for young children, as with older children and adults. In fact, at the end of the last decade, the majority of downloaded educational apps focused on toddlers or preschoolers (Shuler, 2010). While the app rubrics presented in Chapter 1 can be used to evaluate apps for young children, additional, age-specific sources are available that may be more appropriate (More & Travers, 2013). In presenting their framework for integrating apps for young children with disabilities, More and Travers (2013) suggested the following principles must be considered for each app: (a) accessibility, (b) the intersection with "developmentally appropriate practices," (c) suitable content, and (d) relevance to individual child's needs, per his or her IEP or IFSP (p. 17). For accessibility, More and Travers developed a matrix that educators and parents can use to determine whether apps they are considering for young children with disabilities follow the principles of Universal Design for Learning (UDL) in the developmental domains of motor, cognitive, language, and social. Apps that follow developmentally appropriate practices are ones that enable the child to be active in the learning as well as appeal to the interests of the child and meet him or her at his or her developmental level. These apps should also present no violence and avoid stereotypes. A selected app must also relate to a child's goals in his or her IEP or IFSP and challenge the child beyond his or her current level without creating unnecessary frustration. More and Travers presented a guide for evaluating educational apps in early-childhood classes that can be useful when evaluating and selecting apps (see Figure 10.8). Table 10.4 provides a few apps discussed by More and Travers as quality apps for young children, among other examples.

Beyond adherence to best practices for educating young children, apps for early childhood education can and should also be chosen to match a teacher's educational theory or philosophy (Buckleitner, 2015). In recalling the TPACK framework from Chapter 2, technology implemented in education should be consistent with an educator's philosophy and reflect his or her content (Mishra & Koehler, 2009). For example, educators who ascribe to the Montessori philosophy would seek out apps that promote deep learning and aren't focused on rewards. And, of course, educators should not assume any app with Montessori attached to it would adhere to their principles (Buckleitner, 2015).

Figure 10.8 More and Travers's Evaluation Guide for Early-Childhood Apps

Preschool App Evaluation Guide

Directions: Select an app with an educational purpose in mind and explore the app to decide whether it might be useful. Then evaluate the app for these factors. Evaluate several apps to identify the most suitable for the child you are working with.

App Title:_____ Price:_____

1 = Characteristic is Mostly Absent	2=Characteristic is Somewhat Absent	Ratings			
3 = Characteristic is Somewhat Present	4 = Characteristic is Mostly Present				
Accessibility					
App can be used by children with arange of abilities		1	2	3	4
App is easy for children to understand		1	2	3	4
Minimal adult assistance is required		1	2	3	4
Images and sounds are used to present important information		1	2	3	4
App gives positive feedback for correct answers		1	2	3	4
App gives corrective feedback in apositive way		1	2	3	4
App reduces fatigue and maximizes comfort for use		1	2	3	4
App allows enough space on the screen for 1 or more children to use it		1	2	3	4
Accessibility Total					
Content					
App can be used by children with arange of preferences and interests		1	2	3	4
App encourages children to be interactive		1	2	3	4
App has multiple options for children to explore		1	2	3	4
App minimizes rote responses		1	2	3	4
App encourages children to find answers to problems		1	2	3	4
Language is appropriate for young children		1	2	3	4
New vocabulary is taught		1	2	3	4
Music is socially appropriate		1	2	3	4
App is free from violence		1	2	3	4
App avoids cultural stereotyping		1	2	3	4
App promotes diversity		1	2	3	4
App is free from advertisements		1	2	3	4
Content of app is challenging but not frustrating for children		1	2	3	4
Content Total					
Individualization					
App teaches skills the children need in order to use it		1	2	3	4
App is compatible with the child's assistive technology		1	2	3	4
The difficulty of the app can be adjusted or changed based on child's response		1	2	3	4
App has options for *promoting* and other supports that can be turned on and off		1	2	3	4
Content of app addresses multiple skills		1	2	3	4
Use of app can be embedded into daily routine		1	2	3	4
Individualization Total					
Notes:		Overall Score			

Source: More, C. M., & Travers, J. C. (2013) What's app with that? Selecting educational apps for young children with disabilities. Young Exceptional Children , 16(2), 15–32.

Table 10.4 Sample Apps to Consider for Young Children

Name	Description
Dexteria Jr. by BinaryLabs (For purchase)	• Provides exercises for young children's hands and fingers to support motor skills development and readiness for handwriting
Smart Oral Motor by Smarty Ears (For purchase)	• Encourages young children to rehearse oral motor skills
Daniel Tiger's Grr-ific Feelings by PBS KIDS. (For purchase)	• Addresses social-emotional development through learning, playing, and singing about feelings
Breathe, Think, Do with Sesame by Sesame Street (Free)	• Addresses problem-solving of daily activities for young children (e.g., putting on shoes) • Addresses how to handle frustrating situations

Source: More and Travers (2013); Sharapan (2015).

Likewise, educators ascribing to a version of Piagetian constructivism would look for developmentally appropriate apps, not ones that speed up development. They would also seek apps that provide students with increasing challenges based on student success. A Vygotskian might look for apps that involve sharing or communicating among children or those in which a young child engages with another who is more knowledgeable. Finally, educators who take a behaviorist approach, such as that described by Skinner, would consider apps that provide reinforcement, particularly intermittent reinforcement, and promote mastery learning (Buckleitner, 2015).

Web 2.0 Resources and Apps

Even with the concern regarding too much screen time for young children, apps for mobile technologies and Web 2.0 technologies can support young children with disabilities. For young children with disabilities served through Part B of IDEA

(Continued)

(Continued)

(i.e., early childhood special education), educators can use Remind (see https://www .remind.com/) with parents. Remind allows educators to send text messages to parents or students (i.e., secondary students) without giving out their personal cell phone number or students or parents having to give their cell phone number. Text messages can then be sent, which provides a fast way to communicate with parents and older students.

Another technology, albeit for a cost, that supports home–school communication and connections, includes a focus on portfolios, and is geared towards early-childhood programs is Kaymbu (http://www.kaymbu. com). Kaymbu is an iPad system that allows teachers to record and share student work and classroom activities. Teachers can record images or videos for themselves as well as share them with parents.

Concluding Considerations

Assistive technology can support development, independence, access to materials, and interactions with environments for young children with disabilities. However, it is always important that the technology selected be appropriate for the young children, including developmentally appropriate as well as free of bias, violence, and stereotypes (Baker, 2014; Barnyak & McNelly, 2015; More & Travers, 2013). Important in the selection and implementation of assistive technology for young children with disabilities, like all children with disabilities, is using a framework for evaluating and making decisions. IFSP or IEP teams can use the frameworks and tools discussed in Chapter 2 of this textbook to help to make assistive technology decisions; they can also use the Six-Step Framework for Decision-Making (Mistrett, 2004; Mistrett, Lane, & Ruffino, 2005) (see Perspective 10.5). Also important is for early educators *and* parents to be trained on the assistive technology for the young children, including low-tech assistive technology. Low-tech assistive technology can provide an opening for parents to consider assistive technology for their young children if they have reservations (Baker, 2014); low-tech assistive technology is where all considerations of assistive technology should start for all individuals with disabilities because it is often less stigmatizing, easier to implement, and of lower cost (Behrmann & Schaff, 2001; Blackhurst, 1997).

In addition to the assistive technology decision-making frameworks presented in Chapter 2, early childhood educators can also apply the Six-Step Framework for Decision-Making (Mistrett, 2004; Mistrett, Lane, & Ruffino, 2005). The Six-Step Framework was specifically designed for early intervention teams and, aptly, involves six steps: "1.) Collect child/family information; 2.) Identify activities for participation; 3.) Identify observable targets for activity-based assessment and intervention; 4.) Brainstorm AT solutions and action plan; 5.) Conduct trials with AT support; and 6.) Identify what worked" (Sadao & Robinson, 2010, p. 56).

EXTENSION ACTIVITIES

- Show the "Go Baby Go" video on NationSwell (see http://nationswell.com/babiesdrivingracecars/) in class or have students watch individually. Engage in a discussion regarding the repurposing of everyday objects to serve as assistive technology for young children with disabilities.

- Show "Assistive Technology for Young Children: A Parent's Perspective" from the ATP Denver's YouTube Channel (see https://www.youtube.com/watch?v=Y2QToNdic54) in class or have students watch individually. Engage in a discussion regarding what assistive technology is used for Brian and how the assistive technology is used to support this young child with a disability.

APPLICATION ACTIVITIES

- Encourage students to think about how some assistive technology can be made. Considering young children—infants, toddlers, and preschool-aged children with disabilities—have students make an assistive technology device for a young child (most likely low to mid tech). Students can check out Tots 'n Tech for inspiration (see http://tnt.asu.edu/home).

- Have students read More, C. M., & Travers, J. C. (2013). What's app with that? Selecting educational apps for young children with disabilities. *Young Exceptional Children*, 16(2), 15–32. After reading the article, students should use Figures 1 and 2 from the article to evaluate one or more apps designated for young children to determine their appropriateness. Students should share their evaluations of their apps with the class.

- Explore the apps for young children mentioned throughout the chapter (e.g., see Table 10.4). How might these apps help young children with disabilities?

- Visit a local early childhood special education classroom, visit an inclusive or braided preschool classroom, or speak with a local early interventionist. Observe what assistive technology or Universal Design for Learning principles you see in the classroom. Then, discuss with the teacher or interventionist. What assistive technology does he or she use? How does he or she decide what assistive technology or UDL principles to implement, and how does he or she go about implementing them?

DISCUSSION QUESTIONS

1. What are common assistive technologies for young children with disabilities?

2. What are some of the concerns regarding technology for young children and are these concerns valid?

3. What considerations are needed when selecting assistive technology for young children with disabilities?

4. How might an educator help parents aid their special needs child with assistive technology?

5. Explain the differences between early intervention and early childhood special education services when considering the ages served and the focus of the services.

RESOURCES/ADDITIONAL INFORMATION

Please consider the following websites for additional information or resources.

- The National Association for the Education of Young Children (http://www.naeyc.org)

- The Fred Rogers Center for Early Learning and Children's Media (http://www.fredrogerscenter.org/)

- Division for Early Childhood of the Council for Exceptional Children (CEC) (http://www.dec-sped.org/)

- The Division for Early Childhood of CEC YouTube Channel (https://www.youtube.com/user/DECEarlyChildhood)

- The Tots 'n Tech YouTube Channel (https://www.youtube.com/user/TotsnTech/featured)

SUGGESTED ENRICHMENT READINGS

- Blum, C., & Parette, H. P. (2015). Universal Design for Learning and technology in the early childhood classroom. In K. L. Heider, & M. R. Jalongo (Eds.), *Young children and families in the information age: Applications of technology in early childhood* (pp. 165–182). New York, NY: Springer.

- Hume, K., Wong, C., Plavnick, J., & Schultz, T. (2014). Use of visual supports with young children with autism spectrum disorders. In J. Tarbox, D. R. Dixon, P. Sturmey, & J. L. Matson (Eds.), *Handbook of early intervention for autism spectrum disorders: Research, policy, and practice* (pp. 293–313). New York, NY: Springer. doi:10.1007/978-1-4939-0401-3_15

GLOSSARY

abacus: a tool consisting of beads along a wire that is used for calculation

abandonment: stopping the use of assistive technology, for whatever reason

accessible instructional materials: educational materials created or adapted to be accessible for a wide variety of students; accessible instructional materials are generally considered traditional print materials (e.g., books) that are in a different form, such as braille, digital text, audio, or large print

aided communication: a communication system in which the user uses something other than his or her body; a communication system that requires an external tool or device

assistive technology device: "any item, piece of equipment, or product system, whether acquired commercially, modified, or customized, that is used to increase, maintain, or improve functional capabilities of individuals with disabilities" (29 USC § 2202[2])

assistive technology service: "any service that directly assists an individual in the selection, acquisition, or use of an assistive technology device" (Pub. L. 100-407)

assistive technology specialist: individuals within an educational setting who assist students with disabilities in selecting, acquiring, implementing, and maintaining assistive technology

asynchronous: communication between individuals that does not occur at the same time; it can occur at any time (e.g., e-mail or discussion forums)

augmentative and alternative communication: a specific type of assistive technology that supports students with complex communication needs; it is all means of communication other than oral communication

autism spectrum disorder: a disability categorized by impairments in social interactions and communication and limited and/or repetitive interests or behavior; it is generally identified early in one's life

blended course: a course that meets both face to face as well as online

braille: a written communication system consisting of a series of raised dots

cerebral palsy: a disability that is typically related to damage to a baby's brain before or during birth with features involving challenges with muscle coordination

classroom management: effectively managing a classroom; working to prevent behavioral disruptions within a classroom

closed-circuit television: a television that allows one to zoom in on something, such as a document; a television in which the signals are for private use, not public

cochlear implant: a device that is surgically implanted with the goal of improving the hearing in individuals who are deaf

deaf-blind: a disability covered under IDEA in which a student has some level of both visual impairment and hearing impairment

digital speech: the recorded speech of a person

educational technology: technology used in education or for educational purposes; "the application of technology to teaching and learning" (Edyburn, 2013, p. 9)

environmental control units: devices that allow individuals with disabilities to control other devices or tools they may have trouble with otherwise (e.g., appliances or lights)

eText: electronic text; text that is read in a digital or electronic form

flipped classroom: a pedagogical approach to teaching in which a teacher records a lecture, and students watch it at home before class, and then time in class is spent with the teacher helping the students complete their work or students work on projects

hearing impairment: an impairment involving an individual's hearing, which, even with correction, still adversely affects a student's educational attainment; a disability covered under IDEA

hybrid course: a course that meets both face to face as well as online

individualized education program: a written plan that details the educational programming provided to students aged 3 through 21 identified with a disability under IDEA

instructional technology: technology for instruction, including design and delivery

intellectual disability: a disability characterized by below-average IQ and challenges with adaptive behavior

learning management system: a software program that delivers online classes as well as supports face-to-face learning; examples include Blackboard, D2L, Moodle

mobility: the capability to easily or freely move or be moved

occupational therapists: individuals trained to provide occupational therapy, meaning they provide therapy to assist individuals in participating in everyday activities

online learning: learning that occurs without the students and instructor meeting face to face; the course occurs in an online or virtual environment

optical character recognition system: the recognition of letters or a word (i.e., combination of characters) by a computer or computer-like device

physical therapists: individuals trained to provide physical therapy, meaning they provide therapy to support mobility

positioning: refers to an individual's body alignment; involves different positions (e.g., sitting and standing)

print disabilities: students who struggle to access traditional print; generally associated with students with visual impairments, learning disabilities in reading, and, sometimes, students with physical impairments

related service: additional services provided to students with disabilities to benefit from special education; examples include occupational therapy, school social work, and speech-and-language therapy

self-management: the process by which students manage or take responsibility for themselves and their behavior

self-monitoring: the process by which an individual identifies and regulates his or her own behavior

self-operated prompting systems: systems that provide prompts to an individual to complete a task more independently (e.g., picture, audio, and video)

sensory integration: the process by which the body receives and organizes sensory information

sign language: a language or form of communication involving signs and gestures

SMART Board: an interactive whiteboard; involves touch interface for interaction, such as with one's fingers or special markers

social emotional development: development that includes the ability of one to create and maintain healthy positive relationships as well as to experience and express emotions

social skills: skills involving one's ability to effectively interact and communicate with others

speech and language impairment: a category of disability covered under IDEA that encompasses both speech disorders (e.g., articulation disorders or stuttering) and language disorders (e.g., aphasia)

study skills: skills or strategies to support a student in learning or studying supported eText: eText with additional supports or features to benefit the user in terms of access and success in reading

synchronous: communication that occurs at the same time; a student and a teacher communicate at the same time (e.g., speaking face to face, chatting, or texting)

synthesized speech: computer-generated speech

text-to-speech: the conversion of typed text to a spoken form (i.e., printed text is read aloud)

transition services: individualized services a student receives to help him or her transition and achieve his or her postschool goals

unaided communication: a communication system in which nothing is external to the user

Universal Design: designing architectural elements to be accessible to everyone (e.g., curb cuts).

visual impairment: an impairment involving an individual's vision, which, even with correction, still adversely affects a student's educational attainment; a disability covered under IDEA

REFERENCES

1-800-WHEELCHAIR.com. (n.d.). *Sport wheelchairs.* Retrieved from http://www.1800wheelchair.com/category/sports-wheelchairs/

AAC TechConnect. (2014). *Apps summary.* Retrieved from http://www.aactechconnect.com/wp-content/uploads/2011/07/Apps-SummarySummer-6.10.14..pdf

Abbott, M. A., & McBride, D. (2014). AAC decision-making and mobile technology: Points to ponder. *SIG 12 Perspectives on Augmentative and Alternative Communication, 23,* 104–111. doi:10.1044/aac23.2.104

AbleData. (2014). *Corner seats.* Retrieved from http://www.abledata.com/abledata.cfm?pageid=19327&top=13113&ksectionid=19327&productid=215033&trail=0&discontinued=0

AbleNet. (2014). *Switches.* Retrieved from http://webstore.ablenetinc.com/Category.aspx?ss=&c=100&sb=&pgnum=1&pgsize=all

AboutTTY.com. (n.d.). *What is a TTY?* Retrieved from http://www.aboutty.com/

Abreu-Ellis, C., & Ellis, J. B. (2006). The challenge of accommodation in higher education: A survey of adaptive technology use in Ontario universities. *Journal of Teaching and Learning, 4,* 31–41.

Ackerman, A. M., & Shapiro, E. S. (1984). Self-monitoring and work productivity with mentally retarded adults. *Journal of Applied Behavior Analysis, 17,* 403–407.

Adamo-Villani, N., Popescu, V., & Lestina, J. (2013). A non-expert-user interface for posing signing avatars. *Disability and Rehabilitation: Assistive Technology, 8*(3), 238–248. doi:10.3109/17483107.2012.704655

Adamo-Villani, N., & Wilbur, R. (2010). Software for math and science education for the deaf. *Disability and Rehabilitation: Assistive Technology, 5*(2), 115–124.

Agran, M. (1997). *Student directed learning: Teaching self-determination skills.* Pacific Grove, CA: Brooks/Cole.

Ahrens, K. (2011). Build an assistive technology toolkit. *Learning & Leading with Technology, 39*(3), 22–24.

Alajarmeh, N., & Pontelli, E. (2012). A non-visual electronic workspace for learning algebra. In K. Miesenberger, A. Karshmer, P. Penaz, & W. Zagler (Eds.), *Computers helping people with special needs: 13th international conference, ICCHP 2012, Linz, Austria, July 11–13, 2012, proceedings, part I* (pp. 158–165). Heidelberg, Germany: Springer-Verlag.

Allen, K. D., Burke, R. V., Howard, M. R., Wallace, D. P., & Bowen, S. L. (2012). Use of audio cuing to expand employment opportunities for adolescents with autism spectrum disorders and intellectual disabilities. *Journal of Autism and Developmental Disabilities, 42,* 2410–2419. doi:10.1007/s10803-012-1519-7

Alper, S., & Raharinirina, S. (2006). Assistive technology for individuals with disabilities: A review and synthesis of the literature. *Journal of Special Education Technology, 21*(2), 47–64.

Alzrayer, N., Banda, D. R., & Koul, R. K. (2014). Use of iPad/iPods with individuals with autism and other developmental disabilities: A meta-analysis of communication interventions. *Review Journal of Autism and Developmental Disorders, 1,* 179–191. doi:10.1007/s40489-014-0018-5

Amato, S., Hong, S., & Rosenblum, P. L. (2013). The abacus: Instruction by teachers of students with visual impairments. *Journal of Visual Impairment & Blindness, 107,* 262–272.

American Academy of Pediatrics. (2010). Media education. *Pediatrics, 126,* 1012–1017. doi:10.1542/peds.2010-1636

American Foundation for the Blind. (2013). *Reading tools.* Retrieved from http://www.visionaware.org/info/everyday-living/essential-skills/reading-and-writing/reading-tools-and-techniques/1235

American Foundation for the Blind. (2014a). *Screen readers*. Retrieved from http://www.afb.org/prodBrowseCatResults.asp?CatID=49

American Foundation for the Blind. (2014b). *What is Braille?* Retrieved from http://www.afb.org/info/living-with-vision-loss/braille/what-is-braille/123

American Foundation for the Blind. (2014c). *Writing tools for visual readers*. Retrieved from http://www.afb.org/info/living-with-vision-loss/using-technology/reading-and-writing/writing-tools-for-visual-readers/1235

American Occupational Therapy Association. (2014). *About occupational therapy*. Retrieved from http://www.aota.org/about-occupational-therapy.aspx

American Physical Therapy Association. (2014). *Who are physical therapists?* Retrieved from http://www.apta.org/aboutPTs/

American Printing House for the Blind. (2014). *Orion TI-84 Plus Talking Calculator™ user's guide*. Retrieved from http://tech.aph.org/Orion%20TI-84%20Plus%20Documents/gc_doc.htm

American Speech-Language-Hearing Association. (2007). *Scope of practice in speech-language pathologist*. Retrieved from http://www.asha.org/uploadedFiles/SP2007-00283.pdf

American Speech-Language-Hearing Association. (2014a). *Different styles of hearing aids*. Retrieved from http://www.asha.org/public/hearing/Different-Styles-of-Hearing-Aids/

American Speech-Language-Hearing Association. (2014b). *Types of hearing aid technology*. Retrieved from http://www.asha.org/public/hearing/Types-of-Hearing-Aid-Technology/

American Speech-Language-Hearing Association. (n.d.). *Communication services and supports for individuals with severe disabilities: FAQs: Basic information about augmentative and alternative communication*. Retrieved from http://www.asha.org/NJC/faqs-aac-basics.htm

American Speech-Language-Hearing Association. (n.d.a). *Augmentative and alternative communication (AAC)*. Retrieved from http://www.asha.org/public/speech/disorders/AAC/

American Speech-Language-Hearing Association. (n.d.b). Augmentative communication: A glossary. Retrieved from http://www.asha.org/public/speech/disorders/AAC-Glossary/

American Speech-Language-Hearing Association. (n.d.c). Communication services and supports for individuals with severe disabilities: FAQs: Basic information about augmentative and alternative communication. Retrieved from http://www.asha.org/NJC/faqs-aac-basics.htm

Americans with Disabilities Act, 42 U.S.C. § 12101 et seq. (1990).

Anderson-Inman, L., & Horney, M. (2007). Supported eText: Assistive technology through text transformations. *Reading Research Quarterly, 42*(1), 153–160.

Andrade, J. (2010). What does doodling do? *Applied Cognitive Psychology, 24*, 100–106.

Apple. (2013). *Mac basics: Dictation*. Retrieved from http://support.apple.com/kb/HT5449

Apple. (2014). *OS X Mavericks: Control the pointer using mouse keys*. Retrieved from http://support.apple.com/kb/PH14235

Apple. (2015a). *Accessibility—iOS*. Retrieved from https://www.apple.com/accessibility/ios/

Apple. (2015b). *Accessibility—OS X*. Retrieved from https://www.apple.com/accessibility/osx

Apple. (2015c). *Using AssistiveTouch on your iOS device*. Retrieved from http://support.apple.com/en-us/HT202658

Archambault, D., Caprotti, O., Ranta, A., & Saludes, J. (2012). Using GF in multimodal assistants for mathematics. *Digitization and E-Inclusion in Mathematics and Science, 1*(1), 1–10.

ASHA Leader. (2014). Medicare delays new SGD policies. *The ASHA Leader*, *19*, 12. doi:10.1044/leader.NIB4.19102014.12. Retrieved from http://leader.pubs.asha.org/article.aspx?articleid=1912335

Assistive Technology Act of 1998, Pub. L. No. 105-394, 112 Stat. 3627–3662 (1998).

Assistive Technology Act of 2004, Pub. L. No. 108-364, 118 Stat. 1707 (2004).

Assistive Technology Training Online Project. (n.d.). Switch users. Retrieved from http://atto.buffalo.edu/registered/ATBasics/Populations/Switch/printmodule.php

AssistiveWare. (2013). *Proloquo2Go*. Retrieved from https://itunes.apple.com/us/app/proloquo2go/id308368164?mt=8

AssistiveWare®. (2014). Retrieved from http://www.assistiveware.com

Attainment Company. (2014). *GoTalk button*. Retrieved from http://www.attainmentcompany.com/gotalk-button

Ayres, A. J. (1972). *Sensory integration and learning disorders*. Los Angeles, CA: Western Psychological Services.

Ayres, K. M., Mechling, L., & Sansosti, F. J. (2013). The use of mobile technologies to assist with life skills/independence of students with moderate/severe intellectual disability and/or autism spectrum disorders: Considerations for the future of school psychology. *Psychology in the Schools*, *50*(3), 259–271. doi:10.1002/pits.21673

Bagatell, N., Mirigliani, G., Patterson, C., Reyes, Y., & Test, L. (2010). Effectiveness of therapy ball chairs on classroom participation in children with autism spectrum disorder. *American Journal of Occupational Therapy*, *64*, 895–903. doi:10.5014/ajot.2010.09149

Baker, F. S. (2014). Engaging in play through assistive technology: Closing gaps in research and practice for infants and toddlers with disabilities. In B. DaCosta & S. Seok (Eds.), *Assistive technology research, practice, and theory* (pp. 207–221). Hershey, PA: IGI Global.

Banks, D. (2008, December 3). Disney survey shows technology trends for kids. *Wired*. Retrieved from http://archive.wired.com/geekdad/2008/12/disney-survey-s/

Bardach, L. G. (2014). Medicare rules leave patients speechless. *The ASHA Leader*, *19*, 30–31. doi:10.1044/leader.otp.19082014.30. Retrieved from http://leader.pubs.asha.org/article.aspx?articleid=1893874

Barnes, S. B., & Whinnery. K. W. (2002). Effects of functional mobility skills in training for young students with physical disabilities. *Exceptional Children*, *68*, 313–324.

Barnyak, N. C., & McNelly, T. A. (2015). Supporting young children's visual literacy through the use of e-books. In K. L. Heider & M. R. Jalongo (Eds.), *Young children and families in the information age* (pp. 15–41). New York, NY: Springer.

Barr, R., Lauricella, A., Zack, E., & Calvert, S. L. (2010). Infant and early childhood exposure to adult-directed and child-directed television programming: Relations with cognitive skills at age four. *Merrill-Palmer Quarterly*, *56*(1), 21–48. Retrieved from http://www.ericdigests.org/2003-1/assistive.htm

Barrett, B. (2014). Creating protective barriers for students with disabilities in e-learning environments. In B. DaCosta & S. Seok (Eds.), *Assistive technology research, practice, and theory* (pp. 222–231). Hershey, PA: IGI Global.

Barton, E. E., Reichow, B., Schnitz, A., Smith, I. C., & Sherlock, D. (2015). A systematic review of sensory-based treatments for children with disabilities. *Research in Developmental Disabilities*, *37*, 64–80. doi:10.1016/j.ridd.2014.11.006

Bastedo, K., & Vargas, J. (2014). Assistive technology and distance learning: Making content accessible. In B. DaCosta & S. Seok (Eds.), *Assistive technology research, practice, and theory* (pp. 233–251). Hershey, PA: IGI Global.

Batorowicz, B., Missiuna, C. A., & Pollock, N. A. (2012). Technology supporting written productivity in children with learning disabilities: A critical review. *Canadian Journal of Occupational Therapy, 79*(4), 211–224.

Bausch, M. E., & Ault, M. J. (2008). Assistive technology implementation plan: A tool for improving outcomes. *Teaching Exceptional Children, 41*(1), 6–14.

Bausch, M. E., Ault, M. J., & Hasselbring, T. S. (2006). *Assistive technology planner: From IEP consideration to classroom implementation.* Lexington, KY: National Assistive Technology Research Institute.

Bedell, G., Coster, W., Law, M., Liljenquist, K., Kao, Y.-C., Teplicky, R., . . . Khetani, M. A. (2013). Community participation, supports, and barriers of school-age children with and without disabilities. *Archives of Physical Medicine and Rehabilitation, 94,* 315–323. doi:10.1016/j.apmr.2012.09.024

Bedesem, P. L., & Dieker, L. A. (2014). Self-monitoring with a twist: Using cell phones to cellF-monitor on-task behavior. *Journal of Positive Behavior Interventions, 16*(4), 246–254. doi:10.1177/1098300713492857

Behrmann, M., & Jerome, M. (2002). Assistive technology for students with mild disabilities: Update 2002. *ERIC Digest.* Retrieved from http://www .ericdigests.org/2003-1/assistive.htm

Behrmann, M., & Schaff, J. (2001). Assisting educators with assistive technology: Enabling children to achieve independence in living and learning. *Children and Families, 42*(3), 24–28.

Bekele, E. T., Lahiri, U., Swanson, A. R., Crittendon, J. A., Warrend, Z. E., & Sarkar, N. (2013). A step towards developing adaptive robotic-mediated intervention architecture (ARIA) for children with autism. *IEEE Transactions on Neural Systems and Rehabilitation Engineering, 21*(2), 289–299. doi:10.1109/TNSRE.2012.2230188. Retrieved from http://www.ncbi.nlm.nih.gov/pmc/articles/ PMC3860752/

Bell, E. (2010). U.S. national certification in literary braille: History and current administration. *Journal of Visual Impairment & Blindness, 104*(8), 489–498.

Ben-Avie, M., Newton, D., & Reichow, B. (2014). Using handheld applications to improve the transitions of students with autism spectrum disorders. In N. R. Silton (Ed.), *Innovative technologies to benefit children on the autism spectrum* (pp. 105–124). Hershey, PA: IGI Global. doi:10.4018978-1-4666-5792-2.ch007

Beukelman, D. R., & Mirenda, P. (2013). *Augmentative and alternative communication: Management of severe communication disorders in children and adults* (4th ed.). Baltimore, MD: Brooks.

Bhattacharyya, A. (2009). Deaf-blind tech gadgets in educational settings. *Division on Visual Impairment Quarterly, 54*(3). Retrieved from http://documents .nationaldb.org/products/dviqanindya.pdf

Bickford, J. O., & Falco, J. R. (2012). Technology for early braille literacy: Comparison of traditional braille instruction and instruction with an electronic notetaker. *Journal of Visual Impairment & Blindness, 107*(10), 679–693.

Binger, C., & Light, J. (2006). Demographics of preschoolers who require AAC. *Language, Speech, and Hearing Services in Schools, 37,* 200–208.

Bitterman, A., Daley, T. C., Misra, S., Carlson, E., & Markowitz, J. (2008). A national sample of preschoolers with autism spectrum disorders: Special education services and parent satisfaction. *Journal of Autism and Developmental Disorders, 38,* 1509–1517. doi:10.1007/s10803-007-0531-9

Blackhurst, A. (1997). Perspectives on technology in special education. *TEACHING Exceptional Children, 29*(5). 41–48.

Blackhurst, A. (2005a). Historical perspectives about technology applications for people with disabilities. In D. Edyburn, K. Higgins, & R. Boone

(Eds.), *Handbook of special education technology research and practice* (pp. 3–30). Whitefish Bay, WI: Knowledge by Design.

Blackhurst, A. (2005b). Perspectives on applications of technology in the field of learning disabilities. *Learning Disability Quarterly, 28*(2), 175–178.

Bolkan, J. (2012, December 19). Research: IT predictions for 2013. *THE Journal.* Retrieved from http://thejournal.com/articles/2012/12/19/research-it-predictions-for-2013.aspx?admgarea=News1

Bondy, A., & Frost, L. (1994). The Picture-Exchange Communication System. *Focus on Autistic Behavior, 9*(3), 1–19.

Bondy, A., & Frost, L. (2001). The Picture Exchange Communication System. *Behavior Modification, 25,* 725–744.

Bookshare. (n.d.a). Other reading tools. Retrieved from https://www.bookshare.org/cms/help-center/other-reading-tools#applications

Bookshare. (n.d.b). *Reading tools.* Retrieved from https://www.bookshare.org/cms/node/545

Bornman, J. (2011). Low technology. In O. Wendt, R. W. Quist, & L. L. Lloyd (Eds.), *Assistive technology: Principles and applications for communication disorders and special education* (pp. 175–220). Bingley, U.K.: Emerald.

Bottge, B. A. (1999). Effects of contextualized math instruction on problem solving of average and below-average achieving students. *The Journal of Special Education, 33,* 81–92.

Bottge, B. A., Heinrichs, M., Mehta, Z. D., & Hung, Y.-H. (2002). Weighing the benefits of anchored math instruction for students with disabilities in general education classes. *The Journal of Special Education, 35,* 186–200.

Bottge, B. A., Rueda, E., Serlin, R. C., Hung, Y., & Kwon, J. M. (2007). Shrinking achievement differences with anchored math problems: Challenges and possibilities. *The Journal of Special Education, 41,* 31–49.

Bottge, B. A., Rueda, E., & Sivington, M. (2006). Situating math instruction in rich problem-solving contexts: Effects on adolescents with challenging behaviors. *Behavioral Disorders, 31,* 394–407.

Boucenna, S., Narzisi, A., Tilmont, E., Muratori, F., Pioggia, G., Cohen, D., & Chetouani, M. (2014). Interactive technologies for autistic children: A review. *Cognitive Computation, 6,* 722–740. doi:10.1007/s12559-014-9276-x

Bouck, E. C. (2009). Calculating the value of graphing calculators for seventh grade students with and without disabilities: A pilot study. *Remedial and Special Education, 30,* 207–215.

Bouck, E. C. (2010). The impact of calculator type and instructional exposure for students with a disability: A pilot study. *Learning Disabilities: A Multidisciplinary Journal, 16,* 141–148.

Bouck, E. C., & Bouck, M. K. (2008). Does it add up? Calculator use by middle school students with and without disabilities. *Journal of Special Education Technology, 23*(2), 17–32.

Bouck, E. C., & Flanagan, S. M. (in press). Exploring assistive technology and post-school outcomes for students with severe disabilities.

Bouck, E. C., & Flanagan, S. (2009). Assistive technology and mathematics: What is there and where can we go in special education. *Journal of Special Education Technology, 24*(2), 17–30.

Bouck, E. C., Flanagan, S., Joshi, G. S., Sheikh, W., & Schleppenbach, D. (2011). Speaking math: A voice input, speech output calculator for students with visual impairment. *Journal of Special Education Technology, 26*(4), 1–14.

Bouck, E. C., Flanagan, S., Miller, B., & Bassette, L. (2012). Technology in action: Rethinking everyday technology as assistive technology to meet students' IEP goals. *Journal of Special Education Technology, 27*(4), 47–57.

Bouck, E. C., Hunley, M., & Bouck, M. K. (in press). The calculator effect: Understanding the impact of calculators as accommodations for secondary students with disabilities. *Journal of Special Education Technology*.

Bouck, E. C., Jasper, A., Bassette, L., & Shurr, J. (2015). Mobile phone: Repurposed assistive technology for individuals with disabilities. In Z. Yan (Ed.), *Encyclopedia of mobile phone behavior* (Vols. 1, 2, & 3). Hershey, PA: IGI Global.

Bouck, E. C., Jasper, A., Bassette, L., Shurr, J., & Miller, B. (2013). Applying TAPE: Rethinking assistive technology for students with physical disabilities, multiple disabilities, and other health impairment. *Physical Disabilities: Education and Related Services, 32*(1), 31–54.

Bouck, E. C., Joshi, G. S., & Johnson, L. (2013). Calculating the value of calculators: Who uses it and does it help? *Educational Studies in Mathematics, 83,* 369–385.

Bouck, E. C., Maeda, Y., & Flanagan, S. M. (2011). Assistive technology and students with high-incidence disabilities: Understanding the relationship through the NLTS2. *Remedial and Special Education, 33*(5), 298–308. doi:10.1177/0741932511401037

Bouck, E., & Flanagan, S. (2010). Virtual manipulatives: What they are and how teachers can use them. *Intervention in School and Clinic, 45,* 186–191.

Bouck, E., & Meyer, N. (2012). eText, mathematics, and students with visual impairments. *Teaching Exceptional Children, 45*(2), 42–49.

Bouck, E. C., Meyer, N. K., Joshi, G. S., & Schleppenbach, D. (2013). Accessing algebra via MathSpeak: Understanding the potential and pitfalls for students with visual impairments. *Journal of Special Education Technology, 28*(1), 49–63.

Bouck, E. C., Okolo, C. M., & Courtad, C. A. (2007). Learning tools in the private sector for students with disabilities. *Journal of Special Education Technology, 22*(3), 43–56.

Bouck, E. C., Satsangi, R., Bartlett, W., & Muhl, A. (2013). Using audio recorders to promote independence in grocery shopping for students with intellectual disability. *Journal of Special Education Technology, 28*(4), 15–26.

Bouck, E. C., Satsangi, R., Bartlett, W., & Weng, P. (2012). Promoting independence through assistive technology: Evaluating audio recorders to support grocery shopping. *Education and Training in Autism and Developmental Disabilities, 47,* 462–473.

Bouck, E. C., Satsangi, R., Taber-Doughty, T., & Courtney, W. T. (2014). Virtual and concrete manipulatives: A comparison of approaches for solving mathematics problems for students with autism spectrum disorder. *Journal of Autism and Developmental Disabilities, 44,* 180–193.

Bouck, E. C., Shurr, J. C., Tom, K., Jasper, A. D., Bassette, L., Miller, B., & Flanagan, S. M. (2012). Fix it with TAPE: Repurposing technology to be assistive technology for students with high-incidence disabilities. *Preventing School Failure, 56,* 121–128.

Bourgeois-Doyle, R. (2004). *George J. Klein: The great inventor.* Ottawa, Canada: NRC Research Press.

Bowser, G., & Reed, P. (1995). Education TECH points for assistive technology planning. *Journal of Special Education Technology, 12,* 325–338.

Bowser, G., & Reed, P. (2012). *Educational tech points: A framework for assistive technology* (3rd ed.). Winchester, OR: Coalition for Assistive Technology in Oregon.

Briesch, A. M., & Daniels, B. (2013). Using self-management interventions to address general education behavioral needs: Assessment of effectiveness and feasibility. *Psychology in the Schools, 50*(4), 366–381. doi:10.1002/pits.21679

Bright, R. (n.d.). *Kids who can't sit still: Letting them fidget may keep students focused on learning* [Web log post]. Retrieved from http://www.nea.org/tools/47003.htm

Brittain, A. (2007, July 19). Braille literacy flags, even as technology makes it more urgent. *Christian Science*

Monitor. Retrieved from http://www.csmonitor.com/2007/0719/p13s02-legn.html?page51

Brownlee, A. (2014). *Augmentative communication. ALS Association.* Retrieved from http://www.alsa.org/als-care/augmentative-communication/

Bryant, B. R., Seok, S., Ok, M., & Bryant, D. P. (2012). Individuals with intellectual and/or developmental disabilities use of assistive technology devices in support provision. *Journal of Special Education Technology, 27*(2), 41–57.

Bryant, D. P., & Bryant, B. R. (1998). Using assistive technology adaptations to include students with learning disabilities in cooperative learning activities. *Journal of Learning Disabilities, 31*(1), 41–54.

Bryant, D. P., & Bryant, B. R. (2012). *Assistive technology for people with disabilities* (2nd ed.). Boston, MA: Allyn & Bacon.

Bryant, D., & Bryant, B. (2003). *Assistive technology for people with disabilities.* Boston, MA: Allyn & Bacon.

Bryant, D., & Bryant, B. (2012). *Assistive technology for people with disabilities* (2nd ed.). Boston, MA: Allyn & Bacon.

Buckleitner, W. (2015). What would Maria Montessori say about the iPad? Theoretical frameworks for children's interactive media. In C. Donahue (Ed.), *Technology and digital media in the early years: Tools for teaching and learning* (pp. 54–69). New York, NY: Routledge.

Bundonis, J. (2009). *Benefits of early mobility with an emphasis on gait training.* Retrieved from http://www.rifton.com/resources/articles/2011/february/benefits-of-early-mobility-with-an-emphasis-on-gait-training

Burgstahler, S. (2012a). *Making science labs accessible to students with disabilities: Application of universal design to a science lab.* Retrieved from https://www.washington.edu/doit/sites/default/files/atoms/files/Making-Science-Labs-Accessible-Students-Disabilities.pdf

Burgstahler, S. (2012b). *Working together: People with disabilities and computer technology.* Retrieved from http://www.washington.edu/doit/working-together-people-disabilities-and-computer-technology

Calhoon, M., Emerson, R., Flores, M., & Houchins, D. (2007). Computational fluency performance profile of high school students with mathematics disabilities. *Remedial and Special Education, 28*(5), 292–303.

Cannon, L., Dorward, J., Duffin, J., & Heal, B. (2004). National Library of Virtual Manipulatives. *The Mathematics Teacher, 97*(2), 158–159.

Carling, L. Z., & Thompson, K. W. (2011). *Web 2.0 for teaching and learning* [TAM technology fan]. Arlington, VA: Technology and Media Division of the Council for Exceptional Children.

Carr, M. E., Moore, D. W., & Anderson, A. (2014). Self-management interventions on students with autism: A meta-analysis of single-subject research. *Exceptional Children, 81*(1), 28–44.

Carrington, P., Hurst, A., & Kane, S. K. (2013, October). *How power wheelchair users choose computer devices.* Paper presented at the 15th International ACM SIGACCESS Conference on Computers and Accessibility, Bellevue, WA. doi:10.1145/2513383.2513426

Carroll, J. L. (2014). Wheelchairs as assistive technology: What a special educator should know. In Information Resources Management Association (Ed.), *Assistive technologies: Concepts, methodologists, tools, and applications* (pp. 623–633). Hershey, PA: IGI Global. doi:10.4018/978-1-4666-4422-9.ch030

Carroll, L. (2004, October 26). The problem with some 'smart toys': (Hint) Use your imagination. *The New York Times.* Retrieved from http://www.nytimes.com/2004/10/26/health/26toys.html?_r=0

Cass, M., Cates, D., Smith, M., & Jackson, C. (2003). Effects of manipulative instruction on solving area and perimeter problems by students with learning disabilities. *Learning Disabilities Research and Practice, 18*(2), 112–120.

Cassingham, R. (2012). *The Dvorak keyboard: A brief primer*. Retrieved from http://www.dvorak-keyboard.com/

CAST. (2015). *Free learning tools*. Retrieved from http://www.cast.org/our-work/learning-tools.html#.ValbwHjy9p8

Castellani, J. (2010). *Universal Design for Learning* [TAM technology fan]. Arlington, VA: Technology and Media Division of the Council for Exceptional Children.

Cawthon, S. W., & Cole, E. (2010). Postsecondary students who have a learning disability: Student perspectives on accommodations access and obstacles. *Journal of Postsecondary Education and Disability, 23*(2), 112–128.

Center for Assistive Technology and Environmental Access. (2009). *Accessible calculators*. Retrieved from http://atwiki.assistivetech.net/index.php/Accessible_calculators

Center for Parent Information and Resources. (2014a). *Early intervention, then and now*. Retrieved from http://www.parentcenterhub.org/repository/ei-history/

Center for Parent Information and Resources. (2014b). *Writing the IFSP for your child*. Retrieved from http://www.parentcenterhub.org/repository/ifsp/

Center on Online Learning and Students with Disabilities. (2012). *The foundation of online learning for students with disabilities*. Retrieved from http://centerononlinelearning.org/wp-content/uploads/Foundation_7_2012.pdf

Chambers, A. C. (1997). *Has technology been considered? A guide for IEP teams*. Reston, VA: CASE/TAM.

Chen, D., Downing, J., & Rodriguez-Gil, G. (2001). Tactile strategies for children who are deaf-blind: Considerations and concerns from Project SALUTE. *Deaf-Blind Perspectives, 8*(2), 1–6. Retrieved from http://www.projectsalute.net/Learned/Learnedhtml/TactileLearningStrategies.html

Cheney, C. (2014, February 24). Professors create souped-up toy cars for kids with disabilities. *Huffington Post*. Retrieved from http://www.huffingtonpost.com/2014/02/24/toy-store_n_4847954.html

Cheney, C., & Templin, J. (2014, February 5). How one man's trip to Toys 'R' Us brought mobility to hundreds of disabled kids. *Nation Swell*. Retrieved from http://nationswell.com/babiesdrivingracecars/

Cheng, Y., Chiang, H.-C., Ye, J., & Cheng, L.-H. (2010). Enhancing empathy instruction using a collaborative virtual learning environment for children with autistic spectrum conditions. *Computers & Education, 55*(4), 1449–1458. doi:10.1016/j.compedu.2010.06.008

Cheng, Y., & Ye, Y. (2010). Exploring the social competence of students with autism spectrum conditions in a collaborative virtual learning environment: A pilot study. *Computers & Education, 54*(4), 1068–1077. doi:10.1016/j.compedu.2009.10.011

Cihak, D., Fahrenkrog, C., Ayres, K., & Smith, C. (2010). The use of video modeling via a video iPod and a system of least prompts to improve transitional behaviors for students with autism spectrum disorders in the general education classroom. *Journal of Positive Behavior Interventions, 12*, 103–115.

Clements, D. H., & Sarama J. (2007). Effects of a preschool mathematics curriculum: Summative research on the *Building Blocks* project. *Journal for Research in Mathematics Education, 38*(2), 136–63.

Coleman, M. B. (2011). Successful implementation of assistive technology to promote access to curriculum and instruction for students with physical disabilities. *Physical Disabilities: Education and Related Services, 30*(2), 2–22.

Collins, K. (2014, December 2). Stephen Hawking's new speech system is free and open-source. *WIRED*. Retrieved from http://www.wired.co.uk/news/archive/2014-12/02/stephen-hawking-intel-communication-system

Comer, L. (2009). Assistive technology for recreation and leisure. In J. Gierach (Ed.), *Assessing students' needs for assistive technology (ASNAT): A resource manual for school district teams* (5th ed.). Retrieved from http://wati .org/content/supports/free/pdf/Ch10-RecLeisure.pdf

Cook, A. M., & Polgar, J. M. (2015). *Assistive technologies: Principles and practice* (4th ed.). St. Louis, MO: Elsevier.

Council for Exceptional Children. (2005). *Universal Design for Learning: A guide for teachers and education professionals.* Boston, MA: Pearson.

Croser, A. (2013). *Talking Calculator.* Retrieved from https://itunes.apple.com/us/app/talking-calculator/ id424464284?mt=8

Crowl, B., & Franklin, K. (1994). A new and improved "Tech Act." *A. T. Quarterly, 5*(2–3). Retrieved from http://www.resnaprojects.org/nattap/ library/atq/newtech.htm

Cumley, J. (2009). Assistive technology for reading. In J. Gierach (Ed.), *Assessing students' needs for assistive technology (ASNAT): A resource manual for school district teams* (5th ed.). Milton: Wisconsin Assistive Technology Initiative. Retrieved from http:// wati.org/content/supports/free/pdf/Ch7-Reading.pdf

Cumley, J., Maro, J., & Stanek, M. (2009). Assistive technology for communication. In J. Gierach (Ed.), *Assessing students' needs for assistive technology (ASNAT): A resource manual for school district teams* (5th ed.). Retrieved from http://wati.org/content/ supports/free/pdf/Ch3-Communication.pdf

Danielson, C. (2013). *National federation of the blind commends department of education for new guidelines on braille instruction.* Retrieved from https://nfb.org/ national-federation-blind-commends-department- education-new-guidelines-braille-instruction

De Jong, M. T., & Bus, A. G. (2004). The efficacy of electronic books in fostering kindergarten children's emergent story understanding. *Reading Research Quarterly, 39*(4), 378–393. doi:10.1598/RRQ.39.4.2

Deardorff, J. (2012, August 7). Standing desks: The classroom of the future? *Chicago Tribune.* Retrieved from http://articles.chicagotribune.com/2012-08-07/ health/chi-standing-desks-the-classroom-of-the- future-20120807_1_desks-standings-classroom

Dell, A. G. (2010). *Transition: There are no IEP's in college.* Retrieved from http://www.tcnj.edu/~tech nj/2004/transition.htm

Dell, A. G., Newton, D. A., & Petroff, J. G. (2012). *Assistive technology in the classroom: Enhancing the school experience for students with disabilities.* Boston, MA: Pearson.

Diehl, J. J., Cromwell, C. R., Villano, M., Wier, K., Tang, K., Van Ness, M., . . . Shea, N. M. (2013, May). *Humanoid robots as co-therapists in ABA therapy for children with autism spectrum disorder.* Paper presented at the International Meeting for Autism Research, San Sebastián, Spain.

Digital Miracles. (2014). *Digit-Eyes.* Retrieved from https://itunes.apple.com/us/app/digit-eyes/id3764244 90?mt=8

DO-IT. (2012). *Working together: Computers and people with mobility impairments.* Retrieved from http://www .washington.edu/doit/working-together-computers- and-people-mobility-impairments

DO-IT. (2014). *What are environmental control units?* Retrieved from http://www.washington.edu/doit/ what-are-environmental-control-units

DO-IT. (2015). *Legal issues.* Retrieved from http:// www.washington.edu/doit/legal-issues-0

Don Johnston. (2015). Co:Writer (Version 7) [Computer software]. Retrieved from http://www .donjohnston.com/products/cowriter/index.html

Douglas, K. H., Courtad, C. A., Mustian, A. L., & Parette, H. P. (2013). Integrating technology to support emergent reading. In H. P. Parette & C. Blum (Eds.), *Instructional technology in early childhood* (pp. 123–147). Baltimore, MD: Paul H. Brookes Publishing.

Drager, K., Light, J., & McNaughton, D. (2010). Effects of AAC intervention on communication and language for young children with complex communication needs. *Journal of Pediatric Rehabilitation Medicine, 3,* 303–310.

Drescher, P. L. (2009). Access to computers for students with physical disabilities. In J. Gierach (Ed.), *Assessing students' needs for assistive technology (ASNAT): A resource manual for school district teams* (5th ed.). Milton: Wisconsin Assistive Technology Initiative. Retrieved from http://www.wati.org/content/supports/free/pdf/Ch4-ComputerAccess.pdf

Duch, H., Fisher, E. M., Ensari, I., & Harrington, A. (2013). Screen time use in children under 3 years old: A systematic review of correlates. *International Journal of Behavioral Nutrition and Physical Activity, 10*, 102–111.

Dunst, C. J., Trivette, C. M., & Hamby, D. W. (2012). Assistive technology and the communication and literacy development of young children with disabilities. *CELLreviews, 5*(7), 1–13. Retrieved from http://www.earlyliteracylearning.org/cellreviews/cellreviews_v5_n7.pdf

DynaVox. (2014). *Maestro.* Retrieved from http://www.dynavoxtech.com/products/maestro/

Early Childhood Technical Assistance Center. (2014a). *IFSP Process: Planning and implementing family-centered services in natural environments.* Retrieved from http://ectacenter.org/topics/ifsp/ifspprocess.asp

Early Childhood Technical Assistance Center. (2014b). *States' Part C rules, regulations and policies.* Retrieved from http://ectacenter.org/partc/statepolicies.asp

Education of All Handicapped Children Education Act of 1975, 20 U.S.C., § 1401 et seq. (1975).

Educational Resource Center on Deafness. (n.d.). *Overview of assistive listening devices.* Retrieved from http://www.info.texasdhhresources.org/apps/pages/index.jsp?uREC_ID=161096&type=d&pREC_ID=327139

Edyburn, D. (2001). Models, theories, and frameworks: Contributions to understanding special education technology. *Special Education Technology Practice, 4*(2), 16–24.

Edyburn, D. (2004). Rethinking assistive technology. *Special Education Technology Practice, 5*(4), 16–23.

Edyburn, D. (2005). Assistive technology and students with mild disabilities: From consideration to outcomes measurement. In D. Edyburn, K. Higgins, & R. Boone (Eds.), *Handbook of special education technology research and practice* (pp. 239–270). Whitefish Bay, WI: Knowledge by Design.

Edyburn, D. L. (2000). Assistive technology and students with mild disabilities. *Focus on Exceptional Children, 32*(9), 1–24.

Edyburn, D. L. (2004). Rethinking assistive technology. *Special Education Technology Practice, 5*(4), 16–23.

Edyburn, D. L. (2013). Critical issues in advancing the special education technology base. *Exceptional Children, 80*, 7–24.

Edyburn, D. L., Higgins, K., & Boone, R. (2005). Preface. In D. Edyburn, K. Higgins, & R. Boone (Eds.), *Handbook of special education technology research and practice* (pp. xiii–xvi). Whitefish Bay, WI: Knowledge by Design.

Englert, C., Zhao, Y., Dunsmore, K., Collings, N., & Wolbers, K. (2007). Scaffolding the writing of students with disabilities through procedural facilitation: Using an Internet-based technology to improve performance. *Learning Disability Quarterly, 30*(1), 9–29.

Epstein, M. H., Mooney, P., Reid, R., Ryan, J. B., & Uhing, B. M. (2005). A review of self-management interventions targeting academic outcomes for students with emotional and behavioral disorders. *Journal of Behavioral Education, 14*, 203–221.

eType. (2012). eType [Computer software]. Retrieved from http://www.etype.com/

Evmenova, A. S., Graff, H. J., Jerome, M. K., & Behrmann, M. M. (2010). Word prediction programs with phonetic spelling support: Performance comparison and impact on journal writing for students with writing difficulties. *Learning Disabilities Research & Practice, 25*, 170–182.

Fager, S., Bardach, L., Russell, S., & Higginbotham, J. (2012). Access to augmentative and alternative communication: New technologies and clinical decision-making. *Journal of Pediatric Rehabilitation Medicine: An Interdisciplinary Approach, 5*, 53–61. doi:10.3233/PRM-2012-0196

Falcon in Motion LLC. (2014). Magnifying glass with light—digital magnifier with flashlight. Retrieved from https://itunes.apple.com/us/app/magnifying-glass-light-digital/id406048120?mt=8

Federal Communications Commission. (2014). *Closed captioning on television.* Retrieved from http://www.fcc.gov/guides/closed-captioning

Fedewa, A. L., & Erwin, H. E. (2011). Stability balls and students with attention and hyperactivity concerns: Implications for on-task and in-seat behavior. *American Journal of Occupational Therapy, 65*, 393–399. doi:10.5014/ajot.2011.0000554

Feil-Seifer, D., & Matarić, M. J. (2011). Automated detection and classification of positive vs. negative robot interactions with children with autism using distance-based features. *Proceedings of the International Conference on Human–Robot Interaction.* Retrieved from http://robotics.usc.edu/publications/media/uploads/pubs/697.pdf

Fentek. (2014). *Computer keyboard keyguard.* Retrieved from http://www.fentek-ind.com/Keyguard.htm#.VHOSZPTF-1Q

Ferrell, K. A., Bruce, S., & Luckner, J. L. (2014). *Evidence-based practices for students with sensory impairments* (CEEDAR Document No. IC-4). Retrieved from http://ceedar.education.ufl.edu/wp-content/uploads/2014/09/IC-4_FINAL_03-30-15.pdf

Fichten, C. S., Asuncion, J., & Scapin, R. (2014). Digital technology, learning, and postsecondary students with disabilities: Where we've been and where we're going. *Journal of Postsecondary Education and Disability,* 369–379.

Flores, M., Musgrove, K., Renner, S., Hinton, V., Strozier, S., Franklin. S., & Hil, D. (2012). A comparison of communication using the Apple iPad and a picture-based system. *Augmentative and Alternative Communication, 28*, 74–84. doi:10.310907434618.2011.644579

Flower, L., & Hayes, J. (1981). A cognitive process theory of writing. *College Composition and Communication, 32*(4), 365–387.

Flowers, C., Kim, D.-H., Lewis, P., & Davis, V. C. (2011). A comparison of computer-based testing and pencil-and-paper testing for students with a read-aloud accommodation. *Journal of Special Education Technology, 26*(1), 1–12.

Floyd, K. K., & Judge, S. L. (2012). The efficacy of assistive technology on reading comprehension for postsecondary students with learning disabilities. *Assistive Technology Outcomes and Benefits, 8*(1), 48–64.

Fonner, K., & Marfilius, S. (2011). Sorting through AAC apps. Retrieved from http://sccatn.wikispaces.com/file/view/Sorting_AAC_aaps_OCT302011.pdf/289328579/Sorting_AAC_aaps_OCT302011.pdf

Franzone, E., & Collet-Klingenberg, L. (2008). *Overview of video modeling.* Madison: National Professional Development Center on Autism Spectrum Disorders, Waisman Center, University of Wisconsin.

Freedom Scientific. (2015). *Focus Blue family of products.* Retrieved from http://www.freedomscientific.com/Products/Blindness/FocusBlueBrailleDisplays

Fulk, B. M., Watts, E., & Bakken, J. P. (2011). The history of physical and health impairments. In A. F. Rotatori, F. E. Okiakor, & J. P. Bakken (Eds.), *History of special education* (pp. 269–288). Bingley, U.K.: Emerald. doi:10.1108/S0270-4013(2011)0000021014

Fulton, K. P. (2014). *Time for learning: Top 10 reasons why flipping the classroom can change education.* Thousand Oaks, CA: Corwin.

Gable, R. A., Tonelson, S. W., Sheth, M., Wilson, C., & Park, K. L. (2012). Importance, usage, and preparedness to implement evidence-based practices for students with emotional disabilities: A comparison of knowledge and skills of special education and general education teachers. *Education and Treatment of Children, 35*(4), 499–519.

Ganz, J. B. (2014). *Aided augmentative communication for individuals with autism spectrum disorders.* New York, NY: Springer.

Ganz, J. B., Davis, J. L., Lund, E. M., Goodwyn, F. D., & Simpson, R. L. (2012). Meta-analysis of PECS with individuals with ASD: Investigation of targeted versus non-targeted outcomes, participant characteristics, and implementation phase. *Research in Developmental Disabilities, 33,* 406–418. doi:10.1016/j.ridd.2011.09.023

Ganz, J. B., Hong, E. R., & Goodwyn, F. D. (2013). Effectiveness of the PECS Phase II app and choice between the app and traditional PECS among preschoolers with ASD. *Research in Autism Spectrum Disorders, 7,* 973–983.

Gargiulo, R. M. (2015). *Special education in contemporary society: An introduction to exceptionality* (5th ed.). Thousand Oaks, CA: SAGE.

Gentry, T., Kriner, R., Sima, A., McDonough, J., & Wehman, P. (2015). Reducing the need for personal supports among workers with autism using an iPod Touch as an assistive technology: Delayed randomized control trial. *Journal of Autism and Developmental Disabilities, 45,* 669–684. doi:10.1007/s10803-014-2221-8

Gevarter, C., O'Reilly, M. F., Rojeski, L., Sammarco, N., Sigafoos, J., Lancioni, G., & Lang, R. (2014). Comparing acquisition of AAC-based mands in three young children with autism spectrum disorder using iPad® applications with different display and design elements. *Journal of Autism and Developmental Disorders, 44,* 2464–2474. doi:10.1007/s10803-014-2115-9

gh. (2006). *Welcome to the MathSpeak™ initiative.* Retrieved from http://www.gh-MathSpeak.com/

Gierach, J. (Ed.). (2009). *Assessing students' needs for assistive technology (ASNAT): A resource manual for school district teams* (5th ed.). Milton: Wisconsin Assistive Technology Initiative. Retrieved from http://www.wati.org/?pageLoad=content/supports/free/index.php

Gierach, J., & Stindt, K. (2009). Assistive technology for activities of daily living. In J. Gierach (Ed.), *Assessing students' needs for assistive technology (ASNAT): A resource manual for school district teams* (5th ed.). Retrieved from http://wati.org/content/supports/free/pdf/Ch11-ActivitiesDailyLiving.pdf

Ginger Software. (n.d.). Ginger [Computer software] Retrieved from http://www.gingersoftware.com/

Glassy, D., Romano, J., & the Committee on Early Childhood, Adoption, and Dependent Care. (2003). Selecting appropriate toys for young children: The pediatrician's role. *Pediatrics, 111,* 911–913.

Glennen, S. L. (1997). Introduction to augmentative and alternative communication. In S. L. Glennen & D. C. De Coste (Eds.), *Handbook of augmentative and alternative communication* (pp. 3–20). San Diego, CA: Singular Publishing Group.

Glickman, L. B., Geigle, P. R., & Paleg, G. S. (2010). A systematic review of supported standing programs. *Journal of Pediatric Rehabilitation Medicine, 3*(3), 197–213. doi:10.3233/PRM-2010-0129

Goldrick, M., Stevns, T., & Christensen, L. B. (2014). The use of assistive technologies as learning technologies to facilitate flexible learning in higher education. In K. Miesenberg, D. Fels, D. Archambault, P. Peňáz, & W. Zagler (Eds.), *Computers helping people with special needs: 14th international conference, ICCHP 2014, Paris, France, July 9–11, 2014, proceedings, part 2* (pp. 342–349). Cham, Switzerland: Springer International Publishing.

Golinker, L. (2009). Speech generating device funding. *Exceptional Parent Magazine.* Retrieved from http://aac-rerc.psu.edu/index.php/webcasts/show/id/16

Golinker, L. (2011). *Public school students: Who can pay for SGDs?* AAC-RERC Webcast Series. Retrieved from http://aac-rerc.psu.edu/index.php/webcasts/show/id/16

Google. (2015). Android accessibility features. Retrieved from https://support.google.com/accessibility/android/answer/6006564?hl=en&ref_topic=6007234

goQ. (2011). wordQ+speakQ [Computer software]. Retrieved from http://www.goqsoftware.com/products/

Gosnell, J. (2011, October 11). Apps: An emerging tool for SLPs. *The ASHA Leader, 16*, 10–13. Retrieved from http://leader.pubs.asha.org/article.aspx?articleid=2280066

Gray, C. A., & Garand, J. D. (1993). Social stories: Improving responses of students with autism with accurate social information. *Focus on Autistic Behavior, 8*, 1–10.

Green, J. (2014). *Assistive technology in special education: Resources for education, intervention, and rehabilitation* (2nd ed.). Waco, TX: Prufrock Press.

Greer, D., Rowland, A. L., & Smith, S. J. (2014). Critical considerations for teaching students with disabilities in online environments. *Teaching Exceptional Children, 46*(5), 79–91. doi:10.1177/0040059914528105

Gregg, N. (2009). *Assessment and accommodation of adolescents and adults with LD and ADHD*. New York, NY: Guilford.

Gregg, N. (2012). Increasing access to learning for the adult basic education learner with learning disabilities: Evidence-based accommodation research. *Journal of Learning Disabilities, 45*(1), 47–63. doi:10.1177/0022219411426855

Grunwald Associates. (2013). Living and learning with mobile devices: What parents think about mobile devices for early childhood and K–12 learning. Retrieved from http://www.snow.idrc.ocad.ca/content/voice-recognition-speech-text-software

Guerette, P., Furumasu, J., & Tefft, D. (2013). The positive effects of early powered mobility on children's psychosocial and play skills. *Assistive Technology, 25*(1), 39–48. doi:10.1080/10400435.2012.685834

Hanline, M. F., Nunes, D., & Worthy, M. B. (2007). Augmentative and alternative communication in the early childhood years. *Beyond the Journal: Young Children on the Web*, 1–6. Retrieved from https://www.naeyc.org/files/yc/file/200707/BTJHanline.pdf

Hashey, A. I., & Stahl, S. (2014). Making online learning accessible for students with disabilities. *TEACHING Exceptional Children, 46*(5), 70–78. doi:10.1177/0040059914528329

Hattie, J., Rogers, H. J., & Swaminathan, H. (2010). The role of meta-analysis in educational research. In A. Reid, P. Hart, & C. Russell (Eds.), *A companion to research in education* (pp. 197–207). Bath, UK: Springer.

Heckendorf, S. (2009). Assistive technology for individuals who are deaf or hard of hearing. In J. Gierach (Ed.), *Assessing students' needs for assistive technology (ASNAT): A resource manual for school district teams* (5th ed.). Retrieved from http://wati.org/content/supports/free/pdf/Ch13-Hearing.pdf

Heiman, T., & Shemesh, D. O. (2012). Students with learning disabilities in higher education: Use and contribution of assistive technology and website courses and their correlation to students' hope and well-being. *Journal of Learning Disabilities, 45*(4), 308–318. doi:10.1177/0022219410392047

Herold, B. (2014, November 11). Chromebooks gaining popularity in school districts. *EdWeek*. Retrieved from http://www.edweek.org/ew/articles/2014/11/12/12chromebooks.h34.html

Herrick, K. A., Fakhouri, T. H. I., Carlson, S. A., & Fulton, J. E. (2014). TV watching and computer use in U.S. youth aged 12–15, 2012. *NCHS Data Brief 157*. Retrieved from http://www.cdc.gov/nchs/data/databriefs/db157.pdf

Higgins, E., & Raskind, M. (2005). The compensatory effectiveness of the Quicktionary Reading Pen II on the reading comprehension of students with learning disabilities. *Journal of Special Education Technology, 20*(1), 31–40.

Hitchcock, C., Meyer, A., Rose, D., & Jackson, R. (2002). Providing new access to the general curriculum: Universal Design for Learning. *Teaching Exceptional Children, 35*(2), 8–17.

Hoffman, C. (2014, December 5). Why Chromebooks are schooling iPads in education. *PC World*. Retrieved from http://www.pcworld.com/article/2855768/why-chromebooks-are-schooling-ipads-in-education.html

Holland Bloorview Kids Rehabilitation Hospital. (2010). WiViK. Retrieved from http://research.hollandbloorview.ca/Innovations/WiViKOnscreenKeyboardSoftware

Homa, D., & DeLambo, D. (2015). Vocational assessment and job placement. In R. Escorpizo, S. Brage, D. Homa, & G. Stucki (Eds.), *Handbook of vocational rehabilitation and disability evaluation: Application and implementation of the ICF* (pp. 161–186). New York, NY: Springer.

Hoover, J. J., & Patton, P. R. (1995). *Teaching students with learning problems to use study skills: A teacher's guide*. Austin, TX: PRO-ED.

Huang, H., & Galloway, C. (2012). Modified ride-on toy cars for early power mobility: A technical report. *Pediatric Physical Therapy, 24*, 149–154. Retrieved from http://www.ncbi.nlm.nih.gov/pmc/articles/PMC3324847/

Hustad, K., Berg, A., Bauer, D., Keppner, K., Schanz, A., & Gamradt, J. (2005). *AAC interventions for toddlers and preschoolers: Who, what, when, why*. Miniseminar presented at the annual convention of the American Speech Language Hearing Association, San Diego, CA.

Individuals with Disabilities Education Act Amendments of 1997, Pub. L. No. 105-17, 111 Stat. 37 (1997).

Individuals with Disabilities Education Act, 20 U.S.C. § 1400 et seq. (1990).

Individuals with Disabilities Education Improvement Act of 2004, Pub. L. No. 108-446, 150 Stat. 118 (2004).

Ingeno, L. (2013, June 24). Online accessibility a faculty duty. *Inside Higher Ed*. Retrieved from https://www.insidehighered.com/news/2013/06/24/faculty-responsible-making-online-materials-accessible-disabled-students

Inspiration Software. (2012). Kidspiration (Version 3.0) [Computer software]. Retrieved from http://www.inspiration.com/Kidspiration

Institute for Human & Machine Cognition. (n.d.). CmapTools (Version 5.05.0) [Computer software]. Retrieved from http://cmap.ihmc.us/

Jeffs, T., Reed, P., & Warger, C. (2007). *Assistive technology considerations for academic success* [TAM technology fan]. Arlington, VA: Technology and Media Division of the Council for Exceptional Children.

Johnson, C. D., & Seaton, J. B. (2011). *Educational audiology handbook* (2nd ed.). Clifton Park, NY: Cengage Learning.

Johnson, L., Beard, L., & Carpenter, L. (2007). *Assistive technology: Access for all students*. Upper Saddle River, NJ: Pearson Education.

Jones, M. A., McEwen, I. R., & Neas, B. R. (2012). Effects of power wheelchairs on the development and function of young children with severe motor impairments. *Pediatric Physical Therapy, 24*(2), 131–140. doi:10.1097/PEP.0b013e1824c5fdc

Jones, V. L., & Hinesman-Matthews, L. J. (2014). Effective assistive technology considerations and implications for diverse students. *Computers in the Schools, 31*(3), 220–232. doi:10.1080/07380569.2014.932682

Jordan, L., Miller, M. D., & Mercer, C. D. (1998). The effects of concrete to semiconcrete to abstract instruction in the acquisition and retention of fraction concepts and skills. *Learning Disabilities: A Multidisciplinary Journal, 9*(3), 115–122.

Judge, S., Floyd, K., & Jeffs, T. (2015). Using mobile media devices and apps to promote young children's learning. In K. L. Heider & M. R. Jalongo (Eds.), *Young children and families in the information age* (pp. 117–131). New York, NY: Springer.

Kagohara, D. M., Sigafoos, J., Achmadi, D., O'Reilly, M. F., & Lancioni, G. (2012). Teaching children with autism spectrum disorders to check the spelling of words. *Research in Autism Spectrum Disorders, 6*, 304–310.

Kagohara, D. M., van der Meer, L., Ramdoss, S., O'Reilly, M. F., Lancioni, G. E., Davis, T. N., . . . Sigafoos, J. (2013). Using iPods® and iPads® in teaching programs for individuals with developmental disabilities: A systematic review. *Research in Developmental Disabilities, 34*, 147–156. doi:10.1016/j.ridd.2012.07.027

Kamei-Hannan, C., & Lawson, H. (2012). Impact of a Braille Note on writing: Evaluating the process, quality, and attitudes of three students who are visually impaired. *Journal of Special Education Technology, 27*(3), 1–14.

Kander, M. (2013). Bottom line: Will payers cover speech-generating apps? *The ASHA Leader, 18*, 24–25. doi:10.1044/leader.BML.18012013.24

Kander, M., & Satterfield, L. (2014, May). Changes ahead for speech-generating device reimbursement. *The ASHA Leader, 19*, 26–27. doi:10.1044/leader.BML.19052014.26.

Karp, G. (2008). *Life on wheels: The a to z guide to living fully with mobility issues.* New York, NY: Demos Medical Publishing.

Kassardjian, A., Leaf, J. B., Ravid, D., Leaf, J. A., Alcalay, A., Dale, S., . . . Oppenheim-Leaf, M. L. (2014). Comparing the teaching interaction procedure to social stories: A replication study. *Journal of Autism and Developmental Disabilities, 44*, 2329–2340. doi:10.1007/s10803-014-2103-0

Kelly, J., Kratcoski, A., & McClain, K. (2006). The effects of word processing software on the writing of students with special needs. *Journal of the Research Center for Educational Technology, 2*, 32–43.

Kinsell, C. (2014). Technology and disability laws, regulations, and rights. In B. DaCosta & S. Seok (Eds.), *Assistive technology research, practice, and theory* (pp. 75–89). Hershey, PA: IGI Global.

Kitchel, J. E. (n.d.). APH guidelines for print document design. Retrieved from http://www.aph.org/edresearch/lpguide.htm

Knight, V. F., & Sartini, E. (2014). A comprehensive literature review of comprehension strategies in core content areas for students with autism spectrum disorder. *Journal of Autism and Developmental Disorders, 45*, 1213–1229. doi:10.1007/s10803-014-2280-x

Knight, V., Sartini, E., & Spriggs, A. D. (2015). Evaluating visual activity schedules as evidence-based practice for individuals with autism spectrum disorder. *Journal of Autism and Developmental Disabilities, 45*, 157–178. doi:10.1007/s10803-014-2201-z

Koehler, L. J. S. (2011). Assistive technology for daily living. In O. Wendt, R. W. Quist, & L. L. Lloyd (Eds.), *Assistive technology: Principles and applications for communication disorders and special education* (pp. 447–478). Bingley, U.K.: Emerald.

Koehler, M. J., & Mishra, P. (2009). What is technological pedagogical content knowledge? *Contemporary Issues in Technology and Teacher Education, 9*(1), 60–70.

Korat, O., & Shamir, A. (2007). Electronic books versus adult readers: Effects on children's emergent literacy as a function of social class. *Journal of Computer Assisted Learning, 23*(3), 248–259. doi:10.1111/j.1365-2729.2006.00213.x

Krueger, L. J., & Sullivan Coleman, M. J. (2010). Let's stand together: Standing programs for children with disabilities are part of the natural routine at Normandy Park Preschool. *ADVANCE for Physical Therapy & Rehab Medicine, 21*(8), 28–29. Retrieved from http://physical-therapy.advanceweb.com/Archives/Article-Archives/Lets-Stand-Together.aspx

Kurzweil Education. (n.d.). Subscription: Kurzweil 3000-firefly. Retrieved from http://www.kurzweiledu.com/products/k3000-benefits-subscription.html

Kurzweil Technologies. (2015). Kurzweil computer products. Retrieved from http://www.kurzweiltech.com/kcp.html

LaLonde, K. B., MacNeill, B. R., Eversole, L. W., Ragotzy, S. P., & Poling, A. (2014). Increasing physical activity in young adults with autism spectrum disorders. *Research in Autism Spectrum Disorders, 8*(12), 1679–1684. doi:10.1016/j.rasd.2014.09.001

Lancioni, G. E., Sigafoos, J., O'Reilly, M. F., & Singh, N. N. (2013). *Assistive technology: Interventions for individuals with severe/profound and multiple disabilities.* New York, NY: Springer.

Lancoini, G. E., Singh, N. N., O'Reilly, M. F., Sigafoos, J., Oliva, D., & Campodonico, F. (2013). Walker devices and microswitch technology to enhance assisted indoor ambulation by persons with multiple disabilities: Three single case studies. *Research in Developmental Disabilities, 34,* 2191–2194. doi:10.1016/j.ridd.2013.03.025

Lane, S. J., & Mistrett, S. G. (2002). Let's play! Assistive technology intervention for play. *Young Exceptional Children, 5*(2), 19–27.

Lang, R., O'Reilly, M., Healy, O., Rispoli, M., Lydon, H., Streusand, W., . . . Giesbers, S. (2012). Sensory integration therapy for autism spectrum disorders: A systematic review. *Research in Autism Spectrum Disorders, 6,* 1004–1018. doi:10.1016/j. rasd.2012.01.006

Lang, R., Ramdoss, S., Sigafoos, J., Green, V. A., van der Meer, L., Tostanoski, A., . . . O'Reilly, M. F. (2014). Assistive technology for postsecondary students with disabilities. In G. E. Lancioni & N. N. Singh (Eds.), *Assistive technologies for people with diverse abilities* (pp. 53–76). New York, NY: Springer. doi:10.1007/978-1-4899-8029-8_3

Langton, A. J., & Ramseur, H. (2001). Enhancing employment outcomes through job accommodation and assistive technology resources and services. *Journal of Vocational Rehabilitation, 16,* 27–37.

Lee, M. K., Wells, C. S., & Sireci, S. G. (2010). A comparison of linear and nonlinear factor analysis in examining the effect of a calculator accommodation on math performance [Paper 10]. *NERA Conference Proceedings 2010.* Retrieved from http://digitalcommons.uconn.edu/nera_2010/10

Lee, Y., Wehmeyer, M. L., Palmer, S. B., Williams-Diehm, K., Davies, D. K., & Stock, S. E. (2011). The effect of student-directed transition planning with a computer-based reading support program on the self-determination of students with disabilities. *The Journal of Special Education, 45*(2), 104–117. doi:10.1177/0022466909358916

Leong, H. M., Carter, M., & Stephenson, J. R. (2014). Meta-analysis of research on sensory integration therapy for individuals with developmental and learning disabilities [Advanced online publication]. *Journal of Developmental and Physical Disabilities.* doi:10.1007/s10882-14-9408-y

Leseman, P., & de Jong, P. (1998). Home literacy: Opportunity, instruction, cooperation and social-emotional quality predicting early reading achievement. *Reading Research Quarterly, 33*(3), 296–318.

Let's Play! Project. (n.d.). *Special toys: Switch toys: Where to begin.* Retrieved from http://letsplay.buffalo.edu/products/letsplaysheets/Switch.pdf?products/letsplaysheets/Switch-comp.pdf

Lewis, P. H. (1988, August 7). Ex machina; the computer revolution revised. *The New York Times.* Retrieved from http://www.nytimes.com/1988/08/07/education/ex-machina-the-computer-revolution-revised.html

Liang, P., & Johnson, J. (1999). Using technology to enhance early literacy through play. *Computers in the Schools, 15*(1), 55–64. doi:10.1300/J025v15n01_09

Light, J., & McNaughton, D. (2012a). Supporting the communication, language, and literacy development of children with complex communication needs: State of the science and future research priorities. *Assistive Technology, 24,* 34–44. doi:10.1080/10400435.2011.648717

Light, J., & McNaughton, D. (2012b). The changing face of augmentative and alternative communication: Past, present, and future challenges. *Augmentative and Alternative Communication, 28,* 197–204.

Light, J., & McNaughton, D. (2013). Putting people first: Re-thinking the role of technology in augmentative and alternative communication intervention. *Augmentative and Alternative Communication, 29*, 299–309. doi: 10.3109/07434618.2013.848935

Lindstrom, L., Kahn, L. G., & Lindsey, H. (2013). Navigating the early career years: Barriers and strategies for young adults with disabilities. *Journal of Vocational Rehabilitation, 39*(1), 1–12. doi:10.3233/JVR-130637

Lipkin, P., & Schertz, M. (2008). Early intervention and its efficacy. In P. Accardo (Ed.), *Capute & Accardo's neurodevelopmental disabilities in infancy and childhood* (3rd ed., vol. 1) (pp. 519–551). Baltimore, MD: Paul H. Brookes.

Loeding, B. L. (2011). Assistive technology for visual and dual-sensory impairments. In O. Wendt, R. W. Quist, & L. L. Lloyd (Eds.), *Assistive technology: Principles and applications for communication disorders and special education* (pp. 367–412). Bingley, U.K.: Emerald.

Lorah, E. R., Tincani, M., Dodge, J., Gilroy, S., Hickey, A., & Hantula, D. (2013). Evaluating picture exchange and the iPad™ as a speech generating device to teach communication to young children with autism. *Journal of Developmental and Physical Disabilities, 25*, 637–649. doi:10.1007/210882-013-9337-1

Low, S. A., Westcott, S., Beling, J., & Adams, J. (2011). Pediatrics physical therapists' use of support walkers for children with disabilities: A nationwide survey. *Pediatrics Physical Therapy, 23*(4), 381–389. doi:10.1097/PEP.0b012e318235257c

Lusk, K. E. (2012). The effects of various mounting systems of near magnification on reading performance and preferences in school-aged students with low vision. *British Journal of Visual Impairment, 30*, 168–181.

MacArthur, C. (2009). Reflections on research on writing and technology for struggling writers. *Learning Disabilities Research and Practice, 24*(2), 93–103.

Maccini, P., & Gagnon, J. (2000). Best practices for teaching mathematics to secondary students with

special needs. *Focus on Exceptional Children, 32*(5), 1–22.

Maccini, P., & Gagnon, J. (2006). Mathematics instructional practice and assessment accommodations by secondary special and general educators. *Exceptional Children, 72*(2), 217–234.

Maccini, P., & Hughes, C. (2000). Effects of a problem solving strategy on the introductory algebra performance of secondary students with learning disabilities. *Learning Disabilities Research & Practice, 15*(1), 10–21.

Maccini, P., & Ruhl, K. (2000). Effects of graduated instruction sequence on the algebraic subtraction of integers by secondary students with learning disabilities. *Education and Treatment of Children, 23*(4), 465–489.

Madden, M., Lenhart, A., Duggan, M., Cortesi, S., & Gasser, W. (2013). *Teens and technology 2012.* Washington, DC: Pew Research Center. Retrieved from http://www.pewinternet.org/Reports/2013/Teens-and-Tech.aspx

Madraso, J. (1993). Proofreading: The skill we've neglected to teach. *English Journal, 82*, 32–41.

Maggin, D. M., Briesch, A. M., & Chafouleas, S. M. (2013). An application of the What Works Clearinghouse standards for evaluating single-subject research: Synthesis of the self-management literature base. *Remedial and Special Education, 34*(1), 44–58. doi:10.1177/0741932511435176

Mao, T. (2014). Dvorak. Retrieved from https://itunes.apple.com/us/app/dvorak/id920692622?mt=8

Mariage, T., & Bouck, E. (2004). Scaffolding literacy learning for students with mild needs. In A. Rodgers & E. Rodgers (Eds.), *Scaffolding literacy instruction: Strategies for K–4 classrooms* (pp. 36–74). Portsmouth, NH: Heinemann.

Mariage, T., Englert, C., & Garmon, M. (2000). The teacher as 'more knowledgeable other' in assisting literacy learning with special needs students. *Reading and Writing Quarterly, 16*(4), 299–336.

Marino, M., Marino, E., & Shaw, S. (2006). Making informed assistive technology decisions for students with high incidence disabilities. *Teaching Exceptional Children, 38*(6), 18–25.

Mason, L., Harris, K., & Graham, S. (2011). Self-regulated strategy development for students with writing difficulties. *Theory Into Practice, 50*(1), 20–27.

May-Benson, T. A., & Schaaf, R. (2015). Ayres Sensory Integration® intervention. In I. Söderback (Ed.), *International handbook of occupational therapy interventions* (pp. 633–646). New York, NY: Springer. doi:10.1007/978-3-319-08141-1_44

Mayer-Johnson. (2014). What is Boardmaker? Retrieved from http://www.mayer-johnson.com/what-is-boardmaker/

McBride, D. (2014). *AAC apps/device features to consider* [Personal communication].

McDonough, J. T., & Revell G. (2010). Accessing employment supports in the adult system for transitioning youth with autism spectrum disorders. *Journal of Vocational Rehabilitation, 32,* 89–100. doi:10.3233/JVR-2010-0498

McDougall, D., Morrison, C., & Awana, B. (2011). Students with disabilities use tactile cued self-monitoring to improve academic productivity during independent tasks. *Journal of Instructional Psychology, 39*(2), 119–130.

McGregor, G., & Pachuski, P. (1996). Assistive technology in schools: Are teachers ready, able, and supported? *Journal of Special Education Technology, 13,* 4–15.

McNaughton, D., & Light, J. (2013). The iPad and mobile technology revolution: Benefits and challenges for individuals who require augmentative and alternative communication. *Augmentative and Alternative Communication, 29,* 107–116. doi:10.310907434618.2013.784930

Mechling, L. C. (2007). Assistive technology as a self-management tool for prompting students with intellectual disabilities to initiate and complete daily tasks: A literature review. *Education and Training in Developmental Disabilities, 42*(3), 252–269.

Mechling, L. C., Ayres, K. M., Foster, A. L., & Bryant, K. J. (2013). Comparing the effects of commercially available and custom-made video prompting for teaching cooking skills to high school students with autism. *Remedial and Special Education, 34*(6), 371–383. doi:10.1177/0741932513494856

Melichar, J. F., & Blackhurst, A. E. (1993). *Introduction to a functional approach to assistive technology* [Training module]. Lexington, KY: Department of Special Education and Rehabilitation Counseling, University of Kentucky.

Mendelsohn, A. L., Berkule, S. B., Tomopoulos, S., Tamis-LeMonda, C. S., Huberman, H. S., Alvir, J., & Dreyer, B. P. (2008). Infant television and video exposure associated with limited parent–child verbal interactions in low socioeconomic status households. *Archives of Pediatrics & Adolescent Medicine, 162*(5), 411–417.

Merritt, J. M. (2014). Alternative seating for young children: Effects on learning. *American International Journal of Contemporary Research, 4*(1), 12–18.

Messinger-Willman, J., & Marino, M. T. (2010). Universal Design for Learning and assistive technology: Leadership considerations for promoting inclusive education in today's secondary schools. *NASSP Bulletin, 94,* 5–16. doi: 10.1177/0192636510371977

Meyer, N. K., & Bouck, E. C. (2014). The impact of text-to-speech on expository reading for adolescent students with LD. *Journal of Special Education Technology, 29*(1), 21–33.

Microsoft Windows. (2012). Windows Speech Recognition [Computer software]. Retrieved from http://windows.microsoft.com/en-US/windows7/Set-up-Speech-Recognition

Microsoft. (2014). Keyboard shortcuts. Retrieved from http://windows.microsoft.com/en-us/windows/keyboard-shortcuts#keyboard-shortcuts=windows-8

Microsoft. (2015). Accessibility in Windows 8. Retrieved from http://www.microsoft.com/enable/products/windows8

Millar, D. C., Light, J. C., & Schlosser, R. W. (2006). The impact of augmentative and alternative communication intervention on the speech production of individuals with developmental disabilities: A research review. *Journal of Speech, Language, and Hearing Research, 49,* 248–264.

Miller, E. B., & Warschauer, M. (2014). Young children and e-reading: Research to date and questions for the future. *Learning, Media, and Technology, 39*(3), 283–305. doi:10.1080/17439884.2013.867868

Minkel, J. (2011). *A guide to wheelchair selection.* Retrieved from http://www.spinalcord.org/resource-center/askus/index.php?pg=kb.page&id=1412

Minnesota Department of Human Services. (2012). *Assistive technology and independent living aids.* Retrieved from http://www.dhs.state.mn.us/main/idcplg?IdcService=GET_DYNAMIC_CONVERSION&dID=137260

Mishra, P., & Koehler, M. (2009). Too cool for school? No way! Using the TPACK framework: You can have your hot tools and teach with them, too. *Learning & Leading with Technology, 36*(7), 14–18.

Mishra, P., & the Deep-Play Research Group. (2012). Rethinking technology & creativity in the 21st century: Crayons are the future. *Tech Trends, 56*(5), 13–16.

Mistrett, S. (2004). Assistive technology helps young children with disabilities participate in daily activities. *Technology in Action, 1*(4), 1–8.

Mistrett, S. M., Lane, S. L., & Ruffino, A. (2005). Growing and learning through technology: Birth to five. In D. Edyburn, K. Higgins, & R. Boone (Eds.), *The handbook of special education technology research and practice* (pp. 273–307). Whitefish Bay, WI: Knowledge by Design.

Mistrett, S., Ruffino, A., Lane, S., Robinson, L., Reed, P., & Milbourne, S. (2006). *Technology supports for young children* [TAM technology fan]. Arlington, VA: Technology and Media Division of the Council for Exceptional Children.

Moore, D. W., Anderson, A., Glassenbury, M., Lang, R., & Didden, R. (2013). Increasing on-task behavior in students in a regular classroom: Effectiveness of a self-management procedure using a tactile prompt. *Journal of Behavioral Education, 22,* 203–311. doi:10.1007/s10864-013-9180-6

More, C. M., & Travers, J. C. (2013). What's app with that? Selecting educational apps for young children with disabilities. *Young Exceptional Children, 16*(2), 15–32.

Morin, A. (2014). *Understanding executive functioning issues.* Retrieved from https://www.understood.org/en/learning-attention-issues/child-learning-disabilities/executive-functioning-issues/understanding-executive-functioning-issues

Morris, J., & Mueller, J. (2014). Blind and deaf consumer preferences for Android and iOS smartphones. In P. M. Langdon, J. Lazar, A. Heylighen, & H. Dong (Eds.), *Inclusive designing: Joining usability, accessibility, and inclusion* (pp. 69–81). New York, NY: Springer. doi:10.1007/978-3-319-05095-9_7

MOVE International. (n.d.). *How does mobility help?* Retrieved from http://www.move-international.org/stories/storyReader$62

Mulloy, A. M., Gevarter, C., Hopkins, M., Sutherland, K. S., & Ramdoss, S. T. (2014). Assistive technology for students with visual impairments and blindness. In G. E. Lancioni & N. N. Singh (Eds.), *Assistive technologies for people with diverse abilities* (pp. 113–156). New York, NY: Springer. doi:10.1007/978-1-4899-8029-8_5

Nankee, C., Stindt, K., & Lees, P. (2009). Assistive technology for writing, including motor aspects of writing and composing. In J. Gierach (Ed.), *Assessing students' needs for assistive technology (ASNAT): A resource manual for school district teams* (5th ed.). Retrieved from http://wati.org/content/supports/free/pdf/Ch5-WritingMotorAspects.pdf

National Assistive Technology Research Institute. (2001). *What is assistive technology?* Retrieved from http://natri.uky.edu/resources/fundamentals/defined.html

National Assistive Technology Research Institute. (2006). *Assistive technology planner: From IEP consideration to classroom implementation*. Arlington, VA: Technology and Media Division of the Council for Exceptional Children.

National Association for the Education of Young Children and the Fred Rogers Center for Early Learning and Children's Media. (2012). *Technology and interactive media as tools in early childhood programs serving children from birth through age 8*. Retrieved from http://www.naeyc.org/files/naeyc/file/positions/PS_technology_WEB2.pdf

National Association of Special Education Teachers. (2014). IEP goals & objectives with Common Core State Standards [Mobile application software]. Retrieved from https://itunes.apple.com/us/app/iep-goals-objectives-common/id570070557?mt=8

National Association of the Deaf. (2000). *NAD position statement on cochlear implants*. Retrieved from http://nad.org/issues/technology/assistive-listening/cochlear-implants

National Association of the Deaf. (n.d.). *American Sign Language*. Retrieved from http://nad.org/issues/american-sign-language

National Center for Education Statistics. (2011a). *The nation's report card: Mathematics 2011*. Washington, D.C.: U.S. Department of Education.

National Center for Education Statistics. (2011b). *The nation's report card: Reading 2011*. Washington, D.C.: U.S. Department of Education.

National Center for Education Statistics. (2011c). *The nation's report card: Writing 2011*. Washington, D.C.: U.S. Department of Education.

National Center for Education Statistics. (2013). Digest of education statistics 2012. Retrieved from http://nces.ed.gov/programs/digest/d12/

National Center on Accessible Instructional Materials. (2011). *What is the National Instructional Materials Accessibility Standard (NIMAS)?* Retrieved from http://aim.cast.org/learn/policy/federal/what_is_nimas

National Center on Accessible Instructional Materials. (2014). *All about AIM*. Retrieved from http://aim.cast.org/learn/accessiblemedia/allaboutaim

National Center on Universal Design for Learning. (2012). *UDL guidelines—version 2.0: Examples and resources*. Retrieved from http://www.udlcenter.org/implementation/examples/examples2_5

National Commission on Writing for America's Families, Schools, and Colleges. (2005). *Writing: A powerful message from state government*. Retrieved from http://www.nwp.oeg/cs/public/print/resource/2541

National Consortium on Deaf-Blindness. (2007). *Children who are deaf-blind*. Retrieved from http://documents.nationaldb.org/products/population.pdf

National Council of Teachers of Mathematics. (2000). *Principles and NCTM standards for school mathematics*. Reston, VA: Author.

National Dissemination Center for Children with Disabilities. (2012). *Categories of disability under IDEA*. Retrieved September 16, 2014, from http://www.parentcenterhub.org/wp-content/uploads/repo_items/gr3.pdf

National Federation of the Blind. (2009). *The braille literacy crisis in America: Facing the truth, reversing the trend, empowering the blind*. Retrieved from https://nfb.org/images/nfb/documents/pdf/braille_literacy_report_web.pdf

National Federation of the Blind. (2014). *Make Kindle e-books accessible*. Retrieved from https://nfb.org/kindle-books

National Institute on Deafness and Other Communication Disorders. (2011). *NIDCD fact sheet: Assistive devices for people with hearing, voice, speech, or language disorders*. Retrieved from http://www.nidcd

.nih.gov/staticresources/health/hearing/NIDCD-Assistive-Devices-FS.pdf

National Institute on Deafness and Other *Communication Disorders*. (2014a). *American Sign Language*. Retrieved from http://www.nidcd.nih.gov/health/hearing/pages/asl.aspx

National Institute on Deafness and Other Communication Disorders. (2014b). Cochlear implants. Retrieved from http://www.nidcd.nih.gov/health/hearing/pages/coch.aspx

National Joint Committee for the Communicative Needs of Persons with Severe Disabilities. (1992). Guidelines for meeting the communication needs of persons with severe disabilities. *Asha*, 34(Suppl. 7), 2–3.

National Reading Panel. (2000). *Teaching children to read: An evidence-based assessment of the scientific research literature on reading and its implications for reading instruction: Report of the subgroups*. Bethesda, MD: Author.

Nazzaro, J. (1977). *Exceptional timetables: Historic events affecting the handicapped and gifted*. Reston, VA: The Council for Exceptional Children.

Newbutt, N. (2014). The development of virtual reality technologies for people on the autism spectrum. In N. R. Silton (Ed.), *Innovative technologies to benefit children on the autism spectrum* (pp. 230–252). Hershey, PA: IGI Global. doi:10.4018/978-1-4666-5782.2.ch014

Newman, L., Wagner, M., Knokey, A.-M., Marder, C., Nagle, K., Shaver, D., . . . Schwarting, M. (2011). *The post–high school outcomes of young adults with disabilities up to 8 years after high school: A report from the National Longitudinal Transition Study-2 (NLTS2)* (NCSER 2011-3005). Menlo Park, CA: SRI International. Retrieved from http://www.nlts2.org/reports/2011_09_02/index.html

Noble, E. (2011, October 18). Medicaid reimbursement: Making the case for a gait trainer [Web log post]. Retrieved from http://www.rifton.com/adaptive-mobility-blog/blog-posts/2011/october/pediatric-walkers-medicaid-funding

Noel, M. J. (2013). *Does medium matter? Increasing preschoolers' vocabulary during shared storybook reading using electronic and print formats* (Unpublished master's thesis). Western Carolina University, Cullowhee, NC.

Noyes, J. (1983). The QWERTY keyboard: A review. *International Journal of Man-Machine Studies, 18*, 265–281.

Nuance. (2013). Dragon Dictation (Version 2.0.25) [Computer software]. Retrieved from http://www.nuance.com/dragon/index.htm

O'Brien, C., & Aguinaga, N. (2014). Using *Class Dojo* as an interactive whiteboard and iPad projection to promote positive behavior interventions and supports at the classroom level. *Proceedings from the Society for Information Technology & Teacher Education International Conference, 2014*(1), 2931–2933.

Obukowicz, M. (2009). Assistive technology for mathematics. In J. Gierach (Ed.), *Assessing students' needs for assistive technology (ASNAT): A resource manual for school district teams* (5th ed.). Retrieved from http://wati.org/content/supports/free/pdf/Ch8-Mathematics.pdf

Obukowicz, M., Stindt, K., Rozanski, D., & Gierach, J. (2009). Assistive technology for organization. In J. Gierach (Ed.), *Assessing students' needs for assistive technology (ASNAT): A resource manual for school district teams* (5th ed.). Retrieved from http://wati.org/content/supports/free/pdf/Ch9-Organization.pdf

Odom, S. L., Thompson, J. L., Hedges, S., Boyd, B. A., Dykstra, J. R., Duda, M. A., . . . Bord, A. (2014). Technology-aided intervention and instruction for adolescents with autism spectrum disorder. *Journal of Autism and Developmental Disabilities* [Advanced online publication]. doi:10.1007/s10803-014-2320-6

Office of Civil Rights, U.S. Department of Education. (2010, June 29). *Joint "dear colleague" letter: Electronic* book readers. Retrieved from http://www2.ed.gov/about/offices/list/ocr/letters/colleague-20100629.html

Okolo, C. M., & Diedrich, J. (2014). Twenty-five years later: How is technology used in the education of students with disabilities? Results of a statewide survey. *Journal of Special Education Technology*, 29(1), 1–20.

O'Reilly, M. R., Lancioni, G. E., Sigafoos, J., Lang, R., Healy, O., Singh, N. N., . . . Gevarter, C. (2014). Assistive technology for people with behavior problems. In G. E. Lancioni & N. N. Singh (Eds.), *Assistive technologies for people with diverse abilities* (pp. 191–218). New York, NY: Springer. doi:10.1007/978-1-4899-8029-8

Orth, T. (2006). *Visual recipes: A cookbook for non-readers*. Lenexa, KY: Autism Asperger Publishing Company.

Otero, T. L., Schatz, R. B., Merrill, A. C., & Bellini, S. (2015). Social skills training for youth with autism spectrum disorders: A follow-up. *Child and Adolescent Psychiatric Clinics of North America*, 24(1), 99–115. doi:10.1016/j.chc.2014.09.002

Pack, T. G., & Szirony, G. M. (2009). Predictors of competitive employment among persons with physical and sensory disabilities: An evidence-based model. *Work*, 33, 67–79.

Paleg, G., & Livingstone, R. (2015). Outcomes of gait trainer use in home and school settings for children with motor impairments: A systematic review. *Clinical Rehabilitation*. doi:10.1177/0269215514565947

Paleg, G. S., Smith, B. A., & Glickman, L.B. (2013). Systematic review and evidence-based clinical recommendations for dosing of pediatric supported standing programs. *Pediatric Physical Therapy*, 25(3), 232–247. doi:10.1097/PEP.0b13e318299d5e7

Parette, H. P., & Blum, C. (2013). *Instructional technology in early childhood*. Baltimore, MD: Paul H. Brookes.

Parette, H. P., & Blum, C. (2015). Including all young children in the technology-supported curriculum: A UDL technology integration framework for 21st-century classrooms. In C. Donahue (Ed.), *Technology and digital media in the early years: Tools for teaching and learning* (pp. 128–149). New York, NY: Routledge.

Parette, H. P., Blum, C., & Quesenberry, A. C. (2013). The role of technology for young children in the 21st century. In H. P. Parette & C. Blum (Eds.), *Instructional technology in early childhood* (pp. 1–28). Baltimore, MD: Paul H. Brookes Publishing.

Parette, H. P., Huer, M. B., & Brotherson, M. J. (2001). Related service personnel perceptions of team AAC decision-making across cultures. *Education and Training in Mental Retardation and Developmental Disabilities*, 36, 69–82.

Parette, P., VanBiervliet, A., & Hourcade, J. J. (2000). Family-centered decision-making in assistive technology. *Journal of Special Education Technology*, 15(1), 45–55.

Park, A. (2014, September 2). Sitting is killing you. *Time*. Retrieved from http://time.com/sitting/

Pasupathy, M. (2010). Overcoming two obstacles: Technology for students who are deaf-blind. *TECH-NJ*. Retrieved from http://www.tcnj.edu/~technj/2006/deafblind.htm

Patrick, S., Kennedy, K., & Powell, A. (2013). *Mean what you say: Defining and integrating personalized, blended, and competency education*. New York, NY: International Association for K–12 Online Learning. Retrieved from http://www.inacol.org/cms/wp-content/uploads/2013/10/iNACOL-Mean-What-You-Say-October-2013.pdf

Paulsen, K., & Sayeski, K. L. (2013). Using study skills to become independent learners in secondary content classes. *Intervention in School and Clinic*, 49(1), 39–45. doi:10.1177/105345123480026

PBS KIDS. (2010). *PBS KIDS iPod app study: Executive summary*. Retrieved from http://www-tc.pbskids.org/read/files/iPod_Report_ExecSum.pdf

PCD Maltron. (2014). The Maltron letter layout. Retrieved from http://www.maltron.com/keyboard-info/the-maltron-letter-layout-advantage#Maltron%20 Layout

Penuel, W. R., Pasnik, S., Bates, L., Townsend, E., Gallagher, L. P., Llorente, C., & Hupert, N. (2009). *Preschool teachers can use a media-rich curriculum to prepare low-income children for school success: Results of a randomized controlled trial.* New York, NY: Education Development Center. Retrieved from https://secure.edc.org/publications/prodview .asp?2114

Petcu, S. D., Yell, M., & Fletcher, T. (2014). Assistive technology: Legislation and legal issues. *Exceptionality, 22,* 226–236.

Peterson-Karlan, G. R., Parette, H. P., & Blum, C. (2013). Technology problem-solving for children with disabilities. In H. P. Parette & C. Blum (Eds.), *Instructional technology in early childhood* (pp. 95–122). Baltimore, MD: Paul H. Brookes.

Plowman, L., & McPake, J. (2013). Seven myths about young children and technology. *Childhood Education, 89*(1), 27–33. doi:10.1080/00094056.20 13.757490

Plowman, L., McPake, J., & Stephen, C. (2010). The technologisation of childhood? Young children and technology in the home. *Children and Society, 24*(1), 63–74.

Power, C., & Jürgensen, H. (2010). Accessible presentation of information for people with visual disabilities. *Universal Access in the Information Society, 9,* 97–119. doi:10.1007/s10209-009-0164-1

Preece, A., & Burton, D. (2012). A guide to the Read2 Go app for Apple iOS, from Bookshare. *AFB Access World Magazine, 13*(3). Retrieved from http://www.afb.org/AFBPress/pub .asp?DocID=aw130304&Mode=Print

Primavera, J., Wiederlight, P. P., & DiGiacomo, T. M. (2001, April). Technology access for low-income preschoolers: Bridging the digital divide. Paper presented at the American Psychological Association Annual Meeting, San Francisco, CA. Retrieved from www.knowledgeadventure.com/jumpstartworld/_ docs/ChildTechnology_White_Paper.pdf

ProtoGeo. (2015). *Moves* [Version 2.6.6]. Retrieved from https://itunes.apple.com/us/app/moves/ id509204969?mt=8

Ptomey, L. T., Sullivan, D. K., Lee, J., Goetz, J. R., Gibson, C., & Donnelly, J. E. (2015). The use of technology for delivering a weight loss program for adolescents with intellectual and developmental disabilities. *Journal of the Academy of Nutrition and Dietetics, 115*(1), 112–118.

Punch, R., & Hyde, M. B. (2011). Communication, psychosocial, and educational outcomes of children with cochlear implants and challenges remaining for professionals and parents. *International Journal of Otolaryngology, 2011,* 573280-573290. doi:10.1155/2011/573280

QIAT Community. (2012). *Quality indicators for including assistive technology in the IEP.* Retrieved from http://www.qiat.org/docs/3%20QIs%20for%20 Including%20AT%20in%20the%20IEP.pdf

QIAT Consortium. (2012). *Self-evaluation matrices for the Quality Indicators in Assistive Technology services.* Retrieved from http://indicators.knowbility.org/docs/ QIAT%20Matrices%20Explained.pdf

QIAT Leadership Team. (2012). *Quality indicators.* Retrieved from http://www.qiat.org/indicators.html

Quartet Technology. (n.d.). *What is an ECU?* Retrieved from http://www.qtiusa.com/faq-details .aspx?FAQID=13

Queen, B., Lewis, L., & Coopersmith, J. (2011). *Distance education courses for public elementary and secondary school students: 2009–10* [NCES 2012-008]. Washington, D.C.: U.S. Department of Education, National Center for Education Statistics. Retrieved from http://nces.ed.gov/ pubs2012/2012008.pdf

Quinn, B. S., Behrmann, M., Mastropieri, M., Bausch, M. E., Ault, M. J., & Chung, Y. (2009). Who is using assistive technology in schools? *Journal of Special Education Technology*, 24(1), 1–13.

Rafferty, L. A., & Raimondi, S. L. (2009). Self-monitoring of attention versus self-monitoring of performance: Examining the differential effects among students with emotional disturbance engaged in independent math practice. *Journal of Behavioral Education*, 18, 279–299.

Rashid, K. (2010). Identities and locations: Intersecting realities. In S. Burch & A. Kafer (Eds.), *Deaf and disability studies: Interdisciplinary perspectives, part one* (pp. 22–30). Washington, D.C.: Gallaudet Press.

Raskind, M. H., & Higgins, E. L. (1998). Assistive technology for postsecondary students with learning disabilities: An overview. *Journal of Learning Disabilities*, 31, 27–40. doi:10.1177/002221949803100104

Raskind, M., & Bryant, B. R. (2002). *Functional evaluation for assistive technology*. Austin, TX: Psychological Educational Services.

Rayamangalam, A. M. (2013). *Alphabetical keyboard*. Retrieved from https://play.google.com/store/apps/details?id=com.arise.ime.alphakeyboard&hl=en

Reed, F. D. D., Hyman, S. R., & Hirst, J. M. (2011). Applications of technology to teach social skills to children with autism. *Research in Autism Spectrum Disorders*, 5, 1003–1010. doi:10.1016/j.rasd.2011.01.022

Reed, P. (Ed.). (2003). *Designing environments for successful kids*. Oshkosh: Wisconsin Assistive Technology Initiative.

Reed, P., & Bowser, G. (2005). Assistive technology and the IEP. In D. Edyburn, K. Higgins, & R. Boone (Eds.), *Handbook of special education technology: Research and practice* (pp. 61–77). Whitefish Bay, WI: Knowledge by Design.

Reed, P., & Bowser, G. (2012). Consultation, collaboration, and coaching: Essential techniques for integrating assistive technology in schools and early intervention programs. *Journal of Occupational Therapy, Schools, & Early Intervention*, 5(1), 15–30. doi:10.1080/19411243.2012.675757

Reed, P., & Gierach, J. (2009). Overview of the assessment and planning process. In J. Gierarch (Ed.), *Assessing students' needs for assistive technology (ASNAT): A resource manual for school district teams* (5th ed.). Retrieved from http://www.wati.org/content/supports/free/pdf/Ch1-ASNATProcess.doc

Rehabilitation Act of 1973, Pub. L. 93-112, 87 Stat. 355 (1973).

Reid, R. (1996). Research in self-monitoring with students with learning disabilities: The present, the prospects, the pitfalls. *Journal of Learning Disabilities*, 29, 317–331.

Reid, R., Trout, A. L., & Schartz, M. (2005). Self-regulation interventions for children with attention deficit/hyperactivity disorder. *Exceptional Children*, 71, 361–377.

Reynolds, R. (2011). Trends influencing the growth of digital textbooks in US higher education. *Publishing Research Quarterly*, 27, 178–187.

Ricketts, T. A. (2011). Digital hearing aids: Current "state-of-the-art." *ASHA Leader*, 6(14), 8–11. Retrieved from http://leader.pubs.asha.org/article.aspx?articleid=2292572

Rideout, V., Foehr, U., & Roberts, D. (2010). *Generation M2: Media in the lives of 8- to 18-year-olds*. Menlo Park, CA: Henry J. Kaiser Family Foundation.

Riemer-Riess, M. L., & Wacker, R. R. (2000). Factors associated with assistive technology discontinuance among individuals with disabilities. *Journal of Rehabilitation*, 66, 44–50.

Rifton Equipment. (2015). Rifton dynamic standers. Retrieved from http://www.rifton.com/products/standers/dynamic-standers

Robinault, I. P. (1973). *Functional aids for the multiply handicapped*. New York, NY: Harper & Row.

Rogers, S. (2011). Pedagogy and play: A conflict of interests? In S. Rogers (Ed.), *Rethinking play and pedagogy in early childhood education: Concepts, contexts, and cultures* (pp. 5–18). Abingdon, U.K.: Routledge.

Rose, D. H., & Meyer, A. (2002). *Teaching every student in the digital age: Universal Design for Learning*. Alexandria, VA: Association for Supervision and Curriculum Development.

Rose, D. H., Hasselbring, T. S., Stahl, S., & Zabala, J. (2005). Assistive technology and Universal Design for Learning: Two sides of the same coin. In D. Edyburn, K. Higgins, & R. Boone (Eds.), *Handbook of special education technology research and practice* (pp. 507–518). Whitefish Bay, WI: Knowledge by Design.

Rule, A. C., Stefanich, G. P., Boody, R. M., & Peiffer, B. (2011). Impact of adaptive materials on teachers and their students with visual impairments in secondary science and mathematics classes. *International Journal of Science Education*, 33, 865–887.

Sadao, K. C., & Robinson, N. B. (2010). *Assistive technology for young children: Creating inclusive learning environments*. Baltimore, MD: Paul H. Brookes Publishing.

Sanford, C., Newman, L., Wagner, M., Cameto, R., Knokey, A.-M., & Shaver, D. (2011). *The post-high school outcomes of young adults with disabilities up to 6 years after high school: Key findings from the National Longitudinal Transition Study-2 (NLTS2)*. Menlo Park, CA: SRI International. Retrieved from http://www.nlts2.org/reports/2011_09/index.html

Satsangi, R., & Bouck, E. C. (2015). Using virtual manipulative instruction to teach the concepts of area and perimeter to secondary students with learning disabilities. *Learning Disability Quarterly*.

Sauer, A. L., Parks, A., & Heyn, P. C. (2010). Assistive technology effects on the employment outcomes for people with cognitive disabilities: A systematic review. *Disability and Rehabilitation: Assistive Technology*, 5, 377–391.

Savage, M. N. (2014). Self-operated auditory prompting systems: Creating and using them to support students with disabilities. *TEACHING Exceptional Children*, 47(1), 266–275. doi:10.1177/0040059914542763

Scassellati, B., Admoni, H., & Matarić, M. (2012). Robots for use in autism research. *Annual Review of Biomedical Engineering*, 14, 275–294.

Scherer, M., & Craddock, G. (2002). Matching person & technology (MPT) assessment process. *Technology & Disability*, 14(3), 125–131.

Schlosser, R. W., & Wendt, O. (2009). Effects of augmentative and alternative communication intervention on speech production in children with autism: A systematic review. *American Journal of Speech-Language Pathology*, 17, 212–230.

Schmid, R. F., Bernard, R. M., Borokhovski, E., Tamim, R. M., Abrami, P. C., Surkes, M. A., . . . Woods, J. (2014). The effects of technology use in postsecondary education: A meta-analysis of classroom applications. *Computers & Education*, 72, 271–291. doi:10.1016/j.compedu.2012.11.002

Schmidt, M. E., Haines, J., O'Brien, A., McDonald, J., Price, S., Sherry, B., & Taveras, E. M. (2012). Systematic review of effective strategies for reducing screen time among young children. *Obesity*, 20(7), 1338–1354. doi:10.1038/oby.2011.348

Schmitt, A. J., McCallum, E., Hennessey, J., Lovelace, T., & Hawkins, R. O. (2012). Use of reading pen assistive technology to accommodate post-secondary students with reading disabilities. *Assistive Technology*, 24, 229–239. doi:10.1080/10400435.2012.659956

Schmitt, A., McCallum, E., Hennessey, J., Lovelace, T., & Hawkins, R. O. (2012). Use of reading pen assistive technology to accommodate post-secondary students with reading disabilities. *Assistive Technology*, 24, 229–239. doi:10.1080/10400435.2012.659956

Schmitt, A. J., McCallum, E., Rubinic, D., & Hawkins, R. (2011). Reading pen decoding and vocabulary accommodations: Impact on student comprehension accuracy and rate. *Journal of Evidence Based Practices for Schools, 12,* 129–130.

Scruggs, T., Mastropieri, M., & Okolo, C. (2008). Science and social studies for students with disabilities. *Focus on Exceptional Children, 4*(2), 1–24.

Seale, J., Georgeson, J., Mamas, C., & Swain, J. (2015). Not the right kind of 'digital capital'? An examination of the complex relationship between disabled students, their technologies and higher education institutions. *Computers & Education, 82,* 118–128. doi:10.1016/j.compedu.2014.11.007

Sénéchal, M., Pagan, S., Lever, R., & Ouellette, G. (2008). Relations among the frequency of shared reading and 4-year-old children's vocabulary, morphological and syntax comprehension and narrative skills. *Early Education and Development, 19*(1), 27–44.

Senland, A. (2014). Robots and autism spectrum disorder: Clinical and educational applications. In N. R. Silton (Ed.), *Innovative technologies to benefit children on the autism spectrum* (pp. 178–196). Hershey, PA: IGI Global. doi:10.4018/978-1-4666-5782.2.ch011

Sensory Processing Disorder Foundation. (n.d.). *About SPD.* Retrieved from http://www.spdfoundation.net/about-sensory-processing-disorder/

Serianni, B. A., & Coy, K. (2014). Doing the math: Supporting students with disabilities in online courses. *Teaching Exceptional Children, 46*(5), 102–109. doi:10.1177/0040059914528330

Shackelford, J. (2006). State and jurisdictional eligibility definitions for infants and toddlers with disabilities under IDEA. *NECTAC Notes, 21,* 1–16. Retrieved from http://www.nectac.org/~pdfs/pubs/nnotes21.pdf

Shane, H. C., Blackstone, S., Vanderheiden, G., Williams, M., & DeRuyter, F. (2012). Using AAC technology to access the world. *Assistive Technology, 24,* 3–13. doi:10.1080/10400435.2011.648716

Sharapan, H. (2015). Technology as a tool for social-emotional development: What we can learn from Fred Rogers' approach. In C. Donahue (Ed.), *Technology and digital media in the early years: Tools for teaching and learning* (pp. 12–20). New York, NY: Routledge.

Sharpe, M. N., Johnson, D. R., Izzo, M., & Murray, A. (2005). An analysis of instructional accommodations and assistive technologies used by postsecondary graduates with disabilities. *Journal of Vocational Rehabilitation, 22,* 3–11.

Shih, C.-H. (2014). Assisting people with multiple disabilities to improve computer typing efficiency through a mouse wheel and on-screen keyboard software. *Research in Developmental Disabilities, 35,* 2129–2136. doi:10.106/j.ridd.2014.04.030

Shrieber, B., & Seifert, T. (2009). College students with learning disabilities and/or ADHD use of a handheld computer compared to convention planners. In Y. Eshet-Alkalai, A. Caspi, S. Eden, N. Geri, & Y. Yair (Eds.), *Proceedings of the Chais conference on instructional technologies research 2009: Learning in the technological era.* Raanana: The Open University of Israel. Retrieved from http://telem-pub.openu.ac.il/users/chais/2009/noon/2_3.pdf

Shuler, C. (2010). *iLearn: A content analysis of the iTunes app store's education section.* Retrieved from http://www.joanganzcooneycenter.org/Reports-21.html

Shulman, L. (1986). Those who understand: Knowledge growth in teaching. *Educational Researcher, 15*(2), 4–14.

Shulman, L. S. (1987). Knowledge and teaching: Foundations of the new reform. *Harvard Educational Review, 57*(1), 1–22.

Shurr, J., & Taber-Doughty, T. (2012). Increasing comprehension for middle school students with moderate intellectual disability on age-appropriate texts. *Education and Training in Autism and Developmental Disabilities, 47*(3), 359–372.

Shvimer, L., Kerbel, N., & Friedmann, N. (2009). An empirical evaluation of various treatment directions in developmental attentional dyslexia. *Language and Brain, 8,* 87–118.

Simpson, L. A., & Oh, K. (2013). Using circle time books to increase participation in the morning circle routine. *TEACHING Exceptional Children*, *45*(6), 30–36.

Sloan, R. H. (2012). Using an e-textbook and iPad: Results of a pilot program. *Journal of Educational Technology Systems*, *41*(1), 87–104.

Smith, D. W., & Kelly, S. M. (2014). Assistive technology for students with visual impairments: A research agenda. *International Review of Research in Developmental Disabilities*, *46*, 23–53. doi:10.1016/B978-0-12-420039-5.00003-4

Smith, D. W., & Smothers, S. M. (2012). The role and characteristics of tactile graphics in secondary mathematics and science textbooks in braille. *Journal of Visual Impairment and Blindness*, *106*(9), 543–554.

Smith, S. J., & Basham, J. D. (2014). Designing online learning opportunities for students with disabilities. *Teaching Exceptional Children*, *46*(5), 127–137. doi:10.1177/0040059914530102

SNOW. (2013). Voice recognition (speech to text software). Retrieved from http://www.snow.idrc.ocad.ca/content/voice-recognition-speech-text-software

Soft Grup Construct SRL. (2012). Turbo Type (Version 1.39.003) [Computer software]. Retrieved from http://www.easytousetools.com/turbo_type/

Srinivasan, S., & Lloyd, L. L. (2011). Assistive technology for mobility, seating, and positioning. In O. Wendt, R. W. Quist, & L. L. Lloyd (Eds.), *Assistive technology: Principles and applications for communication disorders and special education* (pp. 413–446). Bingley, U.K.: Emerald.

Stachowiak, J. R. (2014). The changing face of assistive technology: From PC to mobile to cloud computer. In B. DaCosta & S. Seok (Eds.), *Assistive technology research, practice, and theory* (pp. 90–98). Hershey, PA: IGI Global.

Stanton, C. M., Kahn, P. H. J., Severson, R. L., Ruckert, J. H., & Gill, B. T. (2008, March). *Robotic animals might aid in the social development of children with autism* [Abstract]. Paper presented at the 3rd ACM/IEEE International Conference on Human–Robot Interaction, Amsterdam, The Netherlands. Retrieved from http://portal.acm.org/citation.cfm?id=1349858

Steinberg, M. A., & Murphy, K. M. (2012). *An annotated review of current research supporting the use of Kurzweil 3000 in higher education*. Retrieved from http://www.kurzweiledu.com/files/pdf/kurzweil-3000-firelfy-higher-ed-summary-of-research-white-paper-final-092112.pdf

Steinman, B. A., Kimbrough, B. T., Johnson, F., & LeJeune, B. J. (2004). Transferring standard English Braille skills to the Unified English Braille code: A pilot study. *Re:View*, *36*, 103–111.

Stephen, C., McPake, J., Plowman, L., & Berch-Heyman, S. (2008). Learning from the children: Exploring preschool children's encounters with ICT at home. *Journal of Early Childhood Research*, *6*(2), 99–117.

Stindt, K. J., Reed, P. R., & Obukowicz, M. (2009). Assistive technology for positioning, seating and mobility. In J. Gierach (Ed.), *Assessing students' needs for assistive technology (ASNAT): A resource manual for school district teams* (5th ed.). Milton: Wisconsin Assistive Technology Initiative. Retrieved from http://wati.org/content/supports/free/pdf/Ch2-PositioningSeatingMobility.pdf

Stodden, R. A., Roberts, K. D., Picklesimer, T., Jackson, D., & Chang, C. (2006). An analysis of assistive technology supports and services offered in postsecondary educational institutions. *Journal of Vocational Rehabilitation 24*, 111–120.

Stodden, R. A., Roberts, K. D., Takahishi, K., Park, H. J., & Stodden, N. J. (2012). Use of text-to-speech software to improve reading skills of high school struggling readers. *Procedia Computer Science, 14*, 359–362.

Strangman, N., & Dalton, B. (2005). Using technology to support struggling readers: A review of research. In D. Edyburn, K. Higgins, & R. Boone (Eds.), *Handbook of special education technology, research, and practice* (pp. 545–569). Whitefish Bay, WI: Knowledge by Design.

Sugai, G., Horner, R. H., Dunlap, G., Hieneman, M., Lewis, T. J., Nelson, C. M., . . . Wilcox, B. (2000). Applying positive behavioral support and functional behavioral assessment in schools. *Journal of Positive Behavioral Interventions, 2*, 131–143.

Sulzer-Azaroff, B., Hoffman, A. O., Horton, C. B., Bondy, A., & Frost, L. (2009). The Picture Exchange Communication System (PECS): What do the data say? *Focus on Autism and Other Developmental Disabilities, 24*, 89–103.

Summers, J., Ruggiero, D., & Quist, R. W. (2011). Computers: History and fundamentals. In O. Wendt, R. W. Quist, & L. L. Lloyd (Eds.), *Assistive technology: Principles and applications for communication disorders and special education* (pp. 23–68). Bingley, U.K.: Emerald.

Supalo, C. A. (2010). *Teaching chemistry and other sciences to blind and low-vision students through hands-on learning experiences in high school science laboratories* (Doctoral dissertation, The Pennsylvania State University). Retrieved from https://etda.libraries.psu .edu/paper/11471/6904

Supercritical Flow. (2015). *Steps pedometer & step counter activity tracker* [Version 1.3]. Retrieved from https://itunes.apple.com/us/app/steps-pedometer-step-counter/id708359518?mt=8

Sutton, M. (2013). *Talking pictures: Visual scene displays.* Retrieved from http://community. advanceweb.com/blogs/sp_6/archive/2013/06/24/ talking-pictures-visual-scene-displays.aspx

Swenson, K., Wirkus, M., & Obukowitz, M. (2009). Assistive technology for the composition of written materials. In J. Gierach (Ed.), *Assessing students' needs for assistive technology (ASNAT): A resource manual for school district teams* (5th ed.). Retrieved from http://wati.org/content/supports/free/pdf/Ch6-CompostionWrittenMaterial.pdf

Szwed, K., & Bouck, E. C. (2013). Clicking away: Using a student response system to self-monitor behavior in a general education classroom. *Journal of Special Education Technology, 28*(2), 1–12.

Taber-Doughty, T. (2005). Considering student choice when selecting instructional strategies: A comparison of three prompting systems. *Research in Developmental Disabilities, 26,* 411–432.

Taber-Doughty, T., & Jasper, A. D. (2012). Does latency in recording data make a difference? Confirming the accuracy of teachers' data. *Focus on Autism and Other Developmental Disabilities, 27*(3), 168–176. doi:10.1177/1088357612451121

Taber-Doughty, T., Bouck, E. C., Tom, K., Jasper, A. D., Flanagan, S. M., & Bassette, L. A. (2011). Video modeling and prompting: A comparison of two strategies for teaching cooking skills to students with mild intellectual disabilities. *Education and Training in Autism and Developmental Disabilities, 46*, 400–513.

Tammaro, M. T., & Jerome, M. K. (2012). Does the app fit? Using the Apps Consideration Checklist. In M. J. Ault & M. E. Bausch (Eds.), *Apps for all students: A teacher's desktop guide* (pp. 23–31). Reston, VA: Technology and Media Division for the Council for Exceptional Children.

Tapus, A., Peca, A., Aly, A., Pop, C., Jisa, A, Pintea, S., . . . David, D. O. (2012). Children with autism social engagement in interaction with Nao, an imitative robot. *Interaction Studies, 13*(3), 315–347. doi:10.1075/is.13.3.01tap

Technical Assistance Center on Positive and Behavioral Interventions and Supports. (n.d.). PBIS and the law. Retrieved from https://www.pbis.org/school/pbis-and-the-law

Technology and Media Division. (2004). *Assistive technology consideration quick wheel.* Arlington, VA: Author.

Technology and Media Division. (2012). Apps Consideration Checklist. In M. J. Ault & M. E. Bausch (Eds.), *Apps for all students: A teacher's desktop guide* (pp. 28–31). Reston, VA: Author.

Technology-Related Assistance for Individuals with Disabilities Act, 29 U.S.C. § 2201 et seq. (1988).

Test, D. W., Aspel, N. P., & Everson, J. M. (2006). *Transition methods for youth with disabilities.* Upper Saddle River, NJ: Pearson Education.

Texthelp. (2012). Read & Write GOLD [Computer software]. Retrieved from http://www.texthelp.com/North-America/our-products/readwrite

Thomas, K. M., & McGee, C. D. (2012). The only thing we have to fear is . . . 120 characters. *TechTrends, 56*(1), 19–33.

Tomopoulos, S., Dreyer, B. P., Berkule, S., Fierman, A. H., Brockmeyer, C., & Mendelsohn, A. L. (2010). Infant media exposure and toddler development. *Archives of Pediatrics & Adolescent Medicine, 164*(12), 1105–1111.

Tots 'n Tech. (2011). Tots 'n Tech helpdesk. Retrieved from http://tnt.asu.edu/tnt-helpdesk

Toussaint, K. A., & Tiger, J. H. (2010). Teaching early Braille literacy skills within a stimulus equivalence paradigm to children with degenerative visual impairments. *Journal of Applied Behavior Analysis, 43,* 181–194.

Trewin, S., Swart, C., & Pettick, D. (2013, October). *Physical accessibility of touchscreen smartphones.* Paper presented to ASSETS '13, Bellevue, WA.

Tufts University. (2008). Visual Understanding Environment (Version 3.1.2) [Computer software]. Retrieved from http://vue.tufts.edu/

Tuthill, J. (2014, June). Get real with visual scene displays. *The ASHA Leader, 19,* 34–35. doi:10.1044/leader.APP.19062014.34

U.S. Department of Education. (n.d.). Building the legacy: IDEA 2004. Retrieved from http://idea.ed.gov/explore/view/p/,root,regs,300,A,300%252E6

U.S. Department of Education. (2013). *35th annual report to Congress on the implementation of the Individuals with Disabilities Education Act.* Retrieved from http://www2.ed.gov/about/reports/annual/osep/2013/parts-b-c/35th-idea-arc.pdf

U.S. National Library of Medicine. (2014). Preventing pressure ulcers. *MedlinePlus Medical Encyclopedia.* Bethesda, MD: Author. Retrieved from http://www.nlm.nih.gov/medlineplus/ency/patientinstructions/000147.htm

Umeda, A., & Deitz, J. (2011). Effects of therapy cushions on classroom behaviors of children with autism spectrum disorder. *The American Journal of Occupational Therapy, 65,* 152–159. doi:10.5014/ajot.2011.000760

University of Kentucky Assistive Technology Project. (2002a). *Human function model.* Lexington, KY: Author. Retrieved from http://serc.gws.uky.edu/www/ukatii/resources/Human_Function_Model.pdf

University of Kentucky Assistive Technology Project. (2002b). Toolkit instructions. Lexington, KY: Author. Retrieved from http://serc.gws.uky.edu/www/ukatii/instruct.pdf

Utah State University. (2015) *National Library of Virtual Manipulatives.* Retrieved from http://nlvm.usu.edu/

van der Meer, L., Sigafoos, J., O'Reilly, M. F., & Lancioni, G. E. (2011). Assessing preferences for AAC options in communication interventions for individuals with developmental disabilities: A review of the literature. *Research in Developmental Disabilities, 32,* 1422–1431.

Van Laarhoven-Myers, T. E., Van Laarhoven, T. R., Smith, T. J., Johnson, H., & Olson, J. (2014). Promoting self-determination and transition planning using technology: Student and parent perspectives [Advanced online publication]. *Career Development and Transition for Exceptional Individuals.* doi:10.1177/2165143414552518

Vanderheiden, G. (1984). High and light technology approaches in the development of communication systems for the severely physically handicapped person. *Exceptional Education Quarterly, 4*(4), 40–56.

Vanderheiden, G. C., & Grilley, K. (1976). *Non-vocal communication techniques and aids for the severely physically handicapped.* Austin, TX: Pro-Ed.

Walker, H. (2010). *Evaluation rubric for iPod apps.* Retrieved from http://learninginhand.com/blog/evaluation-rubric-for-educational-apps.html

Walker, H. (2011). Evaluating the effectiveness of apps for mobile devices: An avalanche of apps. *Journal of Special Education Technology, 26*(4), 59–63.

Walker, M. P. (2007). Standing tall: The benefits of standing devices. *Exceptional Parent, 37*(3), 56–57. Retrieved from http://www.rifton.com/resources/articles/2007/march/standing-tall

Wallen, M., & Hubbard, A. (2013). *The ounce: Blending and braiding early childhood program funding streams toolkit.* Retrieved from http://www.ounceof prevention.org/national-policy/blended-funding-toolkit-nov2013.pdf

Walser, K., Ayres, K. M., & Foote, E. (2012). Effects of a video model to teach students with moderate intellectual disabilities to use key features of an iPhone. *Education and Training in Autism and Developmental Disabilities, 47,* 319–331.

Watson, A. H., Ito, M., Smith, R. O., & Andersen, L. T. (2010). Effect of assistive technology in a public school setting. *The American Journal of Occupational Therapy, 64*(1), 18–29.

Watson, J., Pape, L., Murin, A., Gemin, B., & Vashaw, L. (2014). *Keeping pace with K–12 online learning: An annual review of policy and practice.* Retrieved from http://www.kpk12.com/wp-content/uploads/EEG_KP2014-fnl-lr.pdf

Watts, E. H., O'Brian, M., & Wojcik, B. W. (2004). Four models of assistive technology consideration: How do they compare to recommended educational assessment practices? *Journal of Special Education Technology, 19*(1), 43–56.

WebAIM. (2012). *Motor disabilities: Assistive technology.* Retrieved from http://webaim.org/articles/motor/assistive

WebAIM. (2015). United States laws: Overview of the Rehabilitation Act of 1973 (Sections 504 and 508). Retrieved from http://webaim.org/articles/laws/usa/rehab

Wehman, P., Schall, C., Carr, S., Targett, P., West, M., & Cifu, G. (2014). Transition from school to adulthood for youth with autism spectrum disorder: What we know and what we need to know. *Journal of Disability Policy Studies.* doi: 10.1177/1044207313518071. Retrieved from http://dps.sagepub.com/content/25/1/30

Wehmeyer, M. L. (1996). Self-determination as an educational outcome: Why is it important to children, youth, and adults with disabilities? In D. J. Sands & M. L. Wehmeyer (Eds.), Self-determination across the lifespan: Independence and choice for people with (pp. 15–34). Baltimore, MD: Paul H. Brookes.

Wehmeyer, M. L., Tassé, M. J., Davies, D. K., & Stock, S. (2012). Support needs of adults with intellectual disability across domains: The role of technology. *Journal of Special Education Technology, 27*(2), 11–21.

Wendt, O., & Weed, J. M. (2011). Software and Internet resources for assistive technology and augmentative and alternative communication. In O. Wendt, R. W. Quist, & L. L. Lloyd (Eds.), *Assistive technology: Principles and applications for communication disorders and special education* (pp. 69–94). Bingley, U.K.: Emerald.

Weng, P.-L., & Bouck, E. C. (2014). Using video prompting via iPads to teach price comparison to adolescents with autism. *Research in Autism Spectrum Disorders, 8*(10), 1405–1415.

Weng, P.-L., Savage, M. N., & Bouck, E. C. (2014). iDIY: Video-based instruction using iPads. *TEACHING Exceptional Children, 47*(1), 231–239. doi:10.1177/0040059914542764

Westling, D., & Fox, L. (2009). *Teaching students with severe disabilities* (4th ed.). Upper Saddle River, NJ: Pearson.

WheelchairNet. (2006a). *Funding for wheelchairs.* Retrieved from http://www.wheelchairnet.org/WCN/WCN_ProdServ/Funding/funding.html

WheelchairNet. (2006b). *The history of wheelchairs.* Retrieved from http://www.wheelchairnet.org/WCN_ProdServ/Docs/WCHistory.html

Whinnery, S. B., & Whinnery, K. W. (2011). Effects of functional mobility skills training for adults with severe multiple disabilities. *Education and Training in Autism and Developmental Disabilities, 46,* 436–453.

Wiazowksi, J. (2009). Assistive technology for students who are blind or have low vision. In J. Gierach (Ed.), *Assessing students' needs for assistive technology (ASNAT): A resource manual for school district teams* (5th ed.). Retrieved from http://wati.org/content/supports/free/pdf/Ch12-Vision.pdf

Wiazowski, J. (2013, February). *Audio invasion—Are tactile media in peril?* Paper presented to the First International Conference on Technology for Helping People with Special Needs, Riyadh, Saudi Arabia.

Wilkinson, K. M., & Light, J. (2011). Preliminary investigation of visual attention to human figures in photographs: Potential considerations for the design of aided AAC visual scene displays. *Journal of Speech, Language, and Hearing Research, 54*(6), 1644–1657. doi:10.1044/1092-4388(2011/10-0098)

Willings, C. (2014). *Increase size for students with visual impairments.* Retrieved from http://www.teachingvisuallyimpaired.com/increase-size.html

Willoughby, K. L., Dodd, K. J., Shields, N., & Foley, S. (2010). Efficacy of partial body weight-supported treadmill training compared with overground walking practice for children with cerebral palsy: A randomized control trial. *Archives of Physical Medicine and Rehabilitation, 91,* 333–339. doi:10.1016/j.apmr.2009.10.029

Wissick, C. A., & Gardner, J. E. (2008). Conducting assessments in technology needs: From assessment to implementation. *Assessment for Effective Intervention, 33,* 78–93. doi:10.1177/1534508407311427

Wong, C., Odom, S. L., Hume, K., Cox, A. W., Fettig, A., Kurcharczyk, S., . . . Schultz, T. R. (2014). *Evidence-based practices for children, youth, and young adults with autism spectrum disorder.* Chapel Hill, NC: Frank Porter Graham Child Development Institute. Retrieved from http://autismpdc.fpg.unc.edu/sites/autismpdc.fpg.unc.edu/files/2014-EBP-Report.pdf

Xin, J. F., & Leonard, D. A. (2014, October 8). Using iPads to teach communication skills of students with autism. *Journal of Autism and Developmental Disorders.* Retrieved from http://link.springer.com/article/10.1007/s10803-014-2266-8/fulltext.html

Yell, M. (2012). *The law and special education* (3rd ed.). Boston, MA: Pearson.

York, C. S., & Fabrikant, K. B. (2011). High technology. In O. Wendt, R. W. Quist, & L. L. Lloyd (Eds.), *Assistive technology: Principles and applications for communication disorders and special education* (pp. 221–264). Bringley, U.K.: Emerald.

Zabala, J. (1995). *The SETT framework: Critical areas to consider when making informed assistive technology decisions.* Houston, TX: Region IV Education Service Center.

Zabala, J. (2005). Ready, SETT, go! Getting started with the SETT framework. *Closing the Gap, 23*(6). Retrieved from http://plone.rockyview.ab.ca/Plone/home/21stC/teaching/assistive-technology/atl-assets/Ready-SETT.pdf

Zabala, J., & Carl, D. F. (2005). Quality indicators for assistive technology services in schools. In D. Edyburn, K. Higgins, & R. Boone (Eds.), *Handbook of special education technology: Research and practice* (pp. 179–207). Whitefish Bay, WI: Knowledge by Design.

Zabala, J., Bowser, G., Blunt, M., Hartsell, K., Carl, D., Korsten, J., . . . Reed, P. (2000). Quality indicators for assistive technology services in school settings. *Journal of Special Education Technology*, 15(4), 25–36.

Zentall, S. S. (1975). Optimal stimulation as a theoretical basis of hyperactivity. *American Journal of Orthopsychiatry, 45,* 549–563.

Zentall, S. S. (2005). Theory- and evidence-based strategies for children with attentional problems. *Psychology in the Schools, 42,* 821–836.

Zentall, S. S., & Zentall, T. R. (1983). Optimal stimulation: A model of disordered activity and productivity in normal and deviant children. *Psychological Bulletin, 94,* 446–471.

Zimmer, M., & Desch, L. (2012). Sensory integration therapies for children with developmental and behavioral disorders. *Pediatrics, 129*(6), 1186–1189. doi:10.1542/peds.2012-0876

INDEX

Figures and tables are indicated by f or t following the page number.